Rehabilitation and Re-use of Old Buildings

Rehabilitation and Re-use of Old Buildings

DAVID HIGHFIELD BSc,MPhil,MCIOB
Senior Lecturer in Construction, Leeds Polytechnic

London
E. & F.N. SPON

First published in 1987 by E. & F.N. Spon Ltd
11 New Fetter Lane, London EC4P 4EE

© 1987 David Highfield

Printed in Great Britain at the University Press, Cambridge

ISBN 0 419 13400 X

British Library Cataloguing in Publication Data

Highfield, David
    The rehabilitation and re-use of old
    buildings.
    1. Buildings—Great Britain—
    Repair and reconstruction
    I. Title
    711'.5'0941   TH3401

    ISBN 0-419-13400-X

Contents

Contents

Preface

The rehabilitation and re-use of old buildings has, during the past decade, become a major component of construction activity and currently accounts for over 40% of the industry's workload. Building owners and developers have come to realize the potential value of our vast stocks of old buildings as a means of providing modern accommodation more quickly, and at a lower cost than the alternative of new construction. Generally, the cost of rehabilitating an existing building will be only 50–80% of the cost of new construction, resulting in considerable financial savings.

There has also been a significant increase in attitudes favouring conservation during recent years. The wholesale demolition and redevelopment policies of the 1960s resulted in the replacement of large numbers of attractive, substantial old buildings with buildings of much poorer quality, and it is now widely recognized that it makes far greater sense to retain and rehabilitate the best of these old buildings, rather than to demolish and replace them.

Because of the aforementioned factors, together with the many other advantages to be gained, it is certain that the rehabilitation and re-use of old buildings will continue to represent a major, and increasing, component of construction activity in the foreseeable future. It is therefore vital for all of those associated with building rehabilitation and re-use to be fully aware of the key issues involved. In addressing itself to these key issues, this book should prove to be an invaluable aid to building owners, developers, architects, building surveyors, quantity surveyors, main contractors and specialist sub-contractors involved with building rehabilitation work. It should also be of value to students of architecture, building and surveying in their study of this increasingly important aspect of construction.

The first chapter poses the question 'Why rehabilitation?', and explains the reasons for, and numerous advantages to be gained from, rehabilitating existing buildings. This should enable building owners and developers, and their professional advisers, to take a more analytical approach in appraising potential schemes.

Chapter 2 examines the field of housing rehabilitation, discussing, firstly, the massive national problem of unfit housing and, secondly, the improvement of sub-standard housing, with three illustrated examples showing typical rehabilitation solutions.

Chapter 3 deals with the rehabilitation of non-domestic buildings and discusses the wide range of options available, from 'low key' rehabilitation to that involving

Preface

major structural work. The chapter also provides valuable guidance for developers on where to look for redundant or obsolete buildings that are suitable for rehabilitation, and several useful sources of information are given.

Chapter 4 deals in detail with the practical problems associated with rehabilitation, and the solutions used to overcome them. Aspects covered include upgrading fire resistance, thermal insulation, and sound insulation; upgrading surface finishes; preventing damp and moisture penetration; preventing condensation; eradicating timber decay; repairing decayed timber elements; and strengthening timber floors. The background to each practical problem is discussed, followed by a detailed description of the upgrading technique or method of repair. The text is supplemented by a large number of detailed diagrams which fully explain the recommended technical solutions. The majority of the technical solutions described involve the use of named proprietary products and systems, and, for those wishing to obtain further information, the addresses and telephone numbers of their manufacturers are given at the end of the chapter (see Table 4.6).

Chapter 5 examines the statutory requirements affecting building rehabilitation, and provides guidance on compliance with the relevant acts and regulations. I would like, at this point, to express my sincere thanks to Bill Rimmer, Divisional Building Control Officer with Leeds City Council, for his valuable specialist advice in the preparation of the section on the Building Regulations. It should be pointed out that statutory requirements are constantly being reviewed and updated, and it is essential that the reader is aware of changes in Building Regulations and other legislation that have taken place since the date of publication.

Chapter 6 gives details of the numerous sources of financial aid available for building rehabilitation, and gives valuable information for building owners and developers seeking grants or loans towards the cost of schemes. The availability of financial aid can often make an otherwise uneconomic scheme viable, and owners and developers would therefore be well advised to examine the possibility of obtaining aid from sources given in this chapter.

The reader should be aware that sources of financial aid are subject to regular review and, therefore, some of the sources included in the chapter may, with time, be changed or cease to exist, while new sources may be introduced.

The final chapter gives detailed descriptions of six typical case-studies and illustrates how a wide range of different building types can be successfully rehabilitated to provide modern, high quality accommodation. The case study descriptions are supplemented by drawings and photographs which explain in detail the extent of the rehabilitation work carried out.

There are two further areas of considerable importance in the rehabilitation of old buildings which have not been included in this book. The first concerns the management of rehabilitation schemes, and the second concerns building and structural surveys. Both are highly specialized areas which are dealt with comprehensively by other texts and which, if included in this book, would have merely been duplications of material already available.

The management of rehabilitation schemes is usually far more complex than the management of new construction, and whilst the basic principles of project management still apply, it is vital for both the architect and the main contractor to be aware of the organizational peculiarities and pitfalls of rehabilitation work. In order to assist the reader in this respect, a number of useful texts dealing with project management are included as further reading, headed *Project Management*, at the end of the final chapter.

A further vital component of the rehabilitation process is the initial building and structural survey, without which it would be impossible to accurately assess the nature and extent of the work required, and, more importantly, the likely cost of the scheme. It should be appreciated that the execution of building and structural surveys, for all but the simplest schemes, is a specialized and complex process. It will therefore be necessary to commission a surveyor with the appropriate qualifications and experience. Where structural alterations are envisaged, it may also be necessary to seek the advice of a specialist structural engineer.

There are several textbooks which deal comprehensively with building and structural surveying, and a number of these have been selected for inclusion as further reading, headed *Building and Structural Surveying*, at the end of the final chapter.

Chapter one

Why rehabilitation?

The provision of modern accommodation by rehabilitating old, outdated buildings, rather than constructing new ones, has become increasingly popular with developers, and there are numerous reasons for this. Most of the reasons can be attributed to the specific advantages that can be gained by opting for rehabilitation and re-use, although in some cases there may be legislative constraints which leave the developer with no choice but to retain and re-use an existing building.

Where a developer wishes to provide modern accommodation, and an existing building is available in a suitable location, all of the following points should be carefully considered since it is likely that rehabilitation and re-use may well be a more viable means of providing the accommodation than opting for new construction.

1.1 THE AVAILABILITY OF RAW MATERIAL

Advances in industry and commerce, together with the demand for a more sophisticated interior environment for both work and leisure, have led to large numbers of buildings becoming outdated, redundant or obsolete and this, in turn, has provided an abundance of 'raw material' suitable for rehabilitation and re-use. Examples include large numbers of textile mills in the north of England, old factory and warehouse buildings in industrial centres, out-

dated institutional buildings such as schools and hospitals, older office buildings and pre- and inter-war housing. Another major source of raw material for rehabilitation that has become available relatively recently is the large number of redundant church buildings. There are over 18 000 Anglican churches in the United Kingdom, and many of these, along with churches of other denominations, are becoming redundant because of changing population patterns, and the declining position of the church in people's lives. In the past fifteen years, more than a thousand Anglican churches have been officially declared redundant, and a large proportion of these are still unused. Redundant church buildings, which are likely to increase in their availability in the foreseeable future, have been successfully rehabilitated to provide residential, manufacturing, recreational and office accommodation, and some excellent examples are described in Chapter 7.

In the absence of open sites available for new development, particularly in the prime commercial and residential zones of most towns and cities, developers seeking to provide modern accommodation must therefore look towards those buildings which, because of their age and condition, can often be obtained fairly cheaply. Having focused on a suitable building, the developer must then decide whether to opt for demolition and new construction, or rehabilitation, and the remaining sections of this chapter explain why the latter course is often chosen.

1

1.2 THE QUALITY OF THE RAW MATERIAL

A further major factor in favour of the rehabilitation and re-use of old buildings, in addition to their widespread availability, is that many of these buildings are substantial and structurally sound. Such buildings may well be obsolete, neglected and unfit for modern usage as they stand, but the tried and tested traditional methods of construction used to build them has left potential developers with a legacy of sound, durable structures which provide an ideal basis for improvement and re-use. However, it should not always be assumed, because a building is old and of traditional construction, that its structural quality is high, and it is vital that any building being considered for rehabilitation is subjected to a detailed survey in order either to confirm its structural quality or to ascertain the likely cost of any structural repairs and their effect on the feasibility of going ahead with a rehabilitation scheme.

1.3 THE SHORTER DEVELOPMENT PERIOD

One of the principal advantages of opting for rehabilitation rather than demolition and new construction is that, in the majority of cases, the 'new' accommodation will be available in a much shorter time.

The physical work required to rehabilitate an existing building will normally take considerably less time than the alternative of demolition, site clearance and the construction of a new building, unless, of course, extensive structural alterations or repairs are envisaged. In addition to the time saved during the construction phase, time is also saved during the pre-contract design and planning permission phases, which normally take much longer for new development than for rehabilitation, even where a change of use is proposed for the existing building. These savings, during the pre-contract design, planning and construction phases of development often mean that opting for rehabilitation can provide the new accommodation in only half to three-quarters of the time needed for demolition and new construction, giving the following economic advantages:

- The shorter contract duration reduces the effects of inflation on building costs
- The shorter development period reduces the cost of providing finance for the scheme
- The client obtains the building sooner, and therefore begins to earn revenue from it (for example, rentals or manufacturing profits) at an earlier date.

1.4 THE ECONOMIC ADVANTAGES

The cost of converting a building is generally much less than the cost of new construction, since many of the building elements are already constructed. However, the existing construction and its condition will have a considerable bearing on the conversion costs. For example, if floor to ceiling heights are either too low or too high for the proposed new use, the necessary adjustments may be very expensive. Also, many old industrial buildings have timber floors, supported by timber or cast-iron columns and beams which will require upgrading to comply with current standards of fire protection. In addition, new fire escape stairs and enclosures will almost certainly be required; all of which will add to the cost of conversion. If the building is in a poor physical condition because of neglect and deterioration, the conversion will also involve the expense of repair and restoration work which may have a significant effect on overall costs.

Against costs of this nature, the developer must weigh the potential savings achieved by not having to demolish the building (which would be required if the option of new construction were selected), and the shorter development period with its implications on construction costs and finance charges.

There is little point in rehabilitating and re-using old buildings if the costs are going to be greater than those of new construction, unless, of course, there are overriding environmental benefits as in the case of buildings of architectural or historic interest. Rehabilitation and re-use will only be substantially cheaper than demolition and new construction where a suitable building is chosen which is in a reasonable physical state, and which does not require excessive structural alterations in order to adapt it to its proposed new use.

Thus, the arguments regarding the rehabilitation and re-use of most old buildings inevitably revolve around the economic aspects, and it is vital, therefore, that in the first instance a detailed cost feasibility study is carried out, since this, above all else, will normally decide whether or not rehabilitation is viable.

The most important factors that determine whether or not rehabilitation is viable are:

- The expected rental income (in speculative developments)
- The estimated cost of development
- The cost of acquiring the leasehold or free-hold of the site
- The cost of finance

1.4.1 Expected rental income

The expected rental income from a rehabilitated building will depend upon several factors:
(a) The proposed new use(s) for the building
(b) The location of the building
(c) The relative attractiveness of the area in which the building stands, including the amenity of the surrounding neighbourhood and its accessibility
(d) The quality of the accommodation and services after rehabilitation which, in turn, will depend upon the standard of rehabilitation carried out
(e) The level of demand for such accommodation from new firms setting up or moving into the area, and existing firms wanting to expand or improve their accommodation

(f) The availability of other, similar accommodation in the area.

Details of prevailing rentals, and the extent of demand for different types and levels of accommodation in an area are best obtained from local estate agents.

1.4.2 Estimated cost of development

The development cost for a rehabilitation scheme will depend upon several factors, the most important of which are as follows.

(a) The proposed new use

The proposed new use for the rehabilitated building can have a significant effect upon the development costs. For example, the cost of rehabilitating a late nineteenth century warehouse to provide workshop accommodation for small manufacturing businesses would almost certainly be considerably less than converting it to provide prestige office accommodation.

(b) The standard of rehabilitation envisaged

The standard or quality of the proposed accommodation will affect the final cost of rehabilitation. For example, the existing windows may be in sufficiently good condition to overhaul, strip and repaint, but the developer may wish to replace them with new, double-glazed, mainte-nance-free metal or plastic windows in order to improve the appearance and thermal properties of the building. The latter choice will, clearly significantly increase the development costs.

Decisions regarding services can also have a considerable effect on development costs. For example, where an old building is being rehabilitated to provide modern office accommodation, the developer may choose to save money by opting for a simple hot water radiator heating system, with openable windows to provide the ventilation, rather than the much more expensive alternative of a sophisticated heating, ventilating and air-conditioning system. Costs can also be reduced in taller buildings, by installing fewer passenger lifts, or even no lifts at all in buildings of two or three storeys.

Virtually every design decision that relates to the quality, standard or amenity of the rehabilitated building will have an effect on the development costs: the higher the specification, the higher the overall cost of the building. However, as stated earlier, in the long term, the greater costs incurred by providing a higher standard of rehabilitation can be recouped by the higher rental income that such standards can demand.

(c) The age of the building

Generally, the older the building, and the longer it has been empty, the greater will be the costs of repairing and restoring the existing structure and fabric. Very often dampness, which is the principal agent in most forms of building deterioration, is found to have penetrated old, neglected buildings, resulting in timber decay and other damage. Old, empty buildings often fall victim to vandalism, the results of which may be very expensive to correct. These factors apart, the simple fact that a building is old will mean that certain items will need attention because of their natural deterioration over a long period of time. In addition, items that may still be in good condition will often need replacing because they are obsolete in their design, a good example being sanitary fixtures and fittings, boiler plant, etc.

In many rehabilitation schemes, it will be found that the development costs are directly proportional to the age and degree of neglect of the building, and very careful thought should therefore be given to going ahead with rehabilitation of old, neglected buildings. For this reason, it is vital that the first stage of any feasibility study should comprise a highly detailed survey of the building in order to establish the precise extent of work required to repair and restore the structure and fabric to a reasonable standard.

(d) The construction of the building

The construction of the existing building can have a significant effect on the cost of rehabilitation, particularly with regard to fire protection. Most old buildings have timber stairs and floors which, in large buildings, are often supported by beams and columns of timber or exposed cast-iron, and these will have to be upgraded or replaced to comply with current fire regulations. The upgrading of existing timber and cast-iron or steel elements to comply with current fire regulations, including means of escape, along with the provision of new sanitary accommodation, are usually the most costly items in the rehabilitation of older buildings and, between them, they can account for between 20% and 35% of the overall development costs.

An estimate of the development costs can be made as soon as the rehabilitation proposals have been finalized, and a detailed survey has been carried out to establish the construction and physical condition of the building as it stands. One of the most accurate ways of building up an estimate is on an elemental basis in pounds per square metre of gross floor area, using cost analyses of recent schemes of a similar nature. In this way, the costs of a number of alternative rehabilitation proposals, with different levels of specification, can be estimated for comparative analysis against each other and, of course, against the cost of demolition and new construction, in order to help establish the most viable development option for the existing building.

Testing the financial viability of different alternatives in this way is vital if the best development option is to be selected, and the exercise should always be entrusted to a firm of chartered quantity surveyors, and preferably one that specializes in carrying out feasibility studies of this nature.

1.4.3 The cost of acquiring the freehold or leasehold of the site

The amount paid to acquire a freehold or leasehold interest in a site should never exceed the difference between the capital value of the completed development and the development costs since, if it does, the developer will make a loss. It is therefore very important to assess the proper value of the site which will be determined to a large extent by the following factors:

(a) The location of the site, which will decide the potential users of the rehabilitated building
(b) The uses for which planning permission can be obtained
(c) The expected rental income from the rehabilitated building
(d) The total development costs.

1.4.4 The cost of financing the scheme

The cost of financing a scheme will depend principally on the following factors:

(a) The cost of the work
(b) The duration of the scheme
(c) The level of interest rates prevailing at the time.

Clearly, the total interest payable on money borrowed to finance a rehabilitation scheme will be significantly less than that for new construction, owing to its lower overall cost and shorter development period. In addition, when interest rates are higher, the rehabilitation option will become even more attractive, since this will result in a greater differential between the cost of financing rehabilitation and the higher cost of financing new construction schemes.

Detailed consideration of the four factors discussed above will be essential if the correct decision is to be made on the type and level of rehabilitation or, indeed, whether rehabilitation is viable at all. Of equal importance to examining all of the salient factors, is ensuring that professional designers, building surveyors and building economists with a high level of expertise in rehabilitation work are commissioned to prepare alternative schemes, carry out surveys and complete cost feasibility studies. Only if this

is done can the developer be sure of opting for the scheme that will give the best value for money, while remaining within a realistic budget.

1.5 THE AVAILABILITY OF FINANCIAL AID

The majority of rehabilitation schemes are carried out for economic reasons, and a further major incentive, therefore, and one which can make the rehabilitation option even more attractive, is the availability of financial aid. Financial aid is not available for all rehabilitation schemes, but in many cases, for example where older housing or buildings of architectural interest are concerned, or where jobs are being created, it may be possible to obtain substantial grants towards the cost of the work. The sources of financial aid for building rehabilitation are numerous, and are given detailed consideration in Chapter 6.

It is clear, therefore, that if the rehabilitation option being considered for an existing building is eligible for grant aid, and, if a grant can be obtained, the rehabilitation option will become even more attractive when compared with the alternative of demolition and new construction.

1.6 PLANNING PERMISSION MAY NOT BE REQUIRED

Under the *Town and Country Planning Act 1971*, planning permission is required for "development". However, "the carrying out of works for the maintenance, improvement or other alteration of any building, being works which affect only the *interior* of the building or which *do not materially affect the external appearance* of the building . . ." does not constitute development and therefore does not require planning permission. Thus, if the rehabilitation scheme does not affect the exterior appearance of the building, there may be no need for the developer to obtain planning permission, resulting in a further shortening of the development period, and a corresponding saving in costs.

However, even if the exterior appearance of the building is not affected, planning permission will still be required if a "material change of use" occurs: the *Use Class Order 1973* (Statutory Instrument No. 1385) designates eighteen different use classes, and any proposed change from one of these use classes to another will require planning permission. Thus, many rehabilitation schemes, even though they involve no change to the building's exterior appearance, will still require planning permission. There are, though, many examples of rehabilitation schemes which do not require planning permission, some of the most common examples being the interior upgrading and alteration of old, outdated office buildings to provide modern office accommodation: the rehabilitated building remains in the same use class and it is therefore possible to carry out extensive interior alterations without the need for planning permission, even as far as completely gutting the building and providing a new internal structure, provided the exterior appearance remains the same.

Planning permission and use classes are considered in detail in Chapter 5.

1.7 THE EFFECTS OF PLOT RATIO CONTROL

Plot ratio control, which was introduced by the Ministry of Town and Country Planning in 1948, is a device used by planners to restrict the amount of floor space provided in new buildings in relation to their site areas. For example, a plot ratio of 3:1 will restrict the floor area of a new building to three times the area of its site (see Fig. 1.1). One of the principal reasons for the introduction of plot ratio control was to limit the heights of buildings in towns and cities so as not to impair the amenities and development possibilities of surrounding sites and buildings. It is used by different planning authorities on an *ad hoc* basis to suit their own requirements and is most likely to be applied in the central areas of large towns and cities, where plot ratios are often restricted to between 3:1 and 5:1.

The application of plot ratio control in restricting the size of new developments often makes it advantageous to rehabilitate existing buildings, rather than to demolish and replace them. For example, most Victorian buildings were built to a higher plot ratio than is currently permitted by planners. Some may have a plot ratio as high as 7:1 in areas where the plot ratios for new development may well be restricted to 3 or 4:1. Thus, it is clear that the rehabilitation of such a building could result in the provision of twice as much 'new' floorspace as would be permitted if it were demolished and replaced with a new building. In such cases, where current plot ratio controls would prove restrictive, and where the existing building is suitable for adaptation to provide the accommodation the developer requires, it is therefore usually well worthwhile giving serious consideration to opting for rehabilitation rather than demolition and new construction.

1.8 LISTED BUILDING LEGISLATION

Under the *Town and Country Planning Act 1971*, the Department of the Environment has the power to place buildings of architectural or historic merit on lists, and these listed buildings receive special protection from demolition or insensitive alteration so that they may be preserved as part of our architectural heritage. At present, there are in excess of 300 000 listed buildings in Great Britain, and this number is expected to rise to half a million after the new listing, currently in progress, has been completed. Many of these listed buildings are in established prime commercial and residential locations in our older towns and cities, and it is quite likely, therefore, that a 'developable' building in such a location may have been listed, effectively ruling out demolition and leaving the developer with no choice but to opt for rehabilitation.

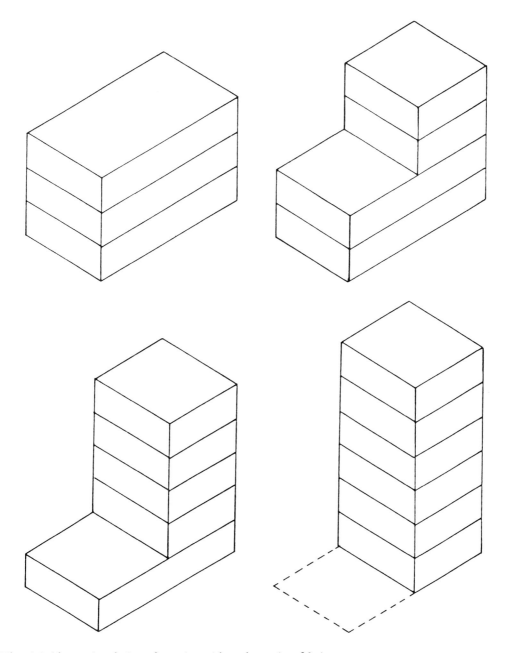

Fig. 1.1 Alternative designs for a site with a plot ratio of 3:1

Why rehabilitation?

Listed building legislation, and the constraints it places on developers, is considered in more detail, along with the other legislation affecting rehabilitation, in Chapter 5.

1.9 THE ARCHITECTURAL ADVANTAGES

There are often architectural advantages, which can be translated into financial advantages, in keeping attractive old buildings and rehabilitating them to provide modern accommodation. Many of our older buildings are far more attractive and possess greater character than their modern counterparts, having been constructed by skilled craftsmen using high quality natural materials. Such buildings are often more attractive to certain users; particularly banks, insurance companies, building societies, etc., which like to project an image of solidity, prestige and prosperity to their customers. In addition, such buildings may stand in areas where they are in close proximity to other architecturally attractive old buildings, and this adds further to their appeal and potential value, provided sensitive rehabilitation is carried out which maintains their architectural character and integrity.

1.10 THE AVAILABILITY OF THE EXISTING INFRASTRUCTURE

The medium and large scale rehabilitation of obsolete housing, carried out mainly by local authorities and housing associations, and also more recently by private developers, achieves substantial financial savings by retaining and re-using not only the houses themselves, but also the existing 'housing infrastructure'. Where new housing development takes place, not only is additional land required, but money must be found to pay for new roads, street lighting, drainage, gas and electricity, water supplies, telephone lines, etc., all of which add considerably to the cost. Where the rehabilitation option is chosen, all or most of this infrastructure already exists, and the expenditure is therefore only concerned with upgrading the houses themselves, a factor which clearly makes the rehabilitation option financially more attractive.

As well as achieving these direct financial savings, the avoidance of having to provide a new housing infrastructure also considerably reduces the development period which results in the further indirect financial savings which are discussed in Section 1.3.

1.11 THE SOCIAL ADVANTAGES

The medium and large scale rehabilitation of existing housing has important sociological advantages. One of the most disruptive aspects of the comprehensive policies of demolition and new construction during the 1960s was that established communities, which had existed for several generations, were broken up permanently. The creation of new communities is now recognized as a complex process, and the rehabilitation of existing houses, by preserving established, stable communities is therefore considered preferable to the alternative of wholesale clearance and new development.

FURTHER READING

Department of the Environment (1977) *Historic Buildings and Conservation Areas – Policy and Procedure*, Circular 23/77, HMSO, London.
Department of the Environment (1981) *Historic Buildings and Conservation Areas*, Circular 12/81, HMSO, London.
Great Britain (1972) *Town and Country Planning Act 1971*, ch. 78, HMSO, London.
Great Britain (1972) *Town and Country Planning (Amendment) Act 1972*, ch. 42, HMSO, London.
Great Britain (1972) *Town and Country Planning (Scotland) Act 1972*, ch. 52, HMSO, London.
Great Britain (1974) *Town and Country Amenities Act 1974*, ch. 32, HMSO, London.
Great Britain (1975) *Town and Country Planning (Listed Buildings and Buildings in Conservation*

Further reading

Areas) (Scotland) Regulations 1975, Statutory Instruments, 1975 No. 2069, HMSO, London.

Great Britain (1977) *Town and Country Planning (Listed Buildings and Buildings in Conservation Areas) Regulations 1977,* Statutory Instruments, 1977 No. 228, HMSO, London.

Lloyd, D. *et al.* (1979) *Save the City,* 2nd edn, Society for the Protection of Ancient Buildings, London.

Ministry of Housing and Local Government and Welsh Office (1968) *Town and Country Planning Act 1968 – Part V. Historic Buildings and Conservation,* Joint Circular 61/68 and 57/68, HMSO, London.

Chapter two

Housing rehabilitation

2.1 THE HOUSING PROBLEM

A number of widely differing reasons for rehabilitating buildings has been given in Chapter 1, but, of all those discussed, the most significant as far as housing is concerned is the poor condition of the existing housing stock. It is the unsatisfactory condition of our housing, whether it be the result of age, neglect or decay, that creates the need for rehabilitation in the first instance. All of the other factors discussed in the previous chapter are therefore secondary.

The enormous scale of the 'housing problem' in England was highlighted by the *English House Condition Survey 1981*. This comprehensive investigation into the state of all categories of permanent dwellings has revealed some alarming statistics, the most significant of which are detailed in this section. It is clear, on examining these statistics, that there is an urgent need to inject large sums of money into upgrading the existing housing stock, both now and in the foreseeable future. Indeed, the problem is so vast that housing rehabilitation has now become, and will remain, as permanent a component of the construction industry as new construction.

2.1.1 The English House Condition Survey 1981

The *English House Condition Survey 1981* was carried out in the autumn of that year by the Department of the Environment, and follows similar surveys conducted in 1976 and 1971. The results of the survey are based on an age-stratified sample of 8243 dwellings, their physical condition being measured against three main criteria: unfitness, lack of amenities, and incidence of disrepair.

In 1981 there were 18.1 million dwellings in England, of which 1.1 million were found to be unfit, 0.9 million lacked basic amenities, and 1.0 million required repairs costing in excess of £7000. Allowing for overlap between these three criteria, the total number of dwellings in 'poor condition' was 2 million. Furthermore, if the threshold for disrepair were lowered from £7000 to £2500, the total number of dwellings in poor condition would rise to 4.3 million, or 24% of all dwellings.

(a) Lack of basic amenities

In 1981, approximately 910 000 dwellings lacked one or more of the five basic amenities and, of these, some 340 000 lacked four or five. The five basic amenities are:

- The exclusive use of a w.c. inside the dwelling
- A fixed bath or shower
- A wash basin
- A kitchen sink
- A hot and cold water system serving a bath, wash basin and sink.

The amenity most frequently lacking was hot and cold water serving three points, this being missing from some 730 000 dwellings. Approximately 550 000 dwellings were without an inside w.c., and a similar number lacked a wash basin. Of those dwellings that lacked amenities 75% were built before 1919. Very few dwellings were without a sink. The absence of amenities is a greater problem in the private rented sector, with 14% of the stock lacking amenities, compared with only 3% of owner-occupied and local authority dwellings.

(b) Unfit dwellings
The *English House Condition Survey 1981* found that approximately 1.1 million dwellings (6% of the total stock) were unfit. An unfit dwelling is one deemed to be so defective in one or more of the following aspects as not to be reasonably suitable for occupation: repair, stability, freedom from damp, internal arrangement, natural lighting, ventilation, water supply, drainage and sanitary conveniences, facilities for the preparation and cooking of food, and the disposal of waste water.

Of the 1.1 million unfit dwellings, 88% were built before 1919, representing some 19% of all existing pre-1919 dwellings. Only 3% of the inter-war housing stock, together with a very small number of post-war dwellings, were adjudged unfit.

The survey revealed that the private rented sector has the greatest problem, over 16% of its dwellings being in an unfit condition, compared with only 5% of the owner-occupied stock.

(c) Dwellings in need of repair
The *English House Condition Survey 1981* found that 3.9 million dwellings, or 22% of the housing stock, needed repairs in excess of £2500, and that just over 1 million needed repairs in excess of £7000 to bring them up to a satisfactory condition. The costs of repairs are the estimated total costs which would be necessary to meet the Ten Point Improvement Grant Standard. For a dwelling to meet this standard, it must:

(i) Be substantially free from damp
(ii) Have adequate natural lighting and ventilation in each habitable room

(iii) Have adequate and safe provision throughout for artificial lighting and have sufficient electrical socket outlets for the safe and proper functioning of domestic appliances
(iv) Be provided with adequate drainage facilities
(v) Be in a stable structural condition
(vi) Have a satisfactory internal arrangement
(vii) Have satisfactory facilities for preparing and cooking food
(viii) Be provided with adequate facilities for heating
(ix) Have proper provision for the storage of food, where necessary
(x) Conform with the specifications applicable to the thermal insulation of roof spaces laid down in the Building Regulations currently in force.

The incidence of disrepair, like the other two condition criteria, is closely associated with the dwelling's age. Around 70% of the 3.9 million dwellings needing over £2500 worth of repairs had been built before 1919, and this represented over half of the pre-1919 stock. On the other hand, only 5% of the total post-war housing stock needed repairs costing over £2500. Again, the private rented housing sector had the highest proportion of dwellings in poor condition, 16% of private rented dwellings needing repairs in excess of £7000, compared with only 5% of the owner-occupied sector.

The repair costs used in the survey were calculated on the basis of mid-1981 tender costs for work in a typical Midland town.

(d) Changes in the condition of dwellings since previous surveys in 1971 and 1976
A component of the *English House Condition Survey 1981* involved revisiting all of the pre-war properties in the 1971 and 1976 surveys, plus a one-in-four sample of post-war properties in the 1976 survey. The data obtained from this part of the survey were used to determine the changes undergone by many individual dwell-

ings between 1971 and 1981, and also between 1976 and 1981. This, in turn, provided an assessment of the overall improvement/deterioration of the nation's housing stock during the period 1971–1981.

There was a significant improvement in the provision of basic amenities in dwellings between 1971 and 1981, the number of dwellings lacking one or more of the basic amenities having fallen by about two-thirds. Much of this reduction took place in the first half of the ten year period, with a fall of over 1.2 million between 1971 and 1976, compared with 0.6 million between 1976 and 1981. Overall, the total number of dwellings lacking one or more of the basic amenities reduced from 2 815 000 in 1971 to 1 531 000 in 1976 to 910 000 in 1981.

Over the country as a whole, there was little change in the number of unfit dwellings between 1971 and 1981. However, trends in the proportion of unfit dwellings were not uniform throughout the country: the northern regions underwent a substantial improvement, the south-east, including London, a deterioration, and the remainder of the country a less significant improvement. Overall, the total number of unfit dwellings reduced from 1 216 000 in 1971, to 1 162 000 in 1976, to 1 116 000 in 1981.

The number of dwellings needing repairs in excess of £7000 (at 1981 prices) increased considerably between 1976 and 1981, following only a slight change between 1971 and 1976. The total number of dwellings in a state of serious disrepair increased by about 200 000 between 1976 and 1981, representing a 22% increase on the 1976 figure. Overall, the total numbers of dwellings needing repairs in excess of £7000 decreased slightly from 864 000 in 1971 to 859 000 in 1976, and then underwent a significant increase to 1 049 000 in 1981.

Figure 2.1 summarizes the overall changes in the condition of dwellings during the period 1971–1981. While there has clearly been a discernible improvement in housing conditions, there remains considerable cause for concern. The large decline in the number of dwellings lacking one or more basic amenities is outweighed by the more serious problems of unfitness and disrepair. As stated above, there has been minimal improvement in the numbers of unfit dwellings and, far more seriously, the numbers of dwellings in serious disrepair have increased considerably. The *English House Condition Survey 1981* revealed that only 76% of all dwellings were in satisfactory condition and fit for habitation, with all amenities present, and the cost of required repairs being below £2500. It has been estimated that the cost of rectifying this problem, and bringing all dwellings up to the Ten Point Improvement Grant Standard, would be in excess of £30 billion. The problem is so severe that, even with the massive increase in Government spending on housing improvement since the results of the survey were published, it is unlikely that a permanent solution will ever be achieved. As previously stated, housing rehabilitation and improvement must therefore remain a permanent, major component of the construction industry.

2.2 THE IMPROVEMENT OF SUB-STANDARD HOUSING

The extent of the work required to improve existing houses which fail to meet modern standards, with regard to fitness, repair and amenities, will vary considerably according to their present condition. Some houses, which are in a generally good state of repair and fitness, may only require minor work, such as the installation of a missing appliance, or the insertion of a new damp-proof course. On the other hand, as the *English House Condition Survey 1981* has shown, large numbers of houses are urgently in need of major improvement.

One of the most common deficiencies requiring major improvement work, particularly in older properties, is the absence of a w.c. and/or a fixed bath. The *English House Condition Survey 1981* revealed that, in 402 000 dwellings, the only w.c. was outside the building, and that 73 000 dwellings had no w.c. at all. The Survey

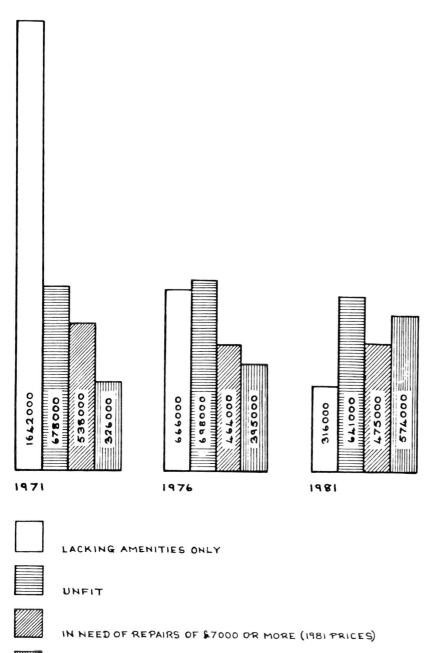

1971   1976   1981

☐ LACKING AMENITIES ONLY

▤ UNFIT

▨ IN NEED OF REPAIRS OF £7000 OR MORE (1981 PRICES)

▥ UNFIT AND IN DISREPAIR

Fig. 2.1 Changes in the condition of dwellings 1971–81

also found that 333 000 dwellings were without a fixed bath. What is required in most cases where these amenities do not exist is the provision of a new bathroom, either within the existing building, or in a purpose-built extension.

Another common deficiency found in older dwellings is the lack of adequate kitchen accommodation for the preparation and cooking of food. Since proper kitchen accommodation is one of the standard criteria by which 'fitness' is assessed, this too will require attention where older houses are the subject of improvement.

Figures 2.2, 2.3 and 2.4 show typical examples of major improvement work to existing dwellings to provide modern amenities where

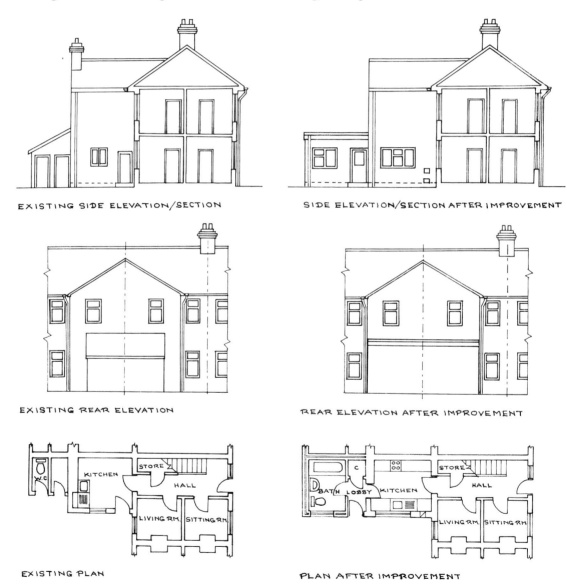

Fig. 2.2 Rehabilitation of adjoining pair of terraced houses

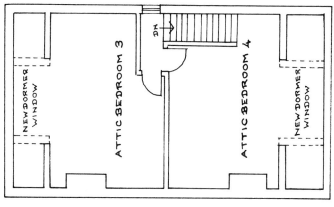

THIRD FLOOR (ATTIC) PLAN

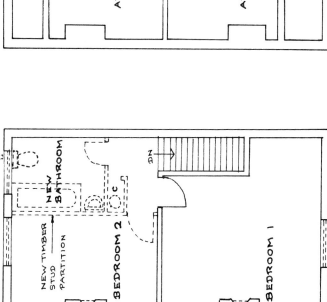

FIRST FLOOR PLAN

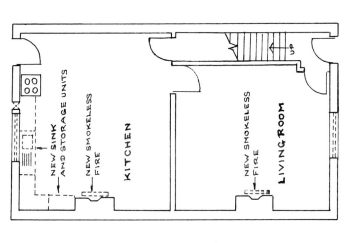

GROUND FLOOR PLAN

Fig. 2.3 Rehabilitation of large terraced house

15

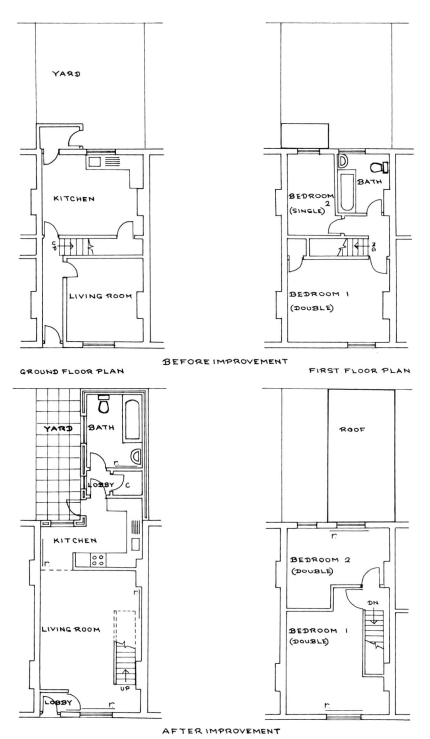

YARD

KITCHEN

cp

LIVING ROOM

GROUND FLOOR PLAN

BEDROOM 2 (SINGLE)

BATH

BEDROOM 1 (DOUBLE)

FIRST FLOOR PLAN

BEFORE IMPROVEMENT

YARD

BATH

LOBBY c

KITCHEN

LIVING ROOM

UP

LOBBY

GROUND FLOOR PLAN

ROOF

BEDROOM 2 (DOUBLE)

DN

BEDROOM 1 (DOUBLE)

FIRST FLOOR PLAN

AFTER IMPROVEMENT

Fig. 2.4 Rehabilitation of small terraced house

previously these were inadequate, unfit or non-existent. Where there is insufficient space within the existing dwelling to provide the new facilities, a purpose-built extension will be necessary and Fig. 2.2 shows such a scheme applied to two adjacent terraced houses. In this example, which is typical of large numbers of dwellings in older towns and cities, the existing outhouses (which included an outside w.c.) have been demolished and replaced by a single storey extension containing the new bathroom and lobby. The existing kitchen has been gutted and fully modernized, and the original window replaced by a larger one.

With larger houses, where there is sufficient internal space available, the new amenities are generally provided within the existing interior. Figure 2.3 shows an improvement scheme in this category, involving a large through-terraced house. The existing kitchen has been re-fitted with modern appliances and storage units, and a new bathroom provided by partitioning one of the existing first floor bedrooms. Additional improvement work, including the provision of new windows and heaters, has also been carried out.

Figure 2.4 shows a more elaborate scheme, where the whole interior of the existing terraced house has been gutted and modernized, with the addition of a built-on extension at the rear. The provision of a new bathroom in the ground floor extension has allowed the second bedroom to be upgraded from a single to a double, therefore increasing the possible occupancy of the house. In addition, a new modern kitchen has been provided, and the living room area enlarged by approximately 60%. A new central heating system has also been installed.

These three examples describe typical designs for major housing improvement work. The actual choice of design will, however, depend on the particular case, and the constraints that the layout of the existing dwelling imposes. There may well be several feasible solutions for any one particular dwelling, and it is desirable that, in reaching a final design decision, practical advice

is sought from a builder who has experience in housing rehabilitation work. In this way, the invaluable technical expertise and knowledge of the builder can be used to achieve the most practicable and cost-effective design.

In addition to providing modern amenities, the improvement of sub-standard housing embraces a wide range of other operations aimed at overcoming problems of unfitness and disrepair. These operations may be designed to upgrade dwellings to, or beyond, the minimum acceptable standards. For example, the minimum standard with regard to thermal insulation is the provision of adequate roof-space insulation, but a higher quality improvement scheme might also involve upgrading the thermal insulation of the external walls. Disrepair is a considerable problem, with, as previously stated, 3.9 million dwellings needing repairs in excess of £2500. In addition, a further 3.1 million dwellings are in need of repairs between £1000 and £2500.

Typical operations commonly associated with the upgrading of sub-standard housing to, or beyond, the minimum acceptable standards of fitness and repair include:

(a) The insertion of new damp-proof courses
(b) Preventing rainwater penetration through walls using a range of internal or external treatments
(c) Total re-roofing of pitched roofs, including the addition of sarking felt, where the existing roof has deteriorated beyond reasonable repair, allowing wind and rainwater penetration
(d) Total re-roofing, or localized repair of flat roofs suffering from rainwater penetration
(e) Upgrading the thermal insulation of roofs, or providing roofspace insulation for the first time.
(f) Upgrading the thermal insulation of external walls using internal dry linings or exterior insulating treatments.
(g) Providing new interior surface finishes to walls, floors and ceilings where the existing

have deteriorated beyond reasonable repair

(h) Preventing condensation within dwellings by means of improved thermal insulation, heating and ventilation, and the addition of vapour barriers

(i) Eradicating fungal and insect attack, including all necessary replacement and/or repair of affected timbers

(j) Strengthening of existing timber floors where they have been weakened by decay, or where increased loads are to be applied.

Clearly, the above list does not embrace the whole spectrum of upgrading operations met in housing rehabilitation. It does, however, cover the most common and important aspects, all of which are described in detail in Chapter 4.

FURTHER READING

Benson, J. *et al.* (1980) *Housing Rehabilitation Handbook,* Architectural Press, London.

Benson, J. *et al.* (1984) Housing rehabilitation: update. *Architects' Journal,* **179** (8–13) 22 February–28 March 1984.

Crook, T. (1984) An enhanced role for the private sector. *The Planner,* **70** (4) April 1984, 19–21.

Department of the Environment (1973) *House Condition Survey 1971 England and Wales,* HMSO, London.

Department of the Environment (1978) *English House Condition Survey 1976,* Part 1. Report of the Physical Condition Survey, HMSO, London.

Department of the Environment (1979) *English House Condition Survey 1976,* Part 2. Report of the Social Survey, HMSO, London.

Department of the Environment (1982) *English House Condition Survey 1981,* Part 1. Report of the Physical Condition Survey, HMSO, London.

Department of the Environment (1983) *English House Condition Survey 1981,* Part 2. Report of the Interview and Local Authority Survey, HMSO, London.

Gibson, M. and Perry J. (1984) Housing renewal in crisis. *The Planner,* **70** (4) April 1984, 8–12.

Jones, P. (1984) Privately funded urban renewal in the north west. *The Planner,* **70** (4) April 1984, 21–22.

Chapter three

Rehabilitation of non-domestic buildings

3.1 THE KEY FACTORS

It was stated in the previous chapter that of all the reasons for rehabilitating buildings, the most significant as far as housing is concerned is the poor physical condition of the existing housing stock. With other building types, however, the need for rehabilitation is more likely to be based on the key factors of obsolescence or redundancy, often in common with poor physical condition.

3.1.1 Obsolescence

One of the principal reasons for the rehabilitation of non-domestic buildings is obsolescence. The majority of old industrial buildings were purpose designed to manufacture specific products using the particular industrial techniques available at the time. Since these buildings were first constructed, the products of industry, and the techniques used to manufacture them, have changed considerably, leaving large numbers of factories obsolete, and unsuitable for the needs of modern manufacturing industry. This has meant that manufacturers have had to update their products and methods and either move out to new purpose-designed factories built outside towns and cities, or rehabilitate their existing obsolete premises. Many of these obsolete industrial buildings may have been well maintained throughout their working lives and, in such cases, their physical condition should not be a problem. Where a building is merely obsolete and there are no (or only a few)

problems with regard to its physical condition, it is likely to be an excellent proposition for economic rehabilitation and re-use, provided its geographical location is suitable. Many obsolete industrial buildings, unlike today's modern factories, are located very close to existing town and city centres and are therefore ideal for a wide range of viable re-uses. The most common re-use of obsolete industrial buildings, particularly where they are close to town and city centres, is for office accommodation. Other uses include shops, sports halls, community centres and housing, and only a small percentage are re-used for manufacturing activities.

In addition to old factories, large numbers of old office buildings have also become obsolete as a result of considerable advances in office technology, and the trend away from permanent interior sub-division in favour of 'open-plan' arrangements. Employees working in offices have also come to expect a far more sophisticated working environment, including a higher standard of interior decor, air conditioning, lifts and quality sanitary accommodation. Many old office buildings, some constructed as recently as the 1950s and 1960s, have therefore become outdated and obsolete and are ripe for economic rehabilitation and re-use. Because of their locations, the majority continue to be used as offices after rehabilitation.

3.1.2 Redundancy

A further major reason for the rehabilitation of

non-domestic buildings, and one which is sometimes confused with that previously discussed, is redundancy. An old factory building that is obsolete because of its age could also be said to have become redundant. However, there is a difference between the two terms, and this is best illustrated by reference to redundant churches. An existing church may be in excellent structural condition, and have a perfectly suitable design and layout, but if it is no longer needed owing to a significant decrease in the local congregation, then it has become redundant or superfluous, despite its suitability as a church. Any building that is no longer needed and is superfluous to requirements, despite its good condition and suitability for the existing purpose, is therefore redundant, and there are large numbers of redundant factories, schools, churches, agricultural buildings, railway stations, mills, warehouses and numerous other types of building that are ripe for economic rehabilitation and re-use.

3.1.3 Poor physical condition

The third major reason for the rehabilitation of non-domestic buildings can be attributed to poor physical condition. As with old housing, many non-domestic buildings are unfit owing to lack of proper maintenance, and must therefore be repaired if they are to continue in use. Generally, occupied buildings tend to be well maintained, and poor physical condition is most often associated with buildings that have been vacated because of obsolescence or redundancy. If such a building stands empty for a long period, then neglect, vandalism and the constant effect of the elements can lead to rapid deterioration. This may often require considerable expenditure in repairing and reinstating the building's structure and fabric, and there can be a significant difference between the cost of rehabilitating a building that has been empty and neglected for several years, and one that has been occupied and properly maintained. It is therefore essential that the developer commissions a detailed survey of

the building under consideration to determine its true condition and likely repair costs, since these could add a considerable amount to the overall cost of rehabilitation.

3.2 THE SCALE OF REDEVELOPMENT OPTIONS

It has been shown in Chapter 1, and in Section 3.1 above, that there are many reasons for, and advantages to be gained from, rehabilitating old buildings. It is understandable, therefore, that developers, whether they be individuals or large property companies, are likely to focus their attention on existing obsolete or redundant buildings as a means of providing 'new' accommodation. The most important and far-reaching decision that the developer must make, once a suitable building has been found, will be the extent, or degree, of rehabilitation. The rehabilitation of existing buildings can be executed in varying degrees, ranging from the least drastic option of 'low key' rehabilitation, where all or most of the existing building is retained and merely upgraded, to the most drastic option of leaving only the facade standing, with the erection of a completely new structure behind. An even more drastic *redevelopment* option, of course, would be to completely demolish the existing building, and erect an entirely new building in its place.

Numerous intermediate solutions exist and their relationships can be shown on a scale of redevelopment options which ranges from the least to the most drastic:

(a) Retention of the entire existing building structure, together with its internal subdivisions, and upgrading of interior finishes, services and sanitary accommodation. In the most low key of rehabilitation schemes, existing stairs would be upgraded in preference to installing lifts, and simple heating systems would be used, in conjunction with natural ventilation.

(b) Retention of the entire existing external

envelope, including the roof, and most of the interior, with minor internal structural alterations, and upgrading of interior finishes, services and sanitary accommodation. The structural alterations might involve the demolition of some interior subdivisions, or the insertion of new staircases, and possibly lift shafts.

Park House, Leeds, described in Chapter 7, is a typical example of this type of 'low key' rehabilitation.

(c) Retention of the entire existing external envelope, including the roof, with major internal structural alterations and upgrading of finishes, services and sanitary accommodation. The major internal structural alterations might include the insertion of new reinforced concrete stairs, lift installations, extensive demolition of interior structural walls, or the insertion of new floors where the original storey heights permit.

(d) Retention of all the building's envelope walls, and complete demolition of its roof and interior, with the construction of an entirely new building behind the retained facade. This option might occur with an isolated building where the entire external facade walls are worthy of retention, but where the developer requires totally new accommodation, unconstrained by existing internal elements.

St Paul's House, Leeds, described in Chapter 7, is an example of this type of very drastic rehabilitation.

(e) Retention of only two or three elevations of the existing building, and complete demolition of the remainder, with the construction of an entirely new building behind the retained facade walls. This option might occur where the building is situated on a corner site.

(f) Retention of only one elevation, a single facade wall, of the existing building, and complete demolition of the remainder with the construction of an entirely new building behind the retained facade. This option

might occur where the building has only one important facade, which is the main street elevation adjoining buildings on each side.

(g) The most drastic *redevelopment* option would be not to opt for rehabilitation, but to totally demolish the existing building and replace it with a new building.

In the vast majority of building rehabilitation schemes, options (a), (b) and (c) are the most common, since these are nearly always the most cost effective. On the other hand, options (d), (e) and (f) can often cost more than total demolition and new construction, and are therefore less economically attractive. These 'facade retention' options are almost exclusively associated with listed buildings, where one or more external elevations *must* be preserved because of their intrinsic architectural or historic interest.

The redevelopment option chosen will depend on a variety of economic, legislative and other constraints, together with the specific requirements of the developer. For example, option (a) on the scale may be, and often is, the most desirable because it will be significantly cheaper than the other options, together with the advantage that it will produce the 'new' accommodation in a much shorter time. On the other hand, option (a) might be the least desirable owing to the design limitations of the existing layout, and the restrictions imposed by having to make the altered building comply with current fire regulations. Another important legislative constraint, mentioned briefly above, is that concerning listed buildings. If the building is contained in the statutory lists of buildings of special architectural or historic interest, then it is certain that the rehabilitation option will be significantly restricted by *having* to preserve certain features, such as the external facade, an ornate staircase, or an ornate plastered ceiling. The effects of listed building legislation and many other statutory constraints are given detailed consideration in Chapter 5.

As with housing, the rehabilitation of the

other building types also involves a range of other operations aimed at overcoming problems of unfitness and disrepair. Typical operations that are commonly associated with the rehabilitation of obsolete and redundant buildings have been listed at the end of the previous chapter and are described in detail in Chapter 4.

3.3 THE AVAILABILITY OF BUILDINGS FOR REHABILITATION

It has already been shown in Chapter 1 that there are considerable advantages to be gained from rehabilitating existing buildings in preference to new construction, and it is clear, therefore, that it will be in the interests of developers to find and give serious consideration to making use of obsolete and redundant buildings.

It is known that there are vast numbers of obsolete and redundant buildings available, and that there are developers seeking suitable properties to rehabilitate. The problem is finding a 'match' between a specific developer and a specific building, and this could best be achieved by the availability to developers of properly compiled and co-ordinated information on the numbers, types and locations of suitable buildings. Unlike housing, where considerable expenditure and effort is put into producing regular, detailed statistics (see Chapter 2), there are no national statistics available on other building types. Quantifying the availability of obsolete and redundant buildings is also aggravated by the fact that there is a very wide range of different building types and sizes, and the production of detailed national statistics would be an enormous task.

In the absence of national statistics, the developer is therefore faced with how to go about finding a suitable building, preferably without having to physically go out and look for one, although in many cases the developer might well have to do this.

Despite the lack of properly compiled and co-ordinated national statistics, certain bodies have succeeded in producing schedules of obsolete and redundant buildings, although these tend to be very restricted, either geographically, or according to building type.

Details of the information provided by a number of different bodies are given below with the aim of indicating possible starting points that developers might consider in their search for buildings suitable for rehabilitation and re-use.

3.3.1 Buildings preservation trusts/local authorities

There are 86 buildings preservation trusts throughout the United Kingdom, and one of their principal concerns is the preservation of threatened historic buildings that have become obsolete or redundant. It is therefore likely that the local trust will know of many of the older buildings within its area that might be suitable for rehabilitation and re-use. The majority of the trusts operate in close liaison with local authorities, and the local planning authority's Conservation Officer is usually a good initial contact for any developer wishing to enquire about available buildings. Alternatively, enquiries about the existence of buildings preservation trusts in particular areas can be made to the Civic Trust, which keeps a register of all trusts throughout the United Kingdom.

Further information:

> Local authority planning department
> Conservation Officer
> or
> The Civic Trust
> 17 Carlton House Terrace
> London SW1Y 5AW
> Tel: 01–930–0914

In the majority of cases, the information provided on the availability of buildings that might be available for rehabilitation and re-use will only be informal and verbal, but a number of the preservation trusts are now, with the help of local authorities, publishing regularly updated schedules of 'threatened' historic buildings. This formal compilation and co-ordination of the relevant information is also becoming more widespread, since it has been found to be highly effective as a means of finding new users for old buildings and providing potential developers with the information they are seeking.

One limitation to the information provided by preservation trusts is that the buildings with which they are concerned are nearly always listed buildings. However, as stated in Chapter 5, when the current process of listing is completed, there will be approximately half a million listed buildings in Great Britain, many of which, as and when they do become obsolete or redundant, are ideal for rehabilitation and re-use. It should also be pointed out that not all of the 'threatened' buildings included in the schedules produced by buildings preservations trusts are necessarily empty or available for purchase, although many of them are, and the schedules are, therefore, a potentially useful source of information for developers.

The schedule of threatened historic buildings produced by Hampshire Buildings Preservation Trust is an excellent example of well co-ordinated, regularly updated relevant information on old buildings. The trust was one of the first to publish a formal schedule of threatened buildings and, for each entry, the following information is given: address, owner, grade of Listing where applicable, nature of threat, preferred use, and, finally, the trust's comments on the current situation. The tenth schedule published by the trust listed some 260 buildings that were unoccupied, in whole or in part, or in need of repair. The schedule is continuously reviewed by updating every two months and is available to any person or organization having a genuine interest.

Further information:

Hampshire Buildings Preservation Trust
The Castle
Winchester
Hampshire
Tel: (0962) 5411

Another preservation trust which produces similar information to the above is the Derbyshire Historic Buildings Trust. Its schedule of historic buildings ". . . thought to be empty, neglected or in need of repair" contains some 150–200 entries, and is updated every 12–18 months. The schedule is available to any person or organization having a genuine interest.

Further information:

Derbyshire Historic Buildings Trust
c/o County Planning Department
County Offices
Matlock
Derbyshire
Tel: (0629) 3411

The Kirklees Historic Buildings Trust, which was initially set up by Kirklees County Council, embarked on a Manpower Services Commission Funded Scheme in early 1986 to produce a schedule of threatened historic buildings within its area. It is intended that the schedule will contain similar information to that produced by the Hampshire Buildings Preservation Trust, with the ultimate aim of 'saving' and finding new uses for all threatened historic buildings within the area covered by the trust.

Further information:

Kirklees Historic Buildings Trust
PO Box B95
Civic Centre
Market Street
Huddersfield, HD1 2NA
Tel: (0484) 22133

Only a relatively small number of buildings preservation trusts produce formal schedules like those described above, and, as stated earlier, in the absence of such information, the local planning authority's Conservation Officer will usually be an excellent source of information on buildings that might be suitable for rehabilitation.

3.3.2 The North West Civic Trust

One of the most ambitious schemes that has been

set up to provide information on buildings suitable for rehabilitation is the North West Civic Trust's Regional Information Service on Vacant Buildings.

The aim of the service is to help the owners of older properties find appropriate purchasers, and to assist those who are looking for buildings in which to invest, in the fields of housing, leisure, commerce and industry. The Information Service provides the following:

(a) A comprehensive Digest is published quarterly giving details of a wide range of vacant properties which are currently on offer and suitable for rehabilitation. The descriptive account of each building includes the current condition of the property, estimated costs of repair where these are known, the planning background, and possible categories of re-use. In most cases, drawings showing the exterior of the building and typical floor plans are also included.

(b) A 'matching up' facility, whereby companies with particular needs in the property market can be directed towards appropriate buildings.

(c) A general advisory service providing information on the sources of grant aid, details of successful restoration schemes, etc.

(d) The preparation of feasibility studies for the restoration or conversion of redundant buildings, providing an assessment of appropriate future uses with estimates of repair costs where these are required.

(e) The opportunity for redundant or vacant buildings to be advertised in the Digest, as a means of reaching a wide variety of prospective purchasers.

(f) The opportunity for companies in the property world (builders, contractors, architects, etc.) to advertise their services through the quarterly Digest.

The information and facilities provided by this service are by far the most comprehensive and potentially valuable to be found throughout the country, and it is hoped that the example set by the North West Civic Trust will be followed elsewhere. Any developer looking for a suitable property in the north-west of England is therefore strongly advised to contact the trust.

The quarterly Digest, and access to the other facilities provided by the Regional Information Service, are available by annual subscription.

Further information:

The North West Civic Trust
The Environmental Institute
Greaves School
Bolton Road
Swinton
Manchester M27 2UX
Tel: 061-794-9314

3.3.3 The Church Commissioners

It was stated in Chapter 1 that more than 1000 Anglican churches have been made redundant during the past 15 years, and that a large proportion of these are still unused. More recently, however, developers have begun to realize the rehabilitation potential of redundant churches, many of which have been converted into housing (see St Lukes Church, Harrogate, Chapter 7), offices (see Headingley Hill Church, Leeds, Chapter 7), recreational buildings, community centres, theatres, art galleries and small manufacturing units.

There is, however, still a large stock of vacant redundant churches, and still more are likely to be declared redundant in the future, and developers would be well advised to examine this source of 'raw material' for rehabilitation.

A list containing the basic details, possible re-uses and planning information for all redundant Anglican churches is kept by the Church Commissioners. The Commissioners will send information from the list to interested parties, along with details of whom to contact in the local Diocesan office for detailed information and negotiations.

Further information:

> The Church Commissioners
> 1 Millbank
> London SW1P 3JZ
> Tel: 01-222-7010

3.3.4 The Methodist Church Property Division

Until recently the number of Methodist churches declared surplus to requirements was approximately 100 annually, but this has now reduced to 60 or 70. As with Anglican churches, Methodist churches often provide an ideal basis for rehabilitation and re-use, situated as they are near to centres of population.

If the managing trustees of a local church decide that it is no longer required, they must seek permission to dispose of it from the Methodist Church Property Division, which meets three times each year. The managing trustees of the church are then responsible for dealing with the sale, which is normally carried out through a local estate agent.

Further information:

> The Methodist Church Property Division
> Central Buildings
> Oldham Street
> Manchester M1 1JQ
> Tel: 061-236-5194

3.3.5 British Rail Property Board

Over 3500 railway stations have been closed throughout Great Britain, and many have been successfully rehabilitated for a wide range of new uses, including restaurants, pubs, sports centres, offices and museums. Many old stations still stand empty and, inevitably, a number of British Rail's vast stock of stations and other buildings are made redundant annually.

'Non-operational' buildings are either let or sold by British Rail's Regional Property Boards, all of which keep detailed records of the properties available. Each Regional Property Board is responsible for marketing its own redundant properties, either itself or through estate agents. Properties are advertised locally or nationally, depending on their size and importance.

Further information:

> British Rail Property Board:
> Eastern Region (London).
> Tel: 01-837-4200 ext 4828
>   01-837-3442 (24 hour service)
> Southern Region (London).
> Tel: 01-922-6284
> South Western Region (Bristol).
> Tel: 0272-24191, ext. 2720
> Midland Region (Birmingham).
> Tel: 021-643-4444, ext. 2293
> North Western Region (Manchester).
> Tel: 061-228-2141, ext. 2400
> North Eastern Region (York).
> Tel: 0904-53022, ext. 2347
> Scottish Region (Glasgow).
> Tel: 041-332-9811, ext. 2366

FURTHER READING

Department of the Environment (1977) *Historic Buildings and Conservation Areas – Policy and Procedure*, Circular 23/77, HMSO, London.

Department of the Environment (1981) *Historic Buildings and Conservation Areas*, Circular 12/81, HMSO, London.

Eley, P. and Worthington, J. (1984) *Industrial Rehabilitation: The Use of Redundant Buildings for Small Enterprises*, Architectural Press, London.

Eley, P. *et al.* (1984) Industrial refurbishment: update *Architects' Journal*, **180** (32, 36–39), 8 August, 5–26 September 1984.

Highfield, D. (1982) *The Construction of New Buildings Behind Historic Facades: the Technical and Philosophical Implications*, M.Phil. thesis, University of York.

Highfield, D. (1983) Keeping up facades. *Building*, **245** (39), 30 September 1983, 40–41.

Highfield, D. (1984) Building behind historic facades. *Building Technology and Management*, **22**(1), January 1984, 18–25.

Chapter four

The technical aspects of building rehabilitation and re-use

4.1 GENERAL

All types of rehabilitation, in adapting buildings to meet new uses and modern standards, will necessarily involve making some physical changes to the existing. In 'low-key' rehabilitation this may only involve relatively minor upgrading of the fabric to produce better quality interior finishes. At the other end of the scale, however, the more drastic forms of rehabilitation, in addition to upgrading the existing fabric, may also involve structural work, such as the removal of loadbearing elements or the insertion of new floors. It may also be necessary to carry out repair and maintenance work, which can be extensive if the building has been neglected over a long period. A further aspect of considerable importance is ensuring that the building complies with current regulations where applicable, and this invariably requires the physical upgrading of certain elements, particularly with regard to fire protection.

The more important technical problems met in rehabilitation work will now be considered, together with the practical solutions that can be used to overcome them.

4.2 UPGRADING THE FIRE RESISTANCE OF EXISTING ELEMENTS OF STRUCTURE

As explained in Chapter 5, it will be necessary to comply with certain parts of the Building Regulations in virtually all categories of rehabilitation work, even where no structural alterations are envisaged.

One part of the Regulations, affecting the vast majority of rehabilitation schemes, is Part B3: (Internal fire spread (structure)). Compliance with Part B3 will almost certainly include upgrading the fire resistance of some existing elements of structure, and in older buildings, with many exposed timber, steel and cast iron elements, the upgrading work and corresponding expenditure can be considerable.

To comply with Regulation B3, loadbearing elements of structure (which include structural frames, beams, columns, internal and external loadbearing walls, floors and galleries), must have at least the fire resistance given in the tables contained in "Approved Document B" to the Regulations (see Section 5.3.1). The tables give required minimum fire resistances from half an hour to four hours, depending on the building's purpose group and size.

A large proportion of older buildings that are suitable for rehabilitation to new uses contain elements of structure which, by today's standards, fall far below the required performance with regard to fire resistance. Such elements will need either to be replaced with new construction of the required fire resistance or, more usually, since it is significantly less expensive, upgraded by some form of additional treatment to ensure that they comply with the Regulations.

Before considering possible upgrading solutions, it is essential to understand the basic principles and meaning of 'fire resistance'.

4.2.1 The principles of fire resistance

British Standard 476 Part 8 : 1972 (*Test methods and criteria for the fire resistance of elements of building construction*) lays down three specific criteria against which the fire resistance of any element can be measured. They are stability, integrity and insulation:

- Stability: for non-loadbearing constructions, failure occurs when the test specimen collapses. For loadbearing constructions, failure is related to collapse and the ability still to carry loads.
- Integrity: failure occurs when cracks and other openings exist through which flame or hot gases can pass.
- Insulation: failure occurs when the temperature of the unexposed (to fire) surface increases by more than 140°C above the initial temperature, or by more than 180°C, regardless of the initial temperature.

The procedures of the various tests, which must be carried out on properly made-up specimens of the constructions being evaluated under strictly controlled conditions, are laid down in BS 476 Part 8 : 1972 and the results are stated in minutes. The fire resistance of an element is the time in minutes until failure first occurs under *any one* of the three criteria. It should be noted that the test methods specified in BS 476 Part 8 : 1972 are currently under revision and in due course will be replaced by BS 476 Parts 20 to 23.

The two most common fire resistance upgrading requirements in rehabilitation work involve timber floors and unprotected beams and columns of steel or, in older buildings, cast iron.

4.2.2 Upgrading the fire resistance of timber floors

The most common example of the need to upgrade existing timber floors occurs in the large numbers of old factory and warehouse buildings of 'traditional' construction that were erected in the latter half of last century and the first part of this century. It has already been stated that such buildings form a large proportion of those that lend themselves to rehabilitation and adaptation to modern uses, and therefore the upgrading of their timber floors is a common problem. In the majority of these utilitarian industrial buildings, the undersides of floors did not receive a ceiling finish and so they merely comprise floorboarding on timber joists left exposed on the underside. Such floors come nowhere near the fire resistance standards required by modern regulations and they therefore require extensive upgrading. In addition, many such floors have plain-edge boarding which is often found to have distorted over the years, leaving gaps, which, in the absence of a ceiling beneath, render the floor almost totally ineffective as a fire barrier. In most cases the fire resistance of the existing timber floors will need to be upgraded to half an hour or one hour, depending on the purpose group and size of the building.

Another rehabilitation example where upgrading of existing timber floors is commonplace, is the conversion of large single dwellings into self-contained flats or maisonettes. Here, the focus for attention is the floors that will separate the newly-created occupancies and these will need to be upgraded to half an hour fire resistance in two-storey buildings and one hour in buildings of three or more storeys. In all cases, any floor over a basement storey must have one hour fire resistance. Where an existing dwelling is being converted, it is clear that the floors requiring upgrading will already have some form of ceiling finish; in many older dwellings, of wood lath and plaster. The existing ceiling will, therefore, already provide some degree of fire resistance and generally the upgrading treatment will not need to be as extensive as with industrial-type floors comprising exposed joists.

(a) Adding a fire resisting layer beneath the existing joists or ceiling

There are numerous techniques and materials available for use in upgrading the fire resistance of existing timber floors. The majority involve providing a new ceiling, where originally the joists were exposed, or an extra layer to the underside of the existing ceiling. In some cases it is also necessary to provide a protective layer on top of the existing floorboards or between the floor joists. Some typical practical upgrading techniques for a variety of existing floor constructions are given in Tables 4.1–4.4 and illustrated in Figs 4.1–4.4, along with the fire resistances that can be achieved. Several of the techniques involve the use of proprietary materials and descriptions of these are also given at the end of this section.

(b) Filling the void between the existing floor surface and ceiling

In many rehabilitation schemes, and particularly those involving buildings of architectural or historic interest, the existing ceilings may comprise ornate plasterwork which must be retained at all costs. The fire upgrading techniques described in (a) above will not, therefore, be suitable, since they would involve either removing or covering up the existing ceiling. The addition of a fire-resisting layer to the floor surface above the ceiling is generally inappropriate and inconvenient, and thus, the only remaining means of providing the required fire resistance is by filling the void between the existing floor surface and ornate ceiling with a suitable fire-resisting material.

Tilcon foamed perlite is a site-mixed material, produced from expanded perlite lightweight aggregate, a water-based aerated foam, inorganic hydraulic binders and special additives, which can be pumped into the floor void to upgrade the fire resistance of existing timber floors. The material is produced on site using a

Table 4.1 Treatments for upgrading the fire resistance of an existing floor construction of plain edge floorboards, 22 mm thick on timber joists not exceeding 38 mm wide; no ceiling

Upgrading treatment		Resulting fire resistance
1.	Expanded metal lathing nailed to joists with gypsum plaster finish 16 mm thick	$\frac{1}{2}$ hour
2.	Expanded metal lathing nailed to joists with vermiculite-gypsum plaster finish 12.5 mm thick	$\frac{1}{2}$ hour
*3.	Plasterboard 12.5 mm thick nailed to joists with gypsum plaster finish 12.5 mm thick	$\frac{1}{2}$ hour
4.	2 layers of plasterboard nailed to joists with joints staggered, total thickness 25 mm	$\frac{1}{2}$ hour
*5.	Hardboard sheet 3 mm thick nailed to floorboards. Supalux board 6 mm thick screwed to joists	$\frac{1}{2}$ hour
*6.	Hardboard sheet 3 mm thick nailed to floorboards. Supalux board 12 mm thick screwed to joists and overlaid with 25 mm mineral wool mat (density 20 kg/m^3)	1 hour
*7.	Vicuclad board 25 mm thick screwed or nailed to joists with Vicuclad strips cemented behind all joists	1 hour

*See Fig. 4.1.

suitable mixer and foam generator, and pump-injected directly into the void after removing selected floorboards. Simple steel tongues are secured to the sides of the floor joists to provide additional retention of the material, which sets

Upgrading the fire resistance

Table 4.2 Treatments for upgrading the fire resistance of an existing floor construction of tongued and grooved floorboards not less than 16 mm thick on timber joists not exceeding 38 mm wide; no ceiling

Upgrading treatment	Resulting fire resistance
1. Expanded metal lathing nailed to joists with gypsum plaster finish 16 mm thick	$\frac{1}{2}$ hour
2. Plasterboard 9.5 mm thick nailed to joists with gypsum plaster finish 12.5 mm thick	$\frac{1}{2}$ hour
*3. Plasterboard 12.5 mm thick nailed to joists with gypsum plaster finish 5 mm thick	$\frac{1}{2}$ hour
*4. 2 layers of plasterboard nailed to joists with joints staggered, total thickness 22 mm	$\frac{1}{2}$ hour
5. Expanded metal lathing nailed to joists with gypsum plaster finish 22 mm thick	1 hour
*6. Expanded metal lathing nailed to joists with vermiculite-gypsum plaster finish 12.5 mm thick	1 hour
7. Plasterboard 9.5 mm thick nailed to joists with vermiculite-gypsum plaster finish 12.5 mm thick	1 hour
*8. Supalux board 12 mm thick screwed to joists and overlaid with 25 mm mineral wool mat (density 20 kg/m³)	1 hour
9. Vicuclad board 25 mm thick screwed or nailed to joists with Vicuclad strips cemented behind all joints	1 hour

*See Fig. 4.2.

Table 4.3 Treatments for upgrading the fire resistance of an existing floor construction of tongued and grooved floorboards not less than 22 mm thick on timber joists not less than 175 mm x 50 mm; no ceiling

Upgrading treatment	Resulting fire resistance
1. Expanded metal lathing nailed to joists with gypsum plaster finish 16 mm thick	$\frac{1}{2}$ hour
*2. Expanded metal lathing nailed to joists with sprayed Limpet mineral-fibre finish 13 mm thick	$\frac{1}{2}$ hour
*3. Plasterboard 9.5 mm thick nailed to joists with gypsum plaster finish 12.5 mm thick	$\frac{1}{2}$ hour
4. Plasterboard 12.5 mm thick nailed to joists with gypsum plaster finish 5 mm thick	$\frac{1}{2}$ hour
5. 2 layers of plasterboard nailed to joists with joints staggered, total thickness 19 mm	$\frac{1}{2}$ hour
*6. Expanded metal lathing nailed to joists with sprayed Limpet mineral-fibre finish 22 mm thick	1 hour
7. Plasterboard 9.5 mm thick nailed to joists with vermiculite-gypsum plaster finish 12.5 mm thick	1 hour
*8. Supalux board 9 mm thick screwed to joists through 12 mm × 75 mm Supalux fillets and overlaid with 25 mm mineral wool mat (density 20 kg/m³)	1 hour
9. Vicuclad board 25 mm thick screwed or nailed to joists with Vicuclad strips cemented behind all joints	1 hour

*See Fig. 4.3.

Table 4.4 Treatments for upgrading the fire resistance of an existing floor construction of plain edge floorboards 22 mm thick on timber joists not exceeding 38 mm wide; wood lath and plaster ceiling 16 mm thick

Upgrading treatment	Resulting fire resistance
*1. Plasterboard 12.5 mm thick nailed to joists through existing ceiling	$\frac{1}{2}$ hour
*2. Hardboard sheet 3 mm thick nailed to floorboards. Supalux board 9 mm thick screwed to joists through existing ceiling	$\frac{1}{2}$ hour
*3. Plasterboard 9.5 mm thick nailed to joists through existing ceiling with gypsum plaster finish 9 mm thick	1 hour
*4. Hardboard sheet 3 mm thick nailed to floorboards. Supalux board 9 mm thick backed by 25 mm mineral wool mat (density 20 kg/m³) screwed through 12 mm × 50 mm Supalux fillets to joists through existing ceiling	1 hour

*See Fig. 4.4.

and cures to a solid light grey honeycombed matrix.

Official fire tests have shown that existing lath and plaster ceilings, even where they have heavy ornate mouldings, give less than half an hour fire resistance. The insertion of Tilcon foamed perlite into the floor cavity, to a depth of 175 mm, will increase the fire resistance of such a floor to one hour (stability, integrity and insulation). The upgrading of an existing timber floor using this technique is illustrated in Fig. 4.5.

Foamed perlite can, of course, be used to upgrade any type of timber floor with a fillable void between the floor surface and ceiling, and the material can also be used for a range of other fire-resisting applications.

Other proprietary fire-resisting materials are described below ((i)–(iv)).

(i) SUPALUX
Description: A rigid laminar board material produced from a calcium silicate matrix reinforced with selected inorganic binders.

Sizes and thicknesses: 1200–3000 mm long × 600 or 1200 mm wide × 6, 9 or 12 mm thick.

Decoration: Boards can be tightly butt-jointed or their edges left slightly apart for filling and sanding. Suitable finishes include paint, paper, tiles or plaster.

(ii) VICUCLAD
Description: A rigid monolithic board material produced from exfoliated vermiculite bonded with inorganic binders. Fixed to timber by nailing or screwing and to steel work by a special non-combustible cement.

Sizes and thicknesses: 1000 mm long × 610 mm wide × 18 and 20–75 mm thick (in 5 mm increments).

Decoration: Vicuclad can be painted, rendered, plastered or finished with proprietary decorative textured coatings.

(iii) LIMPET SPRAYED MINERAL FIBRE
Description: A blend of selected man-made mineral fibres and inorganic binders applied by spraying to form a homogeneous jointless coating.

Finishing/decoration: Can be given a variety of textured finishes using special stippling tools. As an alternative, the material can be finished with a white spray-applied finishing compound,

EXISTING FLOOR CONSTRUCTION: TONGUED AND GROOVED FLOORBOARDS NOT LESS THAN 16 mm THICK. ON TIMBER JOISTS NOT EXCEEDING 38 mm WIDE. NO CEILING.		
DETAIL	UPGRADING TREATMENT	FIRE-RESISTANCE
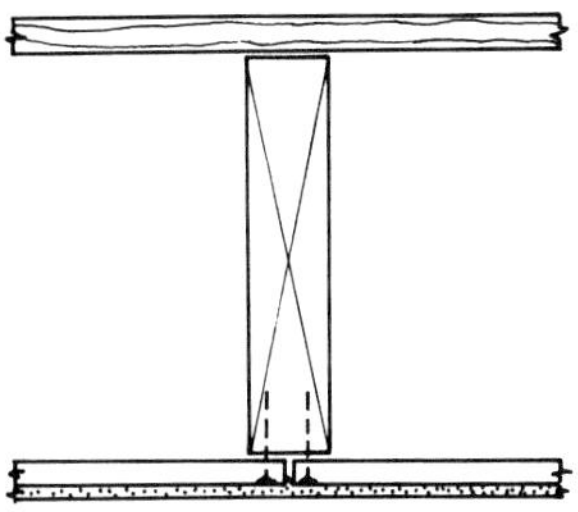	PLASTERBOARD 12.5 mm THICK NAILED TO JOISTS WITH GYPSUM PLASTER FINISH 5 mm THICK	½ HOUR
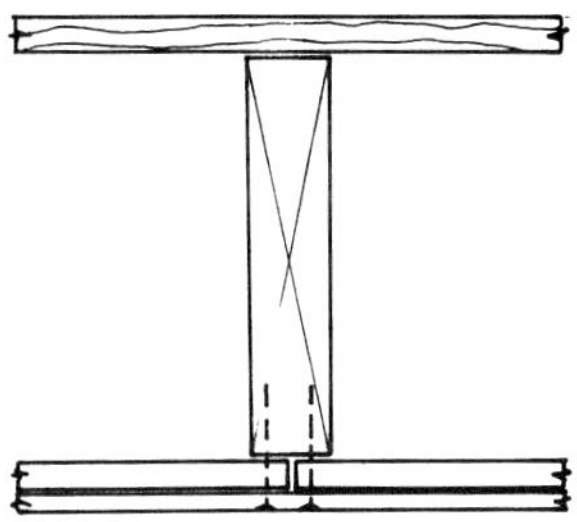	2 LAYERS PLASTERBOARD NAILED TO JOISTS WITH JOINTS STAGGERED. TOTAL THICKNESS 22 mm	½ HOUR
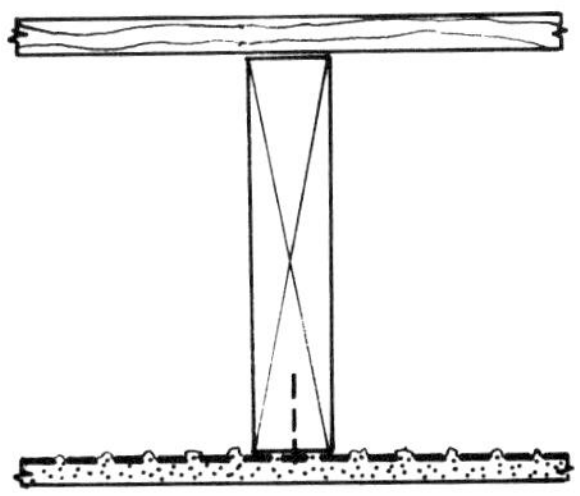	EXPANDED METAL LATHING NAILED TO JOISTS WITH VERMICULITE-GYPSUM PLASTER FINISH 12.5 mm THICK	1 HOUR
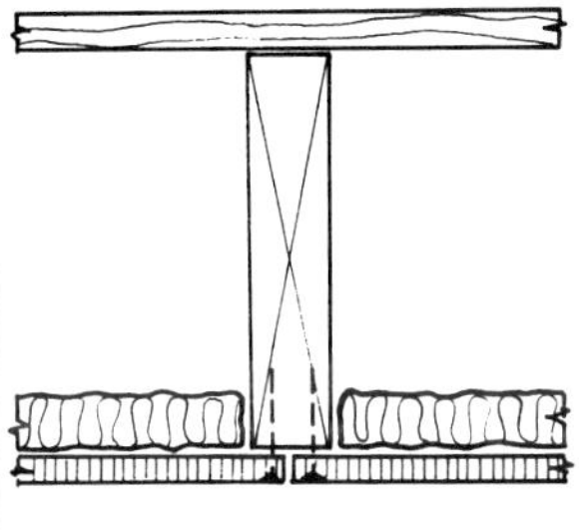	SUPALUX BOARD 12 mm THICK SCREWED TO JOISTS. OVERLAID WITH 25 mm MINERAL WOOL MAT (DENSITY 20 kg m^{-3})	1 HOUR

Fig. 4.1 Upgrading the fire resistance of timber floors

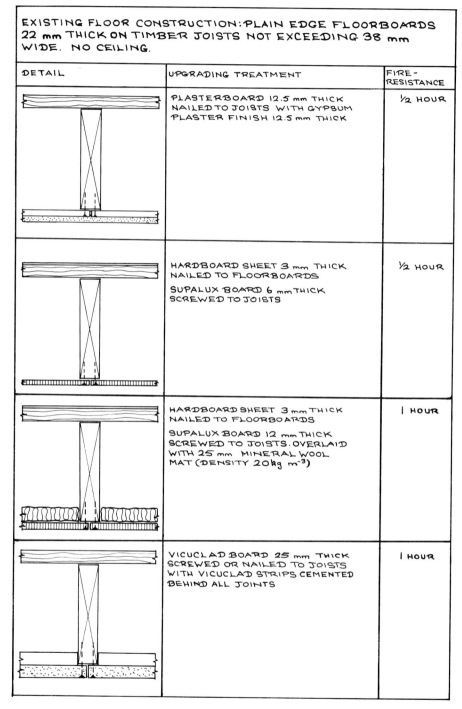

EXISTING FLOOR CONSTRUCTION: PLAIN EDGE FLOORBOARDS 22 mm THICK ON TIMBER JOISTS NOT EXCEEDING 38 mm WIDE. NO CEILING.		
DETAIL	UPGRADING TREATMENT	FIRE-RESISTANCE
	PLASTERBOARD 12.5 mm THICK NAILED TO JOISTS WITH GYPSUM PLASTER FINISH 12.5 mm THICK	½ HOUR
	HARDBOARD SHEET 3 mm THICK NAILED TO FLOORBOARDS SUPALUX BOARD 6 mm THICK SCREWED TO JOISTS	½ HOUR
	HARDBOARD SHEET 3 mm THICK NAILED TO FLOORBOARDS SUPALUX BOARD 12 mm THICK SCREWED TO JOISTS. OVERLAID WITH 25 mm MINERAL WOOL MAT (DENSITY 20 kg m^{-3})	1 HOUR
	VICUCLAD BOARD 25 mm THICK SCREWED OR NAILED TO JOISTS WITH VICUCLAD STRIPS CEMENTED BEHIND ALL JOINTS	1 HOUR

Fig. 4.2 Upgrading the fire resistance of timber floors

EXISTING FLOOR CONSTRUCTION: TONGUED AND GROOVED FLOORBOARDS NOT LESS THAN 22 mm THICK ON TIMBER JOISTS NOT LESS THAN 175 mm × 50 mm NO CEILING		
DETAIL	UPGRADING TREATMENT	FIRE-RESISTANCE
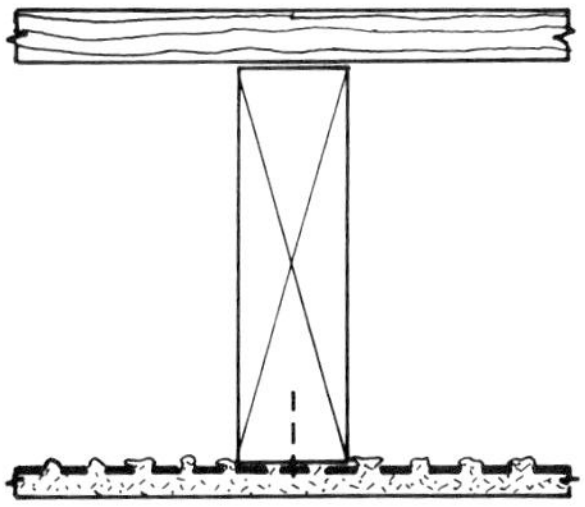	EXPANDED METAL LATHING NAILED TO JOISTS WITH SPRAYED LIMPET MINERAL-FIBRE FINISH 13 mm THICK	1/2 HOUR
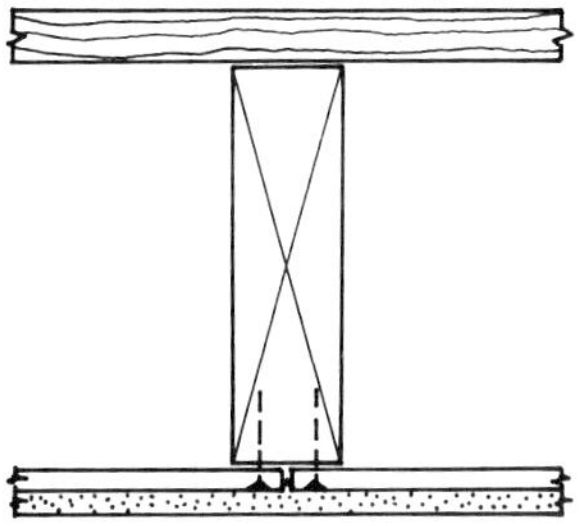	PLASTERBOARD 9.5 mm THICK NAILED TO JOISTS WITH GYPSUM PLASTER FINISH 12.5 mm	1/2 HOUR
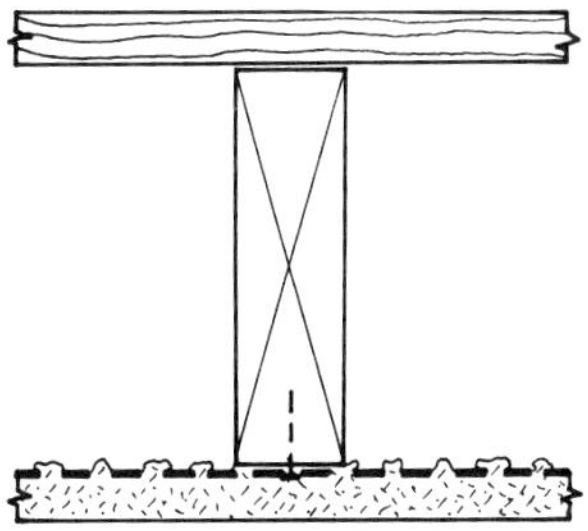	EXPANDED METAL LATHING NAILED TO JOISTS WITH SPRAYED LIMPET MINERAL-FIBRE FINISH 22 mm THICK	1 HOUR
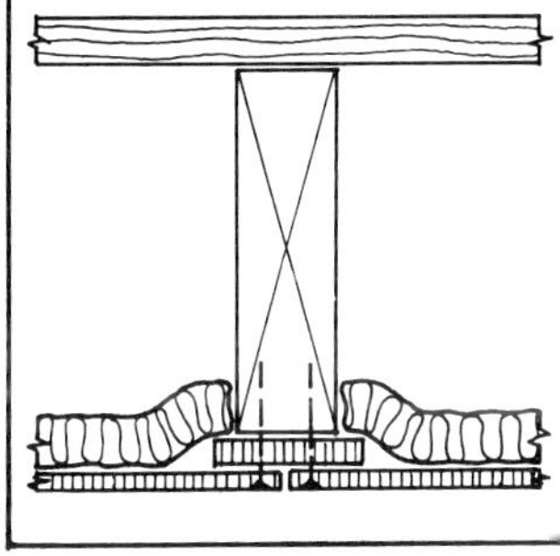	SUPALUX BOARD 9 mm THICK SCREWED TO JOISTS THROUGH 12 mm × 75 mm SUPALUX FILLETS. OVERLAID WITH 25 mm MINERAL WOOL MAT (DENSITY 20 kg m^{-3})	1 HOUR

Fig. 4.3 Upgrading the fire resistance of timber floors

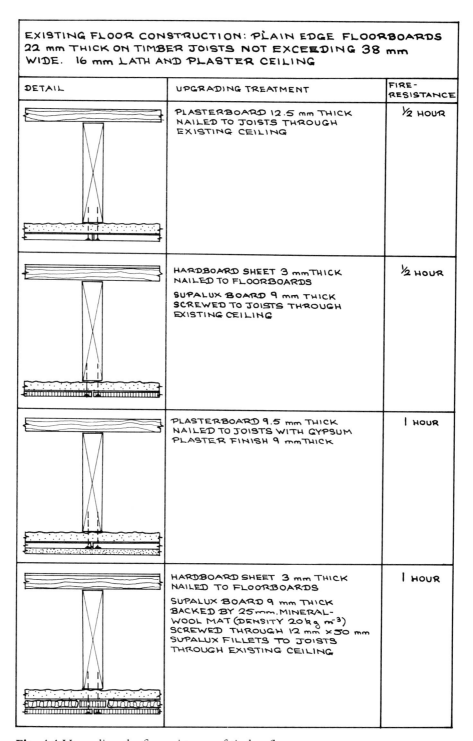

EXISTING FLOOR CONSTRUCTION: PLAIN EDGE FLOORBOARDS 22 mm THICK ON TIMBER JOISTS NOT EXCEEDING 38 mm WIDE. 16 mm LATH AND PLASTER CEILING		
DETAIL	UPGRADING TREATMENT	FIRE-RESISTANCE
	PLASTERBOARD 12.5 mm THICK NAILED TO JOISTS THROUGH EXISTING CEILING	½ HOUR
	HARDBOARD SHEET 3 mm THICK NAILED TO FLOORBOARDS. SUPALUX BOARD 9 mm THICK SCREWED TO JOISTS THROUGH EXISTING CEILING	½ HOUR
	PLASTERBOARD 9.5 mm THICK NAILED TO JOISTS WITH GYPSUM PLASTER FINISH 9 mm THICK	1 HOUR
	HARDBOARD SHEET 3 mm THICK NAILED TO FLOORBOARDS. SUPALUX BOARD 9 mm THICK BACKED BY 25 mm MINERAL-WOOL MAT (DENSITY 20 kg m⁻³) SCREWED THROUGH 12 mm × 50 mm SUPALUX FILLETS TO JOISTS THROUGH EXISTING CEILING	1 HOUR

Fig. 4.4 Upgrading the fire resistance of timber floors

34

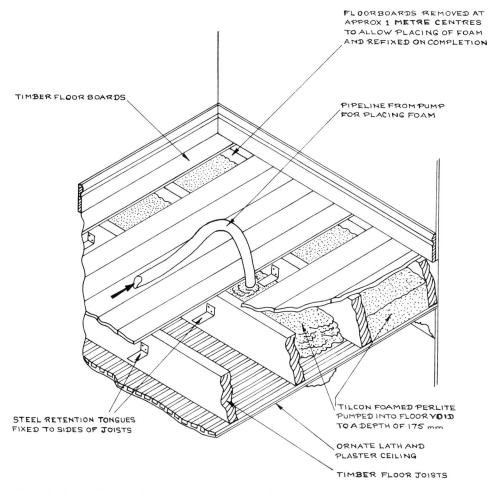

FLOORBOARDS REMOVED AT APPROX 1 METRE CENTRES TO ALLOW PLACING OF FOAM AND REFIXED ON COMPLETION

TIMBER FLOOR BOARDS

PIPELINE FROM PUMP FOR PLACING FOAM

STEEL RETENTION TONGUES FIXED TO SIDES OF JOISTS

TILCON FOAMED PERLITE PUMPED INTO FLOOR VOID TO A DEPTH OF 175 mm

ORNATE LATH AND PLASTER CEILING

TIMBER FLOOR JOISTS

Fig. 4.5 Upgrading the fire resistance of timber floors

Limpet LD3, to produce a textured (as sprayed) finish which can, if required, be overpainted.

(iv) INTUMESCENT MATERIALS
Intumescent materials are applied to surfaces in very thin coatings which, when exposed to fire, expand to form a meringue-like layer 50–75 mm thick which insulates the material beneath from intense heat. (A more detailed description is given in Section 4.2.3(d).) Nullifire WD is a proprietary intumescent material designed specifically for upgrading the fire resistance of timber elements. The material is available in a range of colours, or as a clear coating, which, in addition to the very thin coating required, makes it highly advantageous where the designer wishes to retain the appearance and character of existing timber elements in rehabilitation work. Nullifire WD comprises an intumescent base-coat and a decorative top-sealer, applied by brush, roller or spray, to give a total thickness of less than 1 mm. In the event of fire, the material intumesces, delaying the onset of charring of the timber by an average of 17 minutes. This delay effectively increases the inherent fire resistance of the timber and it is

possible to upgrade existing timber floors with exposed joists to half an hour fire-resistance, provided the existing timber is of adequate thickness.

It should be noted that, as a result of the recent well-founded concern regarding the health risks associated with asbestos, products containing that material should be avoided and none of the proprietary materials described above use asbestos in their manufacture.

4.2.3 Upgrading the fire resistance of cast-iron and steel elements

Large numbers of old buildings that are suitable for rehabilitation and adaptation contain exposed structural beams and columns of cast-iron or steel, and it is often convenient and economical, particularly in the lower-key categories of refurbishment, to retain these elements. However, as with timber floor structures, the fire resistance of exposed iron and steel work does not approach the standards that are required today and some form of upgrading will therefore be necessary. In many of our older industrial buildings, structural frames comprising ornate, circular cast-iron columns and cast-iron main beams support timber secondary beams and floorboarding, and it is often desirable to retain the shape and form of the existing columns as an architectural feature in the refurbished building. In such cases, the materials used in upgrading fire resistance must be capable of application in the form of a very thin coating if the shape and form of the existing sections are to be preserved.

A wide range of techniques and materials are available for upgrading the fire resistance of exposed iron and steel structural elements and all of them are suitable for 'I' section beams and columns. The techniques available for upgrading circular columns, however, are more limited, since some of the materials used are not capable of being applied to circular sections. The techniques and materials used vary considerably in their application and use and fall into four basic categories which are described below, and illustrated in Figs 4.6 and 4.7.

The figures give the fire resistances that can be achieved for various thicknesses of protection, but it should be noted that the data are only approximate and intended to give an indication of requirements for sections of 'typical size' ('I' sections: 406 × 178 mm × 74 kg/m; circular sections: 190 mm diameter × 8 mm thick). In practice, the actual thickness of protection required will vary and is based on the ratio of the section's exposed surface area to the area of its cross-section. The higher the surface area for a given cross-sectional area, the more heat will be absorbed and thus the lower the inherent fire resistance of the section. The actual thickness of the protection required will therefore increase as the ratio of surface area to cross-sectional area increases, and it is necessary to refer to manufacturers' tables, or to use calculations, in order to arrive at the actual thickness of protection required for any particular section. It should also be noted that the thickness of fire protection required for beams is usually less than that required for columns because beams are only exposed to fire on three sides, whereas columns are normally exposed on all four sides.

(a) Solid encasement

Although other materials can be used, solid encasement normally involves casting in-situ concrete around the sections being upgraded. To obtain a good bond between the concrete and the steel or cast-iron elements, steel mesh wrapping fabric is applied to the sections before erecting the temporary formwork and pouring the concrete. The minimum concrete cover to sections being protected must be 25 mm to allow for the maximum coarse aggregate size, and this will give two hours fire resistance to any steel or cast-iron section.

When considering the use of in-situ concrete to upgrade existing cast-iron and steel elements, it should be borne in mind that it is a messy operation, and that erection of temporary formwork within the existing building,

STEELWORK OR CAST-IRON SECTIONS TO WHICH DIFFERENT FORMS OF FIRE PROTECTION CAN BE APPLIED WITH FIXING DETAILS COLUMNS — BEAMS	UPGRADING TREATMENT	FIRE-RESISTANCE
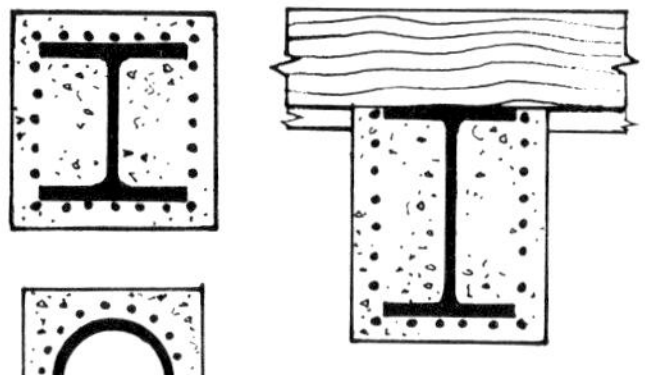 BOARD-TYPE FIRE PROTECTION TO TIMBER FLOOR	SOLID CONCRETE ENCASEMENT 1:2:4 WITH STEEL MESH WRAPPING (NOT LESS THAN 0.48 kg m^{-3} COLUMNS AND BEAMS 25 mm	UP TO 2 HOUR
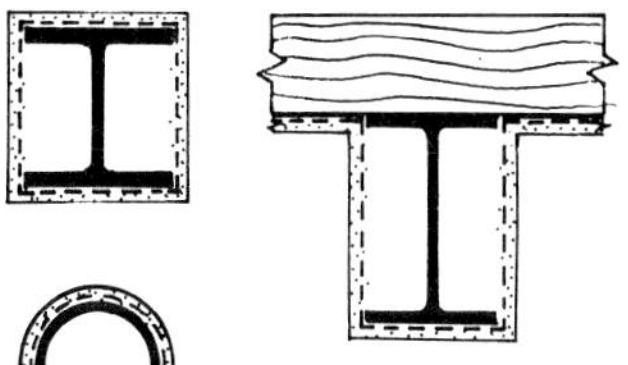 EML AND PLASTER ALSO USED TO PROTECT TIMBER FLOOR	EXPANDED METAL LATHING AND GYPSUM PLASTER THICKNESS: COLUMNS AND BEAMS 12.5 mm COLUMNS 19 mm BEAMS 16 mm COLUMNS 25 mm BEAMS 19 mm EXPANDED METAL LATHING AND VERMICULITE-GYPSUM PLASTER THICKNESS: COLUMNS AND BEAMS 12.5 mm COLUMNS 16 mm BEAMS 12.5 mm	½ HOUR 1 HOUR 1½ HOUR UP TO 1 HOUR 1½ HOUR
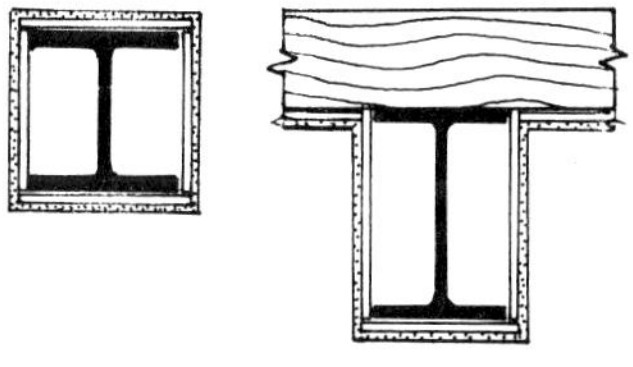 PLASTERBOARD AND PLASTER ALSO USED TO PROTECT TIMBER FLOOR	9.5 mm PLASTERBOARD FIXED TO STEELWORK USING METAL FLANGE CLIPS WITH GYPSUM PLASTER THICKNESS: COLUMNS AND BEAMS 12.5 mm 9.5 mm PLASTERBOARD FIXED TO STEELWORK USING METAL FLANGE CLIPS WITH VERMICULITE-GYPSUM PLASTER THICKNESS: COLUMNS AND BEAMS 7 mm COLUMNS AND BEAMS 10 mm COLUMNS AND BEAMS 12.5 mm	UP TO 1 HOUR ½ HOUR 1 HOUR 1½ HOUR
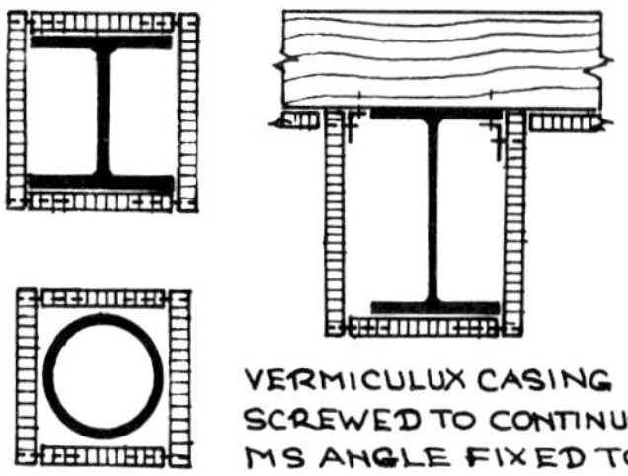 VERMICULUX CASING SCREWED TO CONTINUOUS MS ANGLE FIXED TO SOFFIT OR UNDERSIDE OF BEAM'S TOP FLANGE. VERMICULUX OR SIMILAR BOARD ALSO USED TO PROTECT TIMBER FLOOR	VERMICULUX BOARD ENCASEMENT THICKNESS: COLUMNS AND BEAMS 20 mm COLUMNS AND BEAMS 20 OR 25 mm	UP TO 1 HOUR 1½ HOUR

Fig. 4.6 Upgrading the fire resistance of cast-iron and steel beams and columns

STEELWORK OR CAST-IRON SECTIONS TO WHICH DIFFERENT FORMS OF FIRE-PROTECTION CAN BE APPLIED WITH FIXING DETAILS COLUMNS · BEAMS	UPGRADING TREATMENT	FIRE-RESISTANCE
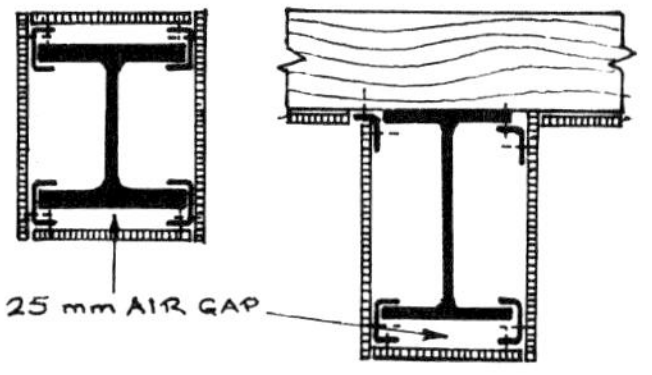 25 mm AIR GAP SUPALUX CASING SCREWED TO CONTINUOUS MS CHANNELS FIXED TO FLANGES. MS ANGLES USED UNDER SOFFIT OR BEAM'S TOP FLANGE. 75mm WIDE SUPALUX STRIPS SCREWED BEHIND ALL JOINTS IN CASING SUPALUX BOARD ALSO USED TO PROTECT TIMBER FLOOR	SUPALUX BOARD ENCASEMENT THICKNESS: COLUMNS AND BEAMS 6 mm COLUMNS AND BEAMS 9 mm COLUMNS 12 mm	½ HOUR 1 HOUR 1½ HOUR 2 HOUR
 VICUCLAD NOGGINGS AT 600 mm CENTRES VICUCLAD NOGGINGS FIXED WITH CEMENT INTO WEB OF STEEL SECTION AT 610 mm CENTRES. VICUCLAD CASING FIXED WITH CEMENT TO FLANGES AND TO NOGGINGS VICUCLAD BOARD ALSO USED TO PROTECT TIMBER FLOOR	VICUCLAD BOARD ENCASEMENT THICKNESS: COLUMNS AND BEAMS 18 mm COLUMNS AND BEAMS 20 - 25 mm	UP TO 1 HOUR 1½ HOUR
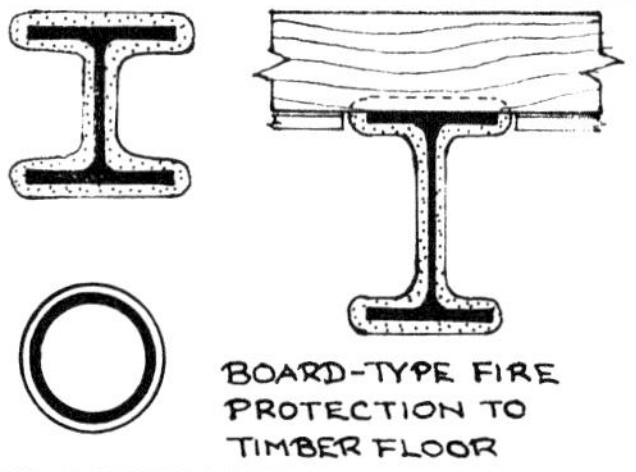 BOARD-TYPE FIRE PROTECTION TO TIMBER FLOOR	LIMPET SPRAYED MINERAL FIBRE THICKNESS: COLUMNS AND BEAMS 10 mm COLUMNS AND BEAMS 12 - 14 mm COLUMNS AND BEAMS 23 - 25 mm	½ HOUR 1 HOUR 1½ HOUR
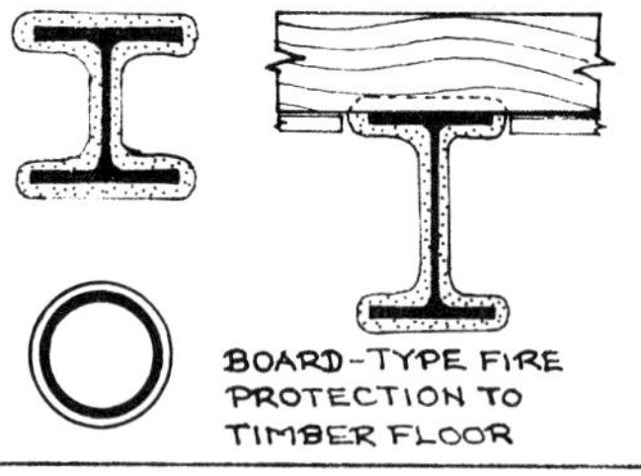 BOARD-TYPE FIRE PROTECTION TO TIMBER FLOOR	MANDOLITE P.20 SPRAYED VERMICULITE-CEMENT THICKNESS: COLUMNS AND BEAMS 8 mm COLUMNS AND BEAMS 16 mm COLUMNS AND BEAMS 22 mm	½ HOUR 1 HOUR 1½ HOUR
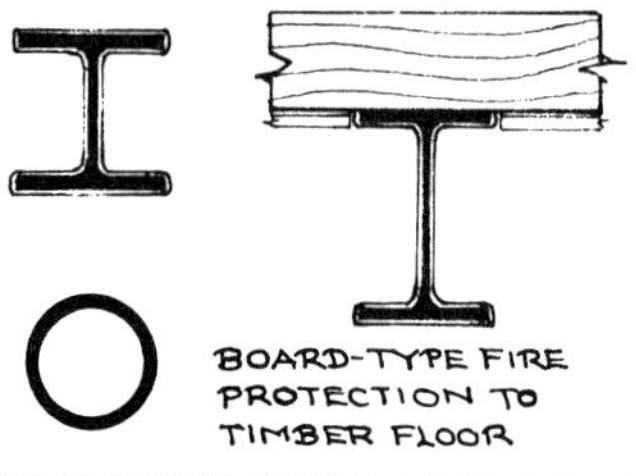 BOARD-TYPE FIRE PROTECTION TO TIMBER FLOOR	NULLIFIRE INTUMESCENT COATING APPLIED BY BRUSH ROLLER OR SPRAY THICKNESS: COLUMNS AND BEAMS 0.6 mm COLUMNS AND BEAMS 1.0 mm	½ HOUR 1 HOUR

Fig. 4.7 Upgrading the fire resistance of cast-iron and steel beams and columns

together with the provision of adequate access into the building for the mixed concrete, may cause considerable difficulties.

(b) Lightweight hollow encasement

Hollow encasement techniques essentially involve 'boxing-in' the columns or beams being upgraded, with fire-resisting materials of various types. Several different materials are available, and a number of them are described below.

(i) EXPANDED METAL LATHING AND PLASTER

Expanded metal lathing is wrapped around the column or beam to form the key for a wet plaster finish. The lathing can be fixed to the steel section using wire clips or steel stirrups, or by spot-welding. With 'I' section columns it is advisable to fix metal angle beads at the arrises to provide additional protection against mechanical damage. Where this method is used for circular columns, the metal lathing follows the column profile and the protection does not, therefore, form a hollow casing (see Fig. 4.6). Fire resistances of up to one and a half hours can easily be obtained using this method, and the thickness of plaster required can be reduced if lightweight vermiculite-gypsum plaster is used. The fire resistances obtainable using this method are given in Fig. 4.6.

(ii) PLASTERBOARD ENCASEMENT

This was the first material to be used for lightweight hollow encasement and it is still by no means uncommon in upgrading work. Lengths of 9.5 mm thick plasterboard are cut to size and fixed to the steel sections by means of special metal flange clips. The plasterboard is then finished with a single coat of wet plaster, its thickness depending on the degree of fire resistance required. Because of the technique used to secure the plasterboard casing to the steelwork, this method cannot be used with circular-section columns. As with the previous method, longer periods of fire resistance can be obtained if vermiculite-gypsum plaster is used (see Fig. 4.6).

(iii) VERMICULUX BOARD ENCASEMENT

Vermiculux is a proprietary board material manufactured from exfoliated vermiculite, other non-organic fibres and fillers and a calcium silicate matrix. The boards (standard size 1220 × 610 mm and 1220 × 1220 mm in thicknesses from 20 to 60 mm) are cut to size on site and fixed around the steel sections using screws. The short edges of Vermiculux boards are supplied rebated to provide a 16 mm wide half-lap at junctions. The completed casing can be finished (after making good countersunk screw fixings, junctions, etc. by filling and sanding) by direct painting, papering or tiling. Alternatively, a wet skim plaster finish may be applied. Where Vermiculux is used to encase beams beneath an existing floor, it is first necessary to fix continuous mild steel angles as shown in Fig. 4.6 to enable the boards enclosing the beam sides to be secured. Figure 4.6 also shows the fire resistances that can be obtained using this material.

(iv) SUPALUX BOARD ENCASEMENT

Supalux board, previously described in Section 4.2.2, is too thin to be edge-screwed and is fixed around the members being upgraded by screwing to mild steel channel and/or angle as shown in Fig. 4.7. Fire resistances up to two hours can be obtained with Supalux (see Fig. 4.7) and the material can be finished as for Vermiculux. The fixing methods used for Supalux encasement rule out its application to circular section columns.

(v) VICUCLAD BOARD ENCASEMENT

Vicuclad board, previously described in Section 4.2.2, is fixed to the existing sections using a non-combustible cement and Vicuclad noggings as shown in Fig. 4.7. Fire resistances of up to one and a half hours can be obtained using this material, which is capable of receiving a variety of surface finishes.

(c) Spray-applied coatings

The majority of spray-applied materials are sprayed directly on to the surfaces of the beams and columns being upgraded and they therefore follow the existing sections' profiles.

(i) LIMPET SPRAYED MINERAL FIBRE

This proprietary material, previously described in Section 4.2.2, is sprayed directly on to the cleaned surface of the section being upgraded in one continuous application until the desired thickness has been obtained. The thicknesses required for various periods of fire resistance are given in Fig. 4.7. Sprayed Limpet mineral fibre can also be used to provide a hollow casing by spraying the material on to expanded metal lathing which has been wrapped around the steel sections.

(ii) MANDOLITE P20 SPRAYED VERMI-CULITE-CEMENT

Mandolite P20 is a pre-mixed material based on vermiculite and Portland cement to which water is added on site. After mixing, it is sprayed directly on to the sections being upgraded, which must be clean and free of any surface impurities that might prevent adhesion. The Mandolite is built up in a series of passes of one or more coats until the required thickness is obtained. After drying, Mandolite P20 forms an off-white textured surface which, if required, may be finished with a proprietary sprayed coloured textured coating. Figure 4.7 gives the fire resistances that can be obtained using Mandolite P20.

(d) Intumescent coatings

Intumescent materials, which are applied in very thin layers, have unique fire-resisting properties and comprise formulations of resinous binders, pigments, blowing agents and fillers (see Fig. 4.7). When exposed to fire, the intumescent coating softens and expands to form a meringue-like layer approximately 50–75 mm thick which insulates the iron or steelwork from intense heat.

Nullifire S60 is a typical proprietary example and consists of an intumescent base-coat and a decorative top-sealing coat, which is available in a wide range of colours. The base-coat provides the fire protection, and the top-coat, in addition to providing a decorative surface, protects the base-coat from mechanical damage and gives a 'wipe clean' surface. Prior to application of the intumescent base-coat, the existing sections being upgraded should be coated with a suitable primer.

One of the principal advantages of using intumescent materials for upgrading existing iron and steelwork is that they are extremely thin (only 1 mm for one hour fire resistance), and they are therefore ideal where, for architectural reasons, the existing profiles of ornate sections need to be preserved.

4.2.4 Upgrading the fire resistance of doors

It is likely where an existing building is improved or undergoes a change of use, that some of the existing internal doors will need either to be replaced or upgraded to comply with the requirements of the Building Regulations. Typical locations where fire doors are required include:

(i)   Doors separating flats or maisonettes from spaces in common use
(ii) Doors penetrating protecting structures (i.e. fire-resisting enclosures to stairwells, lift shafts, etc.)
(iii) Doors penetrating compartment walls (i.e. fire-resisting walls used to subdivide a building into compartments in order to restrict fire spread)

Fire doors will usually need to have a fire resistance of sixty minutes, thirty minutes or twenty minutes (measured against the criterion of 'Integrity', see Section 4.2.1), and most types of existing door constructions are capable of being upgraded to twenty minutes or half an hour with relative ease. However, upgrading an existing door to one hour standard is more difficult, and often produces a rather cumbersome result. Where one hour fire doors are required, therefore, it is usually preferable to replace the existing doors rather than to attempt to upgrade them.

The techniques used to upgrade the fire rating of existing doors, whether they be flush or panelled, are relatively simple and inexpensive. Several proprietary fire-resisting board materials are available in various thicknesses, and these can be nailed or screwed to the existing door's surface to achieve the standard required. Supalux board, previously described in Section 4.2.2, is used for a number of fire upgrading applications and its use in the upgrading of existing doors is illustrated in Fig. 4.8. After fixing to the existing door, all screw/nail holes are filled and the new Supalux surface is painted to complete

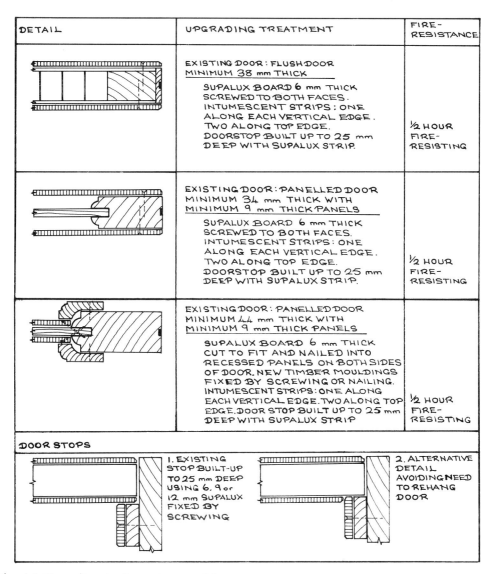

DETAIL	UPGRADING TREATMENT	FIRE-RESISTANCE
	EXISTING DOOR: FLUSH DOOR MINIMUM 38 mm THICK SUPALUX BOARD 6 mm THICK SCREWED TO BOTH FACES. INTUMESCENT STRIPS: ONE ALONG EACH VERTICAL EDGE. TWO ALONG TOP EDGE. DOORSTOP BUILT UP TO 25 mm DEEP WITH SUPALUX STRIP.	½ HOUR FIRE-RESISTING
	EXISTING DOOR: PANELLED DOOR MINIMUM 34 mm THICK WITH MINIMUM 9 mm THICK PANELS SUPALUX BOARD 6 mm THICK SCREWED TO BOTH FACES. INTUMESCENT STRIPS: ONE ALONG EACH VERTICAL EDGE. TWO ALONG TOP EDGE. DOORSTOP BUILT UP TO 25 mm DEEP WITH SUPALUX STRIP.	½ HOUR FIRE-RESISTING
	EXISTING DOOR: PANELLED DOOR MINIMUM 44 mm THICK WITH MINIMUM 9 mm THICK PANELS SUPALUX BOARD 6 mm THICK CUT TO FIT AND NAILED INTO RECESSED PANELS ON BOTH SIDES OF DOOR. NEW TIMBER MOULDINGS FIXED BY SCREWING OR NAILING. INTUMESCENT STRIPS: ONE ALONG EACH VERTICAL EDGE. TWO ALONG TOP EDGE. DOOR STOP BUILT UP TO 25 mm DEEP WITH SUPALUX STRIP	½ HOUR FIRE-RESISTING

DOOR STOPS

	1. EXISTING STOP BUILT-UP TO 25 mm DEEP USING 6, 9 or 12 mm SUPALUX FIXED BY SCREWING		2. ALTERNATIVE DETAIL AVOIDING NEED TO REHANG DOOR

Fig. 4.8 Upgrading the fire resistance of doors

the upgrading of the door. It will be seen from Fig. 4.8 that, in addition to treating the surface of the door, it is also necessary to insert intumescent strips along the edges in order to obtain the required fire rating. In the event of fire, the intumescent strips expand and seal the gaps around the door's edge, preventing the passage of smoke and flames. A further aspect requiring attention is the existing doorstops, which, as shown in Fig. 4.8, must be built up to a depth of 25 mm in order to provide an adequate overlap at the edge of the door.

4.2.5 Upgrading the fire resistance of walls

In the majority of older buildings, the existing walls are normally masonry or brickwork, both of which have excellent fire resistance, and, are therefore, unlikely to need upgrading. For example, an unplastered 100 mm thick brick wall will give a fire resistance of two hours, which is more than adequate in virtually all circumstances. It is quite possible, however, that some of the internal walls within an existing building represent more recent additions which may be of less substantial construction, such as concrete blockwork or timber studding. Unplastered block walls 75 mm and 100 mm thick will give a fire resistance of one hour and two hours respectively and are therefore, like brickwork and masonry, unlikely to need upgrading for fire protection purposes. Many basic timber stud partitions, however, only give half an hour fire resistance and therefore need upgrading if a higher standard is required. One of the simplest ways of upgrading such partitions is to nail an additional layer of 9.5 mm plaster-board to each side, which will give a rating of one hour. If greater periods of fire resistance are required, a wet plaster finish may be added, or thicker plasterboard used.

4.3 UPGRADING INTERNAL SURFACES

The quality of internal surface finishes is an item

that will almost certainly require attention in the majority of refurbishment schemes. If the existing surfaces are in good condition, the upgrading necessary might only involve providing a new coat of paint. On the other hand, in older buildings, the existing surfaces may be in such a poor condition that they need to be completely replaced.

Where existing surfaces need to be upgraded, it will usually be the walls that involve most work, the upgrading of ceilings and floors tending to be less complicated.

4.3.1 Upgrading wall surfaces

In many old buildings, such as factories, mills, warehouses, churches, etc., the wall surfaces never received any applied finishes and therefore consist of exposed masonry or brickwork which, in its present condition, is unlikely to be of an adequate standard. Where plaster finishes have been applied, they may have deteriorated beyond repair because of dampness or general neglect. In such cases, it will therefore be necessary to upgrade the existing wall surfaces to satisfy modern standards. This can be carried out, after suitable preparation, either by applying a new plaster finish, or by applying some form of dry lining.

(a) Plaster finishes
Provided the existing wall is not suffering from dampness, a normal plaster finish can be applied. Any existing surface finish should be removed and the brickwork or masonry joints well raked out to provide a suitable key for the new plaster. The wall should then be brushed down to remove any dust, efflorescence salts or loose particles before applying the new finish. With certain backgrounds, it may also be necessary to apply a bonding agent before plastering. It is quite possible, particularly in older buildings, that the existing wall surfaces may be so uneven that a normal two-coat plaster finish will not be sufficient to give a true surface. In such cases, the application of two undercoats (a render and a

floating coat) will usually be sufficient to fill out the deeper depressions, to give a true and even surface finish to the wall. If this is not possible, then a dry-lining system may be the only solution.

Where the existing walls are suffering from dampness (an extremely common problem in older buildings), a normal plaster finish will be unsuitable. However, provided the source of the dampness can be eliminated, for example by inserting a new damp-proof course, it may be possible to use special moisture-resistant plaster. In cases where the source of dampness in an existing wall has been cured, the use of normal plasters is not recommended since they cannot be used until the residual moisture in the wall has been given time to dry out. Clearly, the resulting delays are undesirable and can add to the overall cost of the rehabilitation work. However, recent developments have resulted in the introduction of special renovating plasters, one such proprietary example being Thistle renovating plaster. This consists of an undercoat with properties which enhance its drying and strength development under damp conditions, and a finishing coat which is resistant to fungal growth. The final strength of the plaster is not adversely affected by dampness. Provided the residual dampness in the existing wall is not excessive and its source has been eliminated, Thistle renovating plaster can be applied immediately, although the longer the delay, the better. However, if the wall is wet and time does not allow for a suitable delay, a first undercoat (or render coat) of Thistle renovating plaster mixed with a water-resisting bonding aid may be used. (Suitable proprietary water-resisting bonding aids include Unibond Universal EVA, Febond SBR and Sika latex.) The render coat, comprising one part waterproofer to two parts plaster, should be applied to the background and, before it has set, the second undercoat of Thistle renovating plaster applied to achieve a plane surface of the required thickness. The new surface is then completed with the application of a 2 mm thick Thistle renovating plaster finish.

(b) Dry linings

Dry linings are a suitable and popular alternative to wet plaster as a means of upgrading wall surfaces in rehabilitation work. If the existing wall is suffering from dampness, its source should be eliminated prior to applying the lining, since basic dry-lining systems are not suitable for use on damp backgrounds. It is possible, however, with certain modifications, to use dry linings on damp backgrounds and this application is considered later in the chapter. A further useful application for dry linings is in upgrading the thermal properties of external walls and this, also, is dealt with later.

Providing a dry-lining wall finish involves the fixing of gypsum plasterboard to the existing wall surface by one of a number of different techniques. Gypsum wallboard, a plasterboard designed to receive direct decoration, is used, thereby eliminating the need for a wet skim coat of plaster. This gives the advantage of allowing the whole finishing process to be dry, involving no wet operations apart from jointing the board edges. Three basic fixing techniques are used to install dry linings, as follows.

(i) TIMBER BATTEN FIXING
Timber battens, 50 mm wide × 25 mm thick, are fixed vertically to the existing wall at 400 mm centres (for 1200 mm wide wallboards), or 450 mm centres (for 900 mm wide wallboards). It is likely that the existing wall surface will be uneven, and it is essential, therefore, that all depressions are packed out with timber or fibreboard pieces in order to achieve correct alignment of the battens. The boards are then nailed to the battens vertically, with 50 mm × 25 mm timber noggings inserted to support their horizonal edges. After the fixings and joints have been made good, the wallboards may be decorated directly by painting, wallpapering or using any other suitable surface finish.

Figure 4.9 shows details of a timber batten dry-lining system.

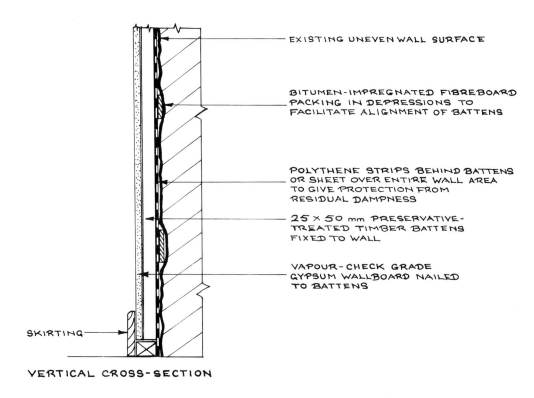

EXISTING UNEVEN WALL SURFACE

BITUMEN-IMPREGNATED FIBREBOARD PACKING IN DEPRESSIONS TO FACILITATE ALIGNMENT OF BATTENS

POLYTHENE STRIPS BEHIND BATTENS OR SHEET OVER ENTIRE WALL AREA TO GIVE PROTECTION FROM RESIDUAL DAMPNESS

25 × 50 mm PRESERVATIVE-TREATED TIMBER BATTENS FIXED TO WALL

VAPOUR-CHECK GRADE GYPSUM WALLBOARD NAILED TO BATTENS

SKIRTING

VERTICAL CROSS-SECTION

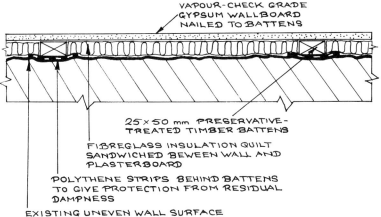

VAPOUR-CHECK GRADE GYPSUM WALLBOARD NAILED TO BATTENS

25 × 50 mm PRESERVATIVE-TREATED TIMBER BATTENS

FIBREGLASS INSULATION QUILT SANDWICHED BEWEEN WALL AND PLASTERBOARD

POLYTHENE STRIPS BEHIND BATTENS TO GIVE PROTECTION FROM RESIDUAL DAMPNESS

EXISTING UNEVEN WALL SURFACE

HORIZONTAL CROSS-SECTION SHOWING THERMAL INSULATION

Fig. 4.9 Dry linings: timber batten fixing

44

Upgrading internal surfaces

(ii) METAL CHANNEL FIXING

As an alternative to fixing the plasterboard dry lining to timber battens, metal furrings may be used. The Gyproc MF system uses 50 mm wide × 9.5 mm deep zinc-coated mild-steel channels which are bonded vertically to the existing wall using a special gypsum adhesive. 200 mm long dabs of the adhesive are applied to the wall at 450 mm centres in vertical rows where each channel is to be fixed. The channels are then pressed on to the adhesive and aligned. The system is capable of accommodating irregularities in the background of up to 25 mm, by using the adhesive to fill out any depressions that exist. When the adhesive has set, each wallboard is screwed to its three vertical channels using a powered screwdriver. The fixings and joints are then made good and a suitable decorative finish applied to complete the upgrading of the wall. Details of the Gyproc MF dry-lining system are shown in Fig. 4.10.

(iii) DIRECT ADHESIVE FIXING

Plasterboard dry linings can be bonded direct to the existing wall surfaces using special gypsum adhesive, thereby ruling out the need to install fixing battens. A widely used proprietary system is the Thistlebond dry-lining system (see Fig. 4.11) which employs bitumen-impregnated fibreboard alignment pads and dabs of adhesive to secure wallboard to the existing surface. Firstly, the fibreboard alignment pads are fixed to the wall in vertical rows 450 mm apart using adhesive. Any depressions in the background are accommodated by the setting-out method. It is essential that the fibreboard pads are properly aligned, since these are used as a base to fix the wallboard against, thereby ensuring that a true, plane surface is obtained. After the pads have set, dabs of adhesive, which must be thick enough to stand proud of the pads, are applied to the background in vertical rows. Wallboards 900 mm wide are then pressed on to the adhesive dabs until an even contact with all of the alignment pads is obtained. The boards are then temporarily secured to the pads with double-headed nails which are withdrawn once the adhesive has set. The joints between the wall-boards can then be made good and the new surface finish applied.

4.3.2 Upgrading ceiling surfaces

The upgrading of existing ceiling finishes is generally less complicated than upgrading walls. Provided the structure above is sound, any conventional ceiling finish can be applied. In older buildings with timber floor structures, this will usually involve removal of the existing ceiling and its replacement with a new plasterboard ceiling. A useful alternative, particularly in buildings with high ceilings and where new services installations need to be concealed, is to install a suspended ceiling system which can be very effective in reducing the room height and providing a generous services void above.

In certain buildings, the upgrading of existing ceilings may be closely associated with other upgrading work. For example, upgrading the fire resistance of timber floors usually involves treatment to the existing ceiling (see Section 4.2.2) and it can therefore be designed to satisfy both upgrading requirements in one single operation.

4.3.3 Upgrading floor surfaces

(a) Re-surfacing with timber

A very wide range of options is available for the upgrading of existing floors, and, provided the structure is sound, any suitable finish can be applied. In many older buildings, the existing floors may be uneven and the first operation will involve re-surfacing the subfloor in order to provide a level base for the new finish. With timber floors, the simplest solution is to overlay the existing floorboards with hardboard, or where the surface is very uneven, plywood. In order to achieve a level surface, it may be necessary to firstly sand down high points and pack out depressions before fixing the new sheeting. In extreme cases, where the existing

45

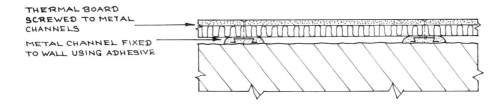

THERMAL BOARD
SCREWED TO METAL
CHANNELS

METAL CHANNEL FIXED
TO WALL USING ADHESIVE

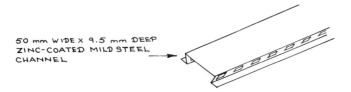

50 mm WIDE x 9.5 mm DEEP
ZINC-COATED MILD STEEL
CHANNEL

THERMAL BOARD FIXED USING
GYPROC M/F MILD STEEL CHANNEL SYSTEM

Fig. 4.10 Dry linings: metal channel fixing

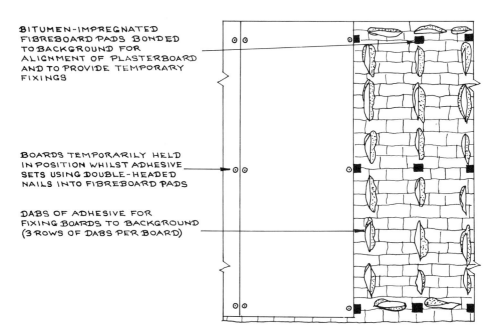

BITUMEN-IMPREGNATED
FIBREBOARD PADS BONDED
TO BACKGROUND FOR
ALIGNMENT OF PLASTERBOARD
AND TO PROVIDE TEMPORARY
FIXINGS

BOARDS TEMPORARILY HELD
IN POSITION WHILST ADHESIVE
SETS USING DOUBLE-HEADED
NAILS INTO FIBREBOARD PADS

DABS OF ADHESIVE FOR
FIXING BOARDS TO BACKGROUND
(3 ROWS OF DABS PER BOARD)

PLASTERBOARD FIXED USING
THISTLEBOND ADHESIVE METHOD

Fig. 4.11 Dry linings: direct adhesive fixing

46

boarding is so uneven that levelling with a new surface is impossible, or where decay has occurred, it will be necessary to remove the boarding completely and replace it with new material. Existing concrete floors are less likely to need upgrading, apart from their surface finishes. However, if necessary, timber grounds or metal fixings can be inserted to receive a new wood surface.

(b) Re-screeding

Where an existing concrete floor surface has deteriorated, an alternative to providing a new timber surface is to re-screed it, or add a new screed where one did not previously exist. This will require an extensive amount of preparation and may involve breaking up and removing an existing deteriorated screed, and treating the exposed concrete surface to provide a suitable key for the new screed. It is also a time-consuming, labour-intensive task, and it may, therefore, be worth considering applying one of the proprietary floor levelling compounds of the type described below.

(c) Proprietary floor levelling compounds

A widely used alternative to the above methods, where an existing floor surface is in poor condition and needs upgrading, is to apply a proprietary synthetic resin-based floor levelling compound. Evo-Stik floor level and fill is a ready-mixed filler and self-levelling compound for preparing old or uneven floors prior to laying new coverings. It can be used over concrete, cement/sand screeds, wood floorboards, timber-based boards, ceramic tiles and asphalt. The material sets to an extremely durable, smooth surface which prevents the unsightly appearance and possible damage caused to the new floorcovering by any irregularities in the existing floor. Existing uneven floors are treated in two stages, as follows.

(i) FILLING

The paste-like compound is applied with a trowel directly from its container in layers up to 20 mm thick to fill any depressions in the floor surface. Each layer must be allowed to dry before the next is applied. The surface is then smoothed with a float, a perfect surface not being necessary if it is intended to level over the top.

(ii) LEVELLING

Any holes deeper than 3 mm should be filled as previously described. Absorbent surfaces should be dampened with water, or in extreme cases, primed with diluted Evo-Bond building adhesive. The level and fill compound, which is diluted for the levelling operation to improve its flow capabilities, is poured on to the floor and spread evenly with a float to give a continuous layer 1 mm thick, and no more than 3 mm at any point. The self-levelling properties allow trowel marks to flow out.

A thin coat will take light foot traffic after drying overnight with good ventilation, and after 24 hours, the new floorcovering can be laid.

4.4 UPGRADING THE THERMAL PERFORMANCE OF EXISTING ELEMENTS

An extremely important consideration, both in new construction and rehabilitation work, is the provision of good thermal insulation to the external envelope in order to minimize heat loss and reduce heating costs. The importance of providing adequate thermal insulation has been reflected in recent changes to the Building Regulations, which now demand considerably greater standards of thermal insulation than were required a few years ago. The construction of many older buildings is not conducive to the retention of heat within their interior spaces. In buildings with thick masonry external walls, heat is absorbed into the walls and therefore lost, satisfactory heating being extremely difficult to achieve, particularly where intermittent heating cycles are operated.

In buildings with thinner, solid masonry or brick walls, heat loss through the structure can be considerable and some form of thermal upgrading will be necessary if heating costs are to be kept within reasonable limits. It should also be noted that untreated cavity walls do not now reach the thermal standards required by current regulations, and thus thermal upgrading of cavity walls is often included in the rehabilitation of more recently constructed buildings.

In addition to upgrading the external walls, it will be prudent also to attend to the existing roof which in most cases will not be insulated to modern standards, and, in some cases, not insulated at all. A wide range of thermal upgrading techniques can be applied to existing roofs, the methods used depending principally on the nature of the existing roof structure.

4.4.1 Upgrading the thermal performance of walls

As explained in the introduction, most categories of rehabilitation will include the addition of thermal insulation to the existing walls. This is usually achieved by applying a layer of insulating material to either the inside face or the outside face, or, in the case of cavity walls, by injecting an insulating fill into the cavity. With solid walled buildings, the choice between internally applied or externally applied insulation will depend on two main factors: firstly, whether the building is heated intermittently or continuously, and, secondly, the thermal capacity of the walls. Internally applied insulation is effective where the building is heated intermittently, since it prevents heat being absorbed by, and lost into, the walls, thereby giving a more rapid warm-up period. However, the addition of internal insulation will cause the existing wall structure to be colder, increasing the risk of condensation on or within it. It is therefore vital that an efficient vapour barrier be provided on the warm side of the new insulation to minimize this risk (see Section 4.7).

Externally applied insulation is effective where the building has thick walls of high thermal capacity, and is heated continuously.

Heat is absorbed into and retained by the walls and 'given back' to the interior, and the risk of condensation is minimized. Externally applied insulation is also effective with thinner walls of low thermal capacity, regardless of whether the heating is intermittent or continuous.

The relative merits and disadvantages of externally and internally applied insulation are given in Table 4.5.

(a) Internally applied insulation

The application of thermal insulation to the internal surfaces of external walls is often combined with the upgrading of their surface finishes, and one of the most convenient ways of achieving this is to incorporate a layer of thermal insulation into a dry-lining system as follows.

(i) SEPARATE SANDWICH INSULATION

With basic timber batten dry linings (see Section 4.3.1), a separate layer of insulation can be sandwiched into the space that has been created between the surface of the existing wall and the plasterboard, as shown in Fig. 4.9. If standard-sized battens are used, the insulation thickness will be limited to 25 mm, higher standards of insulation being obtained by using thicker battens to give a wider space, thereby enabling the insertion of a thicker layer of insulation. Suitable insulation materials include flexible quilts, or semi-rigid batts of fibreglass or rockwool. Rockwool semi-rigid slabs, 40 mm thick, used in conjunction with a timber batten dry-lining system, will upgrade the 'U' value of a 220 mm solid brick wall from 2.17 to 0.59 $W/m^2 K$, which is within the requirements of current regulations.

(ii) LININGS WITH PRE-BONDED INSULATION

The modern alternative to incorporating sandwich insulation is to apply a dry lining comprising plasterboard with a layer of rigid insulation pre-bonded to it. Three proprietary examples are described below.

Table 4.5 The relative merits and disadvantages of externally and internally applied insulation

Externally applied insulation	*Internally applied insulation*
1. Existing wall is kept warm and dry, thus increasing its insulation value and heat storage capacity	1. Application is not affected by weather
	2. Access to surfaces being treated is easier
	3. Has no effect on the external appearance of the building
2. Cold bridging where internal walls and floors abut the facade is eliminated, therefore further reducing heat loss and surface condensation	4. Cheaper than externally applied insulation
	5. Existing wall is not protected
3. The risk of interstitial condensation, within the thickness of the wall, is reduced	6. Does not eliminate structural cold bridging
	7. Causes serious internal disruption
4. No internal work involved	8. Eliminates surface condensation
5. Less disruption to the occupants (where an occupied building is being upgraded)	9. Perimeter floorspace is reduced
	10. Difficult to apply around doors, windows and internal fittings
6. No loss of floorspace	11. Can be applied selectively to various parts of the building
7. Easier to apply around doors and windows	12. Produces similar savings in heat loss and energy consumption (up to 50%) to externally applied insulation.
8. Provides an improved external finish to buildings whose appearance has deteriorated due to weathering and atmospheric pollution	
9. Has a significant effect on the external appearance of the building and is therefore unsuitable for certain historic buildings where the existing appearance must be preserved	
10. More expensive than internally applied insulation	
11. Produces similar savings in heat loss and energy consumption (up to 50%) to internally applied insulation	

Styroliner: Styroliner (see Fig. 4.12) comprises a sheet of plasterboard 9.5 mm thick, factory bonded to a backing of Styrofoam SG closed-cell extruded polystyrene. The product is available with a tapered-edged manilla-faced plasterboard for direct decoration or, alternatively, with a square-edged grey-faced plasterboard for finishing with plaster.

The closed-cell structure of the Styrofoam prevents capillary absorption of moisture and, in addition to thermal insulation, provides an effective moisture barrier and vapour check. Styroliner boards are 1200 mm wide × 2438 mm long and are available in six overall thicknesses, from 22.5 mm to 51.5 mm. Fixing can be directly to the wall using continuous ribbons of adhesive applied either to the wall itself, or to the reverse side of the boards. The boards need only be held in position manually for two minutes, after which the adhesive will be set. However, if required, the boards can be temporarily held by nails lightly driven in to the wall adjacent to the board edges. Styroliner boards can also be fixed by screwing directly to the wall using self-tapping screws, or by nailing to pre-fixed timber battens. The former method is only suitable where the background is fairly even and comprises sound masonry or brick-work capable of allowing the special self-tapping screws to thread in to the background.

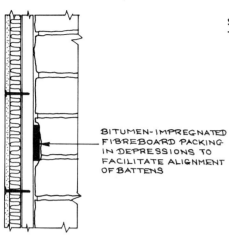

STYROLINER NAILED
TO TIMBER BATTENS

BITUMEN-IMPREGNATED
FIBREBOARD PACKING
IN DEPRESSIONS TO
FACILITATE ALIGNMENT
OF BATTENS

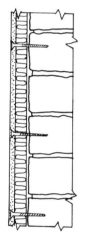

STYROLINER SCREWED
TO WALL USING SELF-
TAPPING SCREWS DIRECTLY
INTO BRICKWORK OR
MASONRY

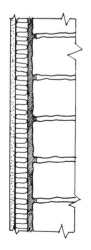

STYROLINER BONDED
DIRECT TO WALL USING
CONTINUOUS RIBBONS
OF ADHESIVE

Fig. 4.12 Styroliner dry lining

50

Timber batten fixing is used where the background is uneven and is similar to the method described in Section 4.3.1, fibreboard pieces being used to pack out any depressions in order to ensure correct alignment of the battens.

The 'U' value of an existing 220 mm solid brick external wall can be upgraded to 0.59 W/m² K by adding a 43.5 mm Styroliner dry lining fixed with adhesive. If timber batten fixing is used, the resulting 'U' value will be better, because of the cavity formed by the battens.

Gyproc thermal board: Gyproc thermal board (see Fig. 4.10) is similar in principle to Styroliner. It comprises gypsum wallboard, 12.7 mm thick, factory bonded to a backing of type A expanded polystyrene insulating board. The boards are supplied in lengths of 2400, 2438 and 2700 × 1200 mm wide and four overall thicknesses from 25 mm to 50 mm. Gyproc thermal board is not suitable for use in continuously damp or humid conditions. The boards can be fixed to the existing wall with adhesive, by screwing to metal channels, or by nailing to timber battens. For adhesive fixing of Gyproc thermal board, the Thistlebond system, previously described in Section 4.3.1 and illustrated in Fig. 4.11, is used, with one modification. In addition to adhesive dabs, nails are also used to secure the boards to special nailable plugs inserted into the wall through the fibreboard alignment pads. For metal channel fixing, the Gyproc MF system, previously described in Section 4.3.1 and illustrated in Fig. 4.10, is used. This entails screwing the Gyproc thermal board to galvanized mild-steel channels which have been fixed vertically to the existing wall with adhesive.

Timber batten fixing of Gyproc thermal board is the same as for plain wallboard, described in Section 4.3.1, screws rather than nails being used to fix the thicker grades. This method is the most suitable for very uneven backgrounds, since fairly deep depressions can easily be packed out to obtain alignment of the battens. The adhesive and metal channel systems, however, can also be used on uneven walls, provided the unevenness is not too excessive. Gyproc thermal board is capable of giving significant improvements to the thermal efficiency of existing walls. A solid 220 mm thick brick external wall, with a 'U' value of 2.17 W/m² K, can be upgraded to 0.65 W/m² K by applying 50 mm thermal board, fixed with adhesive, and 0.58 W/m² K if the boards are fixed to timber battens.

Gyproc urethane laminate: Gyproc urethane laminate is composed of 12.7 mm thick gypsum wallboard, factory bonded to a 13 mm, 20 mm or 28 mm thick backing of paper-faced rigid polyurethane foam insulation. With the exception of the insulant, the laminate is similar in all respects, including its fixing techniques, to Gyproc thermal board, which uses polystyrene, rather than polyurethane, as the insulating material. The thermal performance of polyurethane is superior to that of most other insulating materials, and the paper facing is treated with polyethylene to provide the laminate with a vapour check.

The superiority of the polyurethane insulant is evident when comparing the 'U' values attainable when using Gyproc urethane laminate as an alternative to Gyproc thermal board to upgrade a 220 mm solid brick external wall:

'U' value of existing 220 mm thick solid brick wall	2.17 W/m² K
Upgraded 'U' value using 32 mm Gyproc thermal board fixed with adhesive	0.95 W/m² K
Upgraded 'U' value using 32 mm Gyproc urethane laminate fixed with adhesive	0.69 W/m² K
Upgraded 'U' value using 40 mm Gyproc thermal board fixed with adhesive	0.79 W/m² K
Upgraded 'U' value using 40 mm Gyproc urethane laminate fixed with adhesive	0.56 W/m² K

(b) Externally applied insulation

One of the most important factors that can determine whether externally applied insulation is used in preference to internally applied insulation is the condition and appearance of the existing external wall surfaces. For example, if the facade is constructed from fine, ornate masonry and it possesses architectural and aesthetic merit, then its masking with externally applied insulation will not be appropriate. On the other hand, if the facade is uninteresting, or in poor condition, then externally applied insulation may be the ideal solution, since, in one operation, its thermal performance and its appearance can be significantly improved. A number of other factors must also be considered before deciding whether or not to opt for external insulation, and these have been listed in Table 4.5.

Although the use of externally applied insulation systems rules out the need to disrupt the interior of the building, certain modifications to the exterior will be necessary to allow for the increase in the thickness of the wall. This may involve the extension of window sills, removal and repositioning of rainwater and waste pipes, provision of metal flashings, the accommodation of air bricks, and other work to facilitate addition of the new insulation layer.

There are four basic forms of externally applied thermal insulation, as follows.

(i) THERMAL INSULATION BEHIND CONVENTIONAL CLADDINGS

Where the existing wall has a tile or weatherboard external cladding, it may be possible to insert a layer of rigid or flexible insulation behind. This will involve removal and replacement of the cladding, but has the advantage of maintaining the original exterior appearance of the building.

(ii) LIGHTWEIGHT INSULATING RENDERS

These normally comprise a mixture of cement and lightweight aggregate such as polystyrene, to give a density of about half that of traditional lightweight renders. The Permoglaze Thermarend system (see Fig. 4.13) comprises a cement-based render, incorporating selected aggregates and expanded polystyrene beads. The ingredients are supplied pre-mixed and only water is added on site. The preparation of the background must be as for conventional renders, all loose material being removed before the render is applied. If the background is either very smooth and dense, or highly absorbent, it should be pre-treated with Thermarend pre-coat which acts as a bonding agent. The Thermarend insulating render is applied by trowel or spray-gun to a thickness of 30–60 mm, depending on the degree of thermal upgrading required. Finally, a thin layer of Permoglaze bedding mortar is applied to the surface of the Thermarend and this is finished with either dry dash or a coloured textured coating. The application of a 50 mm thickness of Thermarend will improve the 'U' value of a 220 mm solid brick wall from 2.17 to 0.91 $W/m^2 K$.

(iii) RIGID INSULATION BOARDS WITH RENDER FINISH

This method comprises rigid insulation boards mechanically fixed to the background and finished with a conventional cement/sand render. The Expolath system (see Fig. 4.14) consists of rigid polystyrene insulating boards overlaid with sheets of expanded metal lathing, which provides a key for the render finish. The lathing and insulation boards are secured to the wall with polypropylene fixing pins which pass through the lathing and insulation and into the wall. The render, consisting of cement, white sand and waterproofer, is applied to the expanded metal lathing to a thickness of 10–15 mm, and scratched to provide a key for the finishing coat. The latter may be a traditional cement render with dry or wet dash, or any one of the many proprietary coloured, textured exterior finishes currently available. An Expolath external insulation system, using 50 mm thick boarding, will improve the 'U' value of a

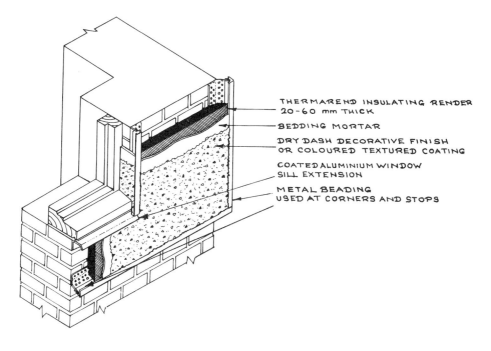

THERMAREND INSULATING RENDER
20-60 mm THICK

BEDDING MORTAR

DRY DASH DECORATIVE FINISH
OR COLOURED TEXTURED COATING

COATED ALUMINIUM WINDOW
SILL EXTENSION

METAL BEADING
USED AT CORNERS AND STOPS

THERMAREND LIGHTWEIGHT INSULATING RENDER

Fig. 4.13 Externally applied insulation

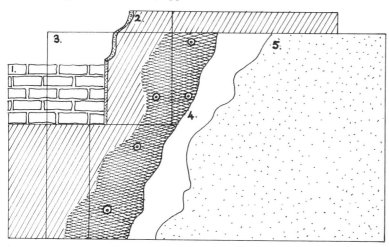

1. EXISTING WALL SURFACE
2. RIGID POLYSTYRENE INSULATION BOARDS 20-100 mm THICK
3. EXPANDED METAL LATH
   (2. AND 3. FIXED TO WALL USING POLYPROPYLENE FIXING PINS ⊙)
4. CEMENT/SAND RENDER 10-15 mm THICK
5. DECORATIVE FINISH

EXPOLATH RIGID INSULATION BOARD AND RENDER

Fig. 4.14 Externally applied
insulation

220 mm solid brick wall from 2.17 to 0.6 W/m² K.

(iv) FLEXIBLE INSULATION WITH RENDER FINISH

This is similar to the previous method with the exception that flexible, rather than rigid, insulation is used, enabling it to be taken around corners and into reveals without the need for cutting and jointing. The Insulath system (see Fig. 4.15) consists of 25 or 50 mm thick high-density flexible fibreglass board, factory bonded to Twil-Lath, a combined breather-paper and wire mesh, which acts as a base for the application of the render finish. The insulation-/Twil-Lath composite is fixed using nylon-sleeved stainless steel fasteners, which penetrate 50 mm into the background. The cement/sand render finish is applied in three coats to a total thickness of 22–25 mm, and finished with dry dash or any other suitable cementitious or resin-based application. As an alternative to applying a traditional render finish, Twil-Fibrerend, produced by the manufacturers of the Insulath system, may be used. This is a fibre-reinforced render system applied in two or three coats on successive days to give an overall thickness of 12–15 mm. It is lighter in weight, stronger, and can be completed in a shorter timescale than traditional rendering. Fibrerend is available with a range of self-coloured top-coats, which can be roller-textured and require no further decoration.

The Insulath system, using 50 mm thick insulation, is capable of upgrading the 'U' value of a 220 mm solid brick wall from 2.17 to 0.51 W/m² K.

(c) Injected cavity fill insulation

This form of insulation was developed specifically for improving the thermal insulation properties of existing cavity-walled buildings in order to reduce energy consumption and fuel costs. The insulation, which is injected into the cavity via holes drilled through the outer skin, may be selected from a number of different proprietary materials. Injected cavity fill materials currently in use include urea-formaldehyde foam, expanded polystyrene beads, and mineral fibres, all of which are capable of reducing the 'U' value of a standard cavity wall to 0.6 W/m² K.

Where a cavity-walled building requires thermal upgrading, this method is the most preferable solution, since it can be applied without affecting the existing exterior or interior surfaces, and with minimal disruption.

4.4.2 Upgrading the thermal performance of roofs

Loss of heat through the roof can represent up to a quarter of a building's total heat loss and thus thermal upgrading of the existing roof structure will be essential if future heating costs are to be minimized. Several techniques are available for use in upgrading roofs and the work can usually be carried out with the minimum of disruption to the building and its occupants.

(a) Thermal upgrading of pitched roofs

Pitched roofs may be upgraded by inserting an additional insulating layer either at ceiling level, or at rafter level, immediately below the roof covering. Where a ceiling exists beneath the roof space, and provided the roof space is not intended for use, the insulation can be inserted at ceiling level to reduce heat loss into the void above and ultimately to the exterior (see Fig. 4.16(a)). If, however, the roof space is to be converted into accommodation in the rehabilitation/alteration scheme, it will be necessary to provide the new insulation at rafter level (see Fig. 4.16(b)). The new insulation may also have to be inserted at rafter level in buildings where no ceiling exists and where the accommodation extends into the roof space. Typical examples of this include redundant churches, where the existing open roof space is retained to preserve the original character; and old factories and warehouses, where ceilings were not normally provided beneath the roof space (see Fig. 4.16(c)).

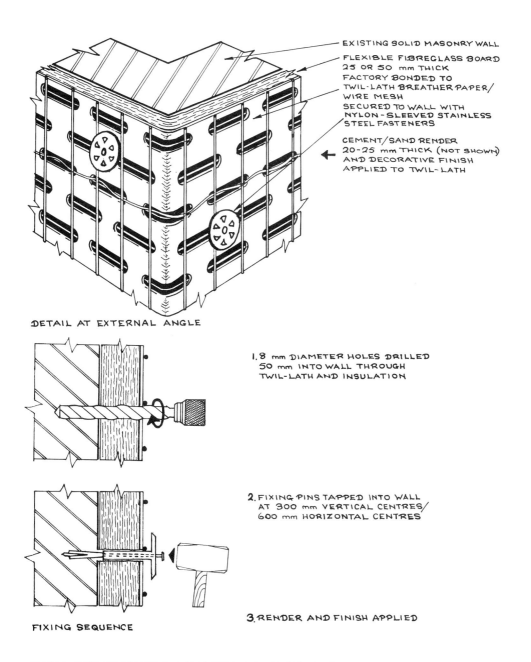

EXISTING SOLID MASONRY WALL

FLEXIBLE FIBREGLASS BOARD
25 OR 50 mm THICK
FACTORY BONDED TO
TWIL-LATH BREATHER PAPER/
WIRE MESH
SECURED TO WALL WITH
NYLON-SLEEVED STAINLESS
STEEL FASTENERS

CEMENT/SAND RENDER
20-25 mm THICK (NOT SHOWN)
AND DECORATIVE FINISH
APPLIED TO TWIL-LATH

DETAIL AT EXTERNAL ANGLE

1. 8 mm DIAMETER HOLES DRILLED
50 mm INTO WALL THROUGH
TWIL-LATH AND INSULATION

2. FIXING PINS TAPPED INTO WALL
AT 300 mm VERTICAL CENTRES/
600 mm HORIZONTAL CENTRES

3. RENDER AND FINISH APPLIED

FIXING SEQUENCE

INSULATH FLEXIBLE INSULATION AND RENDER

Fig. 4.15 Externally applied insulation

55

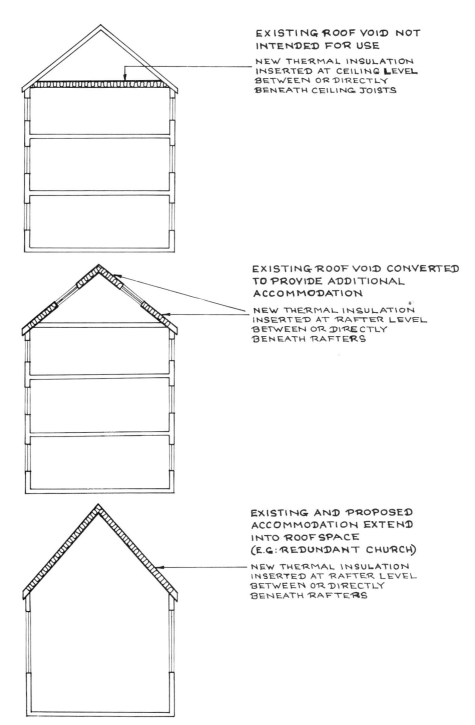

EXISTING ROOF VOID NOT
INTENDED FOR USE

NEW THERMAL INSULATION
INSERTED AT CEILING LEVEL
BETWEEN OR DIRECTLY
BENEATH CEILING JOISTS

EXISTING ROOF VOID CONVERTED
TO PROVIDE ADDITIONAL
ACCOMMODATION

NEW THERMAL INSULATION
INSERTED AT RAFTER LEVEL
BETWEEN OR DIRECTLY
BENEATH RAFTERS

EXISTING AND PROPOSED
ACCOMMODATION EXTEND
INTO ROOF SPACE
(E.G: REDUNDANT CHURCH)

NEW THERMAL INSULATION
INSERTED AT RAFTER LEVEL
BETWEEN OR DIRECTLY
BENEATH RAFTERS

Fig. 4.16 Upgrading the thermal performance of pitched roofs

FLEXIBLE FIBREGLASS
INSULATING QUILT BETWEEN
CEILING JOISTS AND
SUPPORTED BY EXISTING
CEILING

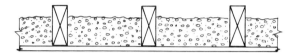

EXPANDED VERMICULITE
POLYSTYRENE BEADS OR
BLOWN MINERAL WOOL
LOOSE-FILL BETWEEN
CEILING JOISTS AND
SUPPORTED BY EXISTING
CEILING

EXISTING CEILING REPLACED
WITH NEW COMPOSITE
THERMAL BOARD CEILING
E.G: GYPROC THERMAL BOARD
OR STYROLINER

**NEW THERMAL INSULATION
AT CEILING LEVEL**

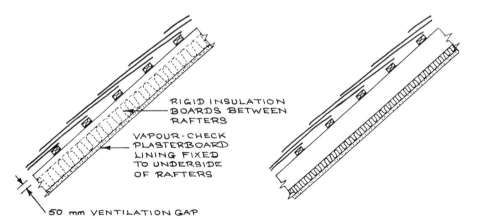

RIGID INSULATION
BOARDS BETWEEN
RAFTERS

VAPOUR-CHECK
PLASTERBOARD
LINING FIXED
TO UNDERSIDE
OF RAFTERS

50 mm VENTILATION GAP

NEW PLASTERBOARD LINING
SUPPORTING SEPARATE RIGID
INSULATION BOARDS
INSERTED BETWEEN RAFTERS

NEW COMPOSITE THERMAL BOARD
LINING (E.G: GYPROC THERMAL
BOARD OR STYROLINER) NAILED
TO UNDERSIDE OF RAFTERS

**NEW THERMAL INSULATION
AT RAFTER LEVEL**

Fig. 4.17 Upgrading the thermal performance of pitched roofs

The various methods that can be used to upgrade the thermal performance of pitched roofs are described below and illustrated in Fig. 4.17.

(i) INSULATING QUILTS AT CEILING LEVEL

Where a ceiling exists beneath the roof space, the simplest and most common solution is to lay the new insulation immediately above the ceiling, between the joists or the lower ties of the roof trusses. Flexible fibreglass insulating quilts, supplied in rolls of varying widths and thicknesses, are a cheap and efficient way of upgrading thermal insulation using this method.

When insulation is provided directly above the existing ceiling in this way, it is essential to ensure that the roof space above the insulation is properly ventilated. Providing better insulation at ceiling level has the effect of reducing the temperature within the roof space which, in turn, increases the risk of condensation. Effective cross-ventilation is therefore essential in order to minimize the condensation risk and avoid potential damage to the roof structure. This can be achieved by forming ventilation openings at the eaves and inserting air-bricks in gable ends.

(ii) LOOSE-FILL MATERIALS AT CEILING LEVEL

As an alternative to laying insulating quilts above the existing ceiling, loose-fill insulating materials may be used. These include expanded vermiculite, expanded polystyrene beads and blown mineral wool, all of which can be inserted in varying thicknesses according to the degree of thermal upgrading required. One disadvantage of using these materials is that their loose, lightweight nature can cause problems such as leakage via ventilation openings and inadvertent blocking of services ducts, flues, etc. As with insulating quilts, it will also be necessary to ventilate the roof space in order to minimize the risk of condensation (see (i)).

(iii) THERMAL BOARDS AT CEILING LEVEL

Where the existing ceiling is in poor condition and is beyond economic repair, its replacement with a proprietary thermal board such as Gyproc thermal board or Styroliner (see Section 4.4.1) will be a viable solution. In this way, a new plasterboard ceiling, capable of receiving direct decoration, and an additional insulating layer are provided in a single operation. A further advantage is that thermal boards can be obtained with an integral vapour barrier, sandwiched between the plasterboard and the factory-bonded insulation, therefore significantly reducing the risk of condensation in the roof space above.

(iv) RIGID INSULATION AT RAFTER LEVEL

Thermal insulation must be provided at rafter level where the roof is to be converted into usable accommodation or where no ceiling exists and the upper rooms extend into the roof space. In most cases, a rigid internal lining of plasterboard or similar material will be fixed to the rafters and the insulation can therefore be sandwiched between the lining and the roof covering. The insulating material will need to be held in position to prevent settlement or slipping down the roof slope which could result in gaps opening between sections. This rules out the use of loose-fill materials, the most preferable being rigid insulation boards supported at regular intervals down the roof slope by cross-battens between the rafters. Suitable materials include rigid boards of glass-fibre, rock-fibre, expanded polystyrene or polyurethane foam, all of which are available in a range of sizes and thicknesses to suit individual requirements.

Where sandwiched insulation of this type is used, it is essential that a ventilation gap of at least 50 mm is provided between the insulation and the sarking felt in order to minimize the risk of condensation. The condensation risk can also be reduced by using vapour-check plasterboard, such as Gyproc Duplex plasterboard, for the internal lining.

A suitable alternative to using a plasterboard lining and separate sandwiched insulation is to use one of the proprietary thermal boards described earlier (see (iii) above). Styroliner, or Gyproc vapour-check thermal board (see Section 4.4.1) fixed to the underside of the rafters, provides an internal lining, thermal insulation and a vapour check in one operation.

(b) Thermal upgrading of flat roofs

The method used to upgrade an existing flat roof will depend to some extent on its construction. Concrete flat roofs can only be upgraded by adding the new insulation either beneath the slab at ceiling level or on top of the slab. With timber flat roofs, a third option is available, this being to insert the insulation within the void between the ceiling and the roof covering. A number of methods can be used to upgrade flat roofs, as follows.

(i) THERMAL BOARDS AT CEILING LEVEL

The simplest and most cost effective means of upgrading a flat roof is to provide thermal boards at ceiling level. Proprietary boards, such as Gyproc thermal board or Styroliner (see (a)(iii) above) can either be fixed directly beneath the existing ceiling or be used to replace the existing ceiling if it is in a poor state of repair. The use of thermal board for upgrading rules out the need to gain access to the void (in the case of timber roofs), does not involve external work, and provides a new ceiling capable of direct decoration. However, it does involve some internal disruption and inconvenience to occupants, and it may also be inappropriate where the existing ceiling has ornate plasterwork.

The provision of additional insulation on the underside of the roof structure in this way produces a 'cold roof', i.e. the temperature of the roof structure is at or near that of the outside air. This condition significantly increases the risk of condensation within the roof construction and it is therefore essential that precautions are taken to reduce this risk. The use of thermal board with an integral vapour barrier sandwiched between the plasterboard and insulation will minimize the occurrence of condensation,

and, if the roof is of timber, the void should also be ventilated.

(ii) INSULATING QUILTS OR BOARDS AT CEILING LEVEL

This method is only applicable to timber flat roofs and involves inserting the new insulation in the void between the ceiling and roof covering. It is therefore only appropriate in cases where the existing ceiling is in a poor condition and needs replacing, and involves inserting insulating quilt or rigid insulation boards between the roof joists prior to fixing a new plasterboard ceiling. This method has the advantage of allowing a much thicker layer of insulation to be provided, since the void between the ceiling and roof covering will be at least 100 mm. As with the previous method, however, a cold roof will result and it will therefore be necessary to use a vapour-check plasterboard and to ventilate the roof void.

(iii) RIGID INSULATION BOARDS ON TOP OF THE EXISTING ROOF COVERING

In some cases, it may be necessary to remove and replace the exterior roof covering if it has deteriorated beyond repair, and in this event, new, rigid insulation can be provided before laying the new covering. If, however, the existing roof covering is waterproof and in good physical condition, the new thermal insulation can be added without having to take up the existing covering. Roofmate* is a proprietary closed-cell, water-resistant insulation board specifically developed for the external insulation of flat roofs. It can be used to upgrade both timber and concrete roofs finished with built-up felt, asphalt and other materials, the procedure being as follows.

Any loose chippings are removed and the existing roof surface swept clean. Roofs with bonded gravel toppings should be covered with a levelling layer such as Ethafoam* extruded polyethylene foam sheet applied loose. The

*Trademarks of the Dow Chemical Company.

Roofmate* insulation boards are laid loose and tightly butted with staggered joints prior to covering with a 50 mm layer of 20–30 mm gravel or paving slabs, as for new roofs. It is essential that the capability of the roof structure to take the extra weight is checked, particularly if paving slabs are to be used. An uninsulated flat roof with an existing 'U' value of 1.3 W/m² K can be upgraded to 0.55 W/m² K using 50 mm thick Roofmate*, and to 0.38 W/m² K using 75 mm thick Roofmate*.

An alternative to the above, produced by the same manufacturer, is Roofmate* LG insulation. This system comprises Roofmate* insulation boards, with an integral mortar topping and interlocking tongued and grooved edging. Roofmate* LG does not require Ethafoam* underlay, nor does it require a heavy layer of gravel or paving slabs to hold it down, therefore significantly reducing its overall weight.

Although these methods involve external work, there are a number of significant advantages:

- Adding the insulation externally produces a 'warm roof', which minimizes the risk of condensation within the roof construction
- There is no disruption to interior finishes and fittings
- The occupants of the building undergo minimal inconvenience since no interior work is necessary.

4.4.3 Upgrading the thermal properties of floors

Heat loss through the floor of a building is minimal in relation to heat loss via the external walls and roof, and, for this reason, the floor is often ignored. However, in some situations, it may also be worth while upgrading the thermal insulation value of the floors.

Generally, the heat loss through ventilated raised timber floors is greater than that through solid concrete floors and, if the building has a

*Trademarks of the Dow Chemical Company.

timber ground floor, consideration should be given to thermal upgrading. Raised timber and solid concrete floors can both be upgraded fairly easily using proprietary insulating materials: Thermafloor laminated flooring panels consist of moisture-resistant Styrofoam closed-cell insulation board with a high compressive strength, bonded to flooring-grade chipboard, which can be laid on existing floors to provide added insulation and a new floor finish in a single operation. The adhesive used in manufacturing the panels is moisture and vapour-resistant and provides an integral vapour check on the warm side of the insulation. Where the Thermafloor panels are used to upgrade a solid floor, the surface should be dry and free of loose material. If the base is particularly uneven, a blinding layer of sand can be used to level the floor. The panels are laid with their cross joints staggered, and PVA or mastic adhesive is used to bond their edges. With timber floors, the panels are nailed to the floorboards or joists in the conventional manner. In all cases, an expansion gap should be left between the edges of the outer panels and the perimeter walls.

The panels are 2440 × 600 mm and tongued and grooved on all four edges. The chipboard thickness is 18 mm, with insulation thicknesses of 16, 20, 25 or 50 mm, giving overall panel thicknesses of 34, 38, 43 and 68 mm respectively.

4.5 UPGRADING THE ACOUSTIC PERFORMANCE OF EXISTING ELEMENTS

The need to upgrade the acoustic performance of the elements of a building will depend mainly on its proposed usage. If, after rehabilitation, the building is intended for industrial or commercial use, sound insulation may not be important, since relatively high levels of noise are generally acceptable in such builings. However, upgrading may be desirable, for example, to reduce sound transmission between workshops and offices, or between general offices and directors' offices.

The most common need for acoustic upgrading in rehabilitation work occurs in schemes involving the conversion of existing buildings into self-contained flats or maisonettes. In such cases it will normally be desirable to upgrade the sound insulation value of walls and floors which separate different occupancies in order to prevent or reduce noise nuisance between them.

It should be made clear at this point that acoustic upgrading, whether in industrial, commercial, residential or any other class of rehabilitation, is *not* statutorily required by the Building Regulations under the "material change of use" clause: Regulation 6 requires that certain specified parts of the Regulations must be complied with when the purpose for which a building will be used is changed. Several parts of the Regulations must be complied with, but Part E: "Resistance to the passage of sound", is not included. However, sound insulation of elements, particularly between residential occupancies, is extremely important if noise nuisance is to be avoided. It is advisable, therefore, that serious consideration be given to improving the acoustic properties of certain walls and floors if a good overall standard of rehabilitation is to be achieved.

In the case of residential rehabilitation, the most appropriate means of dealing with acoustic upgrading is to use Part E of the Building Regulations as a guide, even though there is no statutory obligation to comply.

In order to comply with the sound insulation requirements of Part E of the Building Regulations, walls and floors may either be constructed in accordance with one of the specifications contained in Approved Document E to the Regulations, *or* comply with specified sound transmission values.

It should be understood at this point that floors and walls may need to be resistant to the passage of one or both of the following types of sound:

- Airborne sound: i.e. sound waves in the air striking the wall or floor

- Impact sound: i.e. sound waves initiated in the wall or floor itself as a result of a direct impact

4.5.1 Upgrading the acoustic performance of party walls

Building Regulation E1 requires that any wall separating one dwelling from another dwelling or from another building, *or* any wall separating a habitable room in a dwelling from any other part of the same building which is not used exclusively with that dwelling "shall have reasonable resistance to *airborne* sound".

Thus, in rehabilitation work it will be desirable to ensure that such walls are constructed or upgraded to comply with the guidance contained in Approved Document E to the Regulations. Existing walls are generally difficult to upgrade owing to their constructional integration with floors which allow 'flanking transmission' of sound. Thus, a wall which has been constructed to provide good sound insulation may have its effectiveness significantly reduced because of flanking transmission of sound via the floors with which it connects.

One of the most effective treatments, where the sound insulation of an existing wall must be improved, is to add a separate leaf on one, or preferably both sides of the wall to give a 100 mm air gap. This can be carried out in any of the following ways (see Fig. 4.18).

(a) Timber studding finished with plasterboard and with a 50 mm layer of glass-fibre quilt inserted in the cavity. It is essential that the timber studding is fixed only to the existing floor and ceiling, and *not* to the wall itself, since any contact with the wall will adversely affect the degree of sound reduction obtained. The best procedure is to fix the head and sole plates to the existing ceiling and floor respectively, and insert the vertical studs between them to give a continuous gap between the stud framing and the wall.

A double layer of 12.7 mm plasterboard

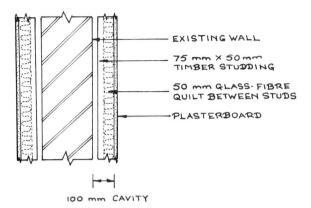

EXISTING WALL

75 mm x 50 mm TIMBER STUDDING

50 mm GLASS-FIBRE QUILT BETWEEN STUDS

PLASTERBOARD

100 mm CAVITY

TIMBER STUDDING AND PLASTERBOARD
WITH 50 mm GLASS-FIBRE QUILT IN CAVITY

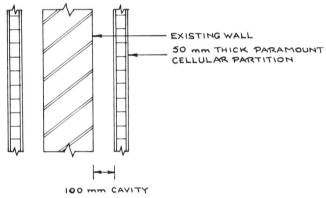

EXISTING WALL

50 mm THICK PARAMOUNT CELLULAR PARTITION

100 mm CAVITY

PARAMOUNT PARTITIONING

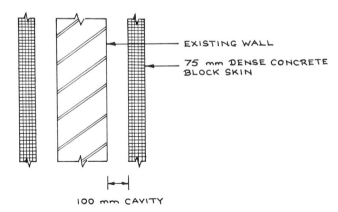

EXISTING WALL

75 mm DENSE CONCRETE BLOCK SKIN

100 mm CAVITY

BRICKWORK OR BLOCKWORK

Fig. 4.18 Upgrading the acoustic performance of party walls

62

should be applied to the studding, and the space between the back of the plasterboard and the existing wall face should be 100–125 mm wide. As an alternative to inserting the 50 mm glass-fibre quilt between the studs, as shown in Fig. 4.18, it can be hung against the existing wall face, a timber fixing batten along the top being sufficient to hold the quilt in position.

Ideally, if the best possible sound reduction is to be obtained, studding, plasterboard and quilt should be provided on both sides of the existing wall as shown in the figure. However, where this is inconvenient or undesirable, the treatment can be applied to one side only, and this will give a typical improvement of from 5 dB to 10 dB sound reduction across the frequency range 100 Hz to 3150 Hz.

(b) Proprietary Paramount partitioning (a composite, comprising two sheets of plasterboard separated by, and bonded to, a cellular core).

(c) An additional brickwork or blockwork skin.

All of these methods significantly increase the overall thickness of the existing wall and, in turn, reduce the usable floor area. Where loss of floorspace is a problem, the new, sound-reducing constructions can be positioned nearer

to the existing wall, and, if necessary, the treatment can be provided on one side of the wall only, but it should be appreciated that this, or the narrowing of the cavity, will be less effective in reducing sound transmission through the party wall.

4.5.2 Upgrading the acoustic performance of party floors

The basic requirements of Building Regulation E2 and E3 are as follows:

- A floor which separates two dwellings must provide adequate resistance to both *airborne and impact sound*.
- A floor which separates a dwelling above that floor from any other part of the building which is *not* a dwelling, is only required to provide adequate resistance to *airborne sound*.

This is illustrated in Fig. 4.19: the party floor separating the two dwellings must resist the transmission of airborne sound emanating from *both* dwellings *and* the transmission of impact sound from the upper to the lower dwelling caused by footsteps. On the other hand, where the part of the building below the floor is not a dwelling, the floor need only be resistant to airborne sound emanating from the space below.

Fig. 4.19 Acoustic performance of party floors: Building Regulations requirements

Methods of upgrading the sound insulation of existing floors are given below ((a)–(e)).

(a) Carpets

The provision of carpets with underlay makes a significant improvement to insulation against impact sound. In addition, where gaps exist between badly fitting floorboards, these should be sealed by fixing hardboard sheeting over the whole floor area, since such gaps can drastically reduce the sound insulation properties of the floor.

(b) 'Pugging'

Pugging is the insertion of 'sound-deadening' materials within the thickness of the floor between the existing floorboards and ceiling. The most effective and commonly used pugging material is sand inserted in the void to a density of 80 kg/m². This is normally too heavy to be supported directly by the existing ceiling and is therefore supported by 'pugging boards' and battens fixed between the joists (see Fig. 4.20.). Slag wool pellets and mineral wool may also be used as pugging but both are much less effective than sand.

(c) Floating floor

One of the most effective ways of upgrading a floor's sound insulation is to lift the existing floorboards and convert it into a floating floor. The conversion involves 'floating' the floor on a 25 mm layer of resilient quilt draped over the joists. The materials most commonly used are glass wool or mineral wool. Figure 4.20 shows two methods of producing a floating floor, as follows.

(i) FIRST METHOD

In the first method, which raises the level of the floorboards by approximately 10 mm, the surface is made up in 500–1000 mm wide sections with battens projecting beyond them to enable adjacent sections to be screwed together when laid. The 25 mm quilt crushes down to approximately 10 mm over the joists, resulting in a minimal increase in the level of the floor surface. The battens should be 50 mm × 50 mm in section and the floating surface should *not* be nailed or screwed to the joists. In addition, it is essential that the quilt is taken up round the edges of the floorboards to prevent flanking transmission of sound via the adjoining walls.

(ii) SECOND METHOD

The second method of producing a floating floor is more conventional and simpler to construct. It does, however, raise the level of the existing floor's surface by a greater amount, approximately 60 mm (50 mm battens *plus* 10 mm crushed quilt). The 50 mm × 50 mm battens are positioned directly over the joists with the quilt in between. In order for this type of floating floor to be successful it is vital that the nails, which secure the floorboards to the battens, only penetrate the battens and *not* the quilt and the joists. As with the previous method, it is also essential to take the quilt up round the edges of the floorboards, to rule out flanking transmission.

(iii) ALTERNATIVE METHOD

As an alternative to the above methods, a completely new floor surface can be floated on top of the existing floorboards in conjunction with the insertion of a sound-absorbent material between the joists. This involves the following operations:

- Lift existing floorboards and insert glass–fibre or rockwool quilt, not less than 100 mm thick, (density not exceeding 36 kg/m³) between joists.
- Re-lay floorboards. If the existing boarding was plain-edged, or in poor condition, it should be replaced with new.
- Lay 25 mm glass–fibre or rockwool quilt (density 60 to 80 kg/m³) over floorboards.
- Lay 19 mm plasterboard sheets on top of quilt, laid loose and with gap at perimeter walls.
- Lay 19 mm tongued and grooved chipboard,

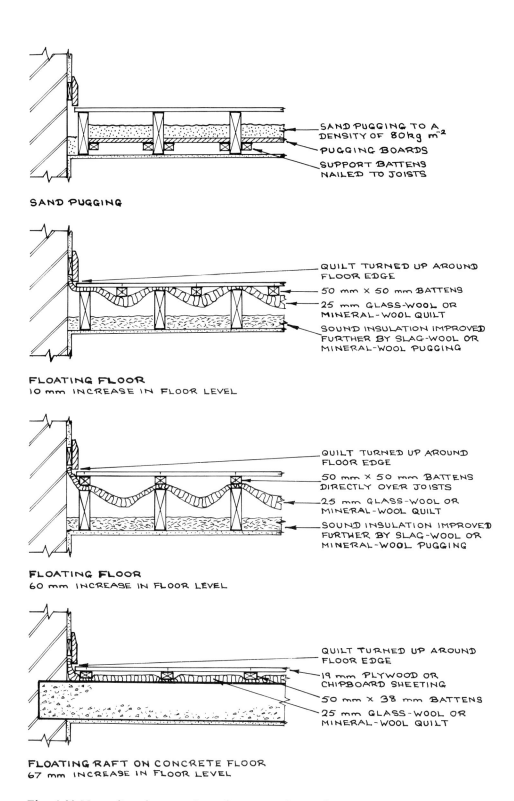

SAND PUGGING TO A DENSITY OF 80kg m⁻²

SAND PUGGING TO A
DENSITY OF 80kg m⁻²
PUGGING BOARDS
SUPPORT BATTENS
NAILED TO JOISTS

SAND PUGGING

QUILT TURNED UP AROUND
FLOOR EDGE
50 mm x 50 mm BATTENS
25 mm GLASS-WOOL OR
MINERAL-WOOL QUILT
SOUND INSULATION IMPROVED
FURTHER BY SLAG-WOOL OR
MINERAL-WOOL PUGGING

FLOATING FLOOR
10 mm INCREASE IN FLOOR LEVEL

QUILT TURNED UP AROUND
FLOOR EDGE
50 mm x 50 mm BATTENS
DIRECTLY OVER JOISTS
25 mm GLASS-WOOL OR
MINERAL-WOOL QUILT
SOUND INSULATION IMPROVED
FURTHER BY SLAG-WOOL OR
MINERAL-WOOL PUGGING

FLOATING FLOOR
60 mm INCREASE IN FLOOR LEVEL

QUILT TURNED UP AROUND
FLOOR EDGE
19 mm PLYWOOD OR
CHIPBOARD SHEETING
50 mm x 38 mm BATTENS
25 mm GLASS-WOOL OR
MINERAL-WOOL QUILT

FLOATING RAFT ON CONCRETE FLOOR
67 mm INCREASE IN FLOOR LEVEL

Fig. 4.20 Upgrading the acoustic performance of party floors

65

with all joints glued but not nailed down, leaving a perimeter gap of at least 10 mm.

- Fix ceiling coving to eliminate airborne sound transmission at perimeter, or seal gaps with a flexible sealant.
- Re-fix skirting boards to cover the 10 mm gap at perimeter of new chipboard floor surface, ensuring that a slight gap is also left between the lower edge of the skirting and the floor surface.

The use of this method to add a new floating floor over the existing will raise the floor level by about 65 mm and, like methods (i) and (ii), will require the alteration of skirtings, doors and their frames, services, sanitary fittings, stairs, etc.

In the majority of rehabilitation schemes which involve acoustic upgrading, the floors will be of timber, to which all the above techniques apply. However, in some schemes the floors may be of concrete and, although this material generally provides good sound reduction in its own right, it might still be desirable to improve it further, especially where flanking transmission or impact sound is a problem.

(d) Floating raft

This technique, illustrated in Fig. 4.20, involves providing a floating raft of floorboards or timber sheeting on top of the existing concrete floor. The raft is made up in sections using 50 mm × 38 mm timber battens and laid on the concrete floor over a 25 mm thick layer of resilient quilt. If flanking transmission of sound is to be avoided, it is essential that the resilient layer is turned up at the edges, to isolate the raft from the existing walls, and that a gap is left between the raft and the skirting board.

(e) Independent ceiling

The methods described above all involve treating the existing floor surface and/or the floor void in some way. An alternative means of upgrading the acoustic performance of a party floor is to add a new ceiling beneath it. This should be carried on its own set of joists, and

spaced as far below the existing ceiling as possible, with an acoustically absorbent quilt inserted between the new and existing ceilings. The addition of an independent ceiling involves the following operations:

- Fix new ceiling joists beneath existing ceiling. They can be supported by fixing timber bearers to the walls and notching the joist-ends over them; or by using metal joist hangers.
- Lay 25 mm thick glass-fibre or rockwool quilt over the new joists, ensuring that it is not compressed between the new joists and existing ceiling.
- Fix two layers of 12.7 mm plasterboard beneath the new joists to form the new ceiling.
- If the floorboards in the upper room are plain-edged, they should be covered with hardboard sheeting to seal all gaps.

The principal advantage of this technique, which should improve sound insulation by 5 dB to 10 dB over the frequency range 100 Hz to 3150 Hz, is that it does not affect the floor level and create the problems referred to in (c)(iii) above. However, it should be borne in mind that the addition of an independent ceiling will affect existing light fittings, plaster covings, etc., and it will not be acceptable where an existing ornate plaster ceiling has to be preserved.

4.5.3 Upgrading the acoustic performance of external walls

Upgrading the sound insulation of external walls is rarely necessary, unless the building faces a noisy roadway, factory or other excessive noise source. The importance of upgrading the external walls will also depend to some extent upon the acceptable noise levels within the building.

External noise usually enters a building via the windows, since single glazing is a very poor sound reducer. Relatively insignificant gaps around ill-fitting casements also adversely affect their acoustic performance, and, if a window is opened only slightly, its sound reduction capability will be drastically reduced.

The most effective means of upgrading the acoustic performance of an external wall, therefore, is to deal with the windows. If the existing windows are in good condition, they can be converted into double windows, by adding new glazing internally with an intervening airspace of 150 to 200 mm. A narrower airspace will result in a much poorer sound reduction performance. If double windows are installed, it must be ensured that the casements and frames fit tightly, all gaps being properly sealed. Ideally, the double windows should not be openable since, as previously stated, opening windows drastically reduces their sound insulation capability. This may, in turn, require the installation of mechanical ventilation which will significantly increase the cost of the rehabilitation work. In view of this, and the expense of providing and sealing the double windows, acoustic upgrading of external walls in this way should normally only be carried out where external noise sources would cause severe problems.

4.6 PREVENTING DAMP PENETRATION INTO THE BUILDING

The most common single cause of building deterioration is dampness, and it has been estimated that over 1.5 million dwellings in the UK are seriously affected by dampness problems. The principal sources of dampness are rainwater penetration through roofs and external walls, rising damp, through walls and solid floors, and condensation. Because its causes and prevention are different from the other sources of dampness, condensation is dealt with separately in Section 4.7.

4.6.1 Preventing rainwater penetration through external walls

The majority of old buildings have solid stone or brick external walls which are inherently vulnerable to rainwater penetration, often resulting in permanent dampness and deterioration of plasterwork and internal finishes. The severity of the problem varies and, at best, might only result in a few damp patches over the internal surface of the wall. In some cases, however, the dampness may be so severe as to cause total deterioration of plasterwork and finishes over large areas of the wall.

A number of different techniques can be used to overcome the problems of rainwater penetration through solid walls, as follows.

(a) Internal treatments

(i) DRY LININGS
The use of dry linings for upgrading internal wall surfaces is described in detail in Section 4.3.1. In cases where the external walls are suffering only from slight dampness, a traditional timber batten dry lining, used in conjunction with an externally applied water-repellent solution, is an appropriate means of overcoming the problem. The dry lining is fixed as described in Section 4.3.1 to provide a new, dry wall surface, and additional precautions are taken to protect it from the penetrating dampness. The vertical timber battens must be pressure impregnated with preservative to prevent the risk of fungal attack, and they should be secured to the wall over strips of polythene sheeting or bitumen felt to isolate them from the damp wall. If the dampness is widespread, the whole wall surface should be lined with sheet polythene, properly lapped and jointed, and secured to the wall by the timber battens.

If the damp penetration is more severe, a dry lining fixed directly to the wall will itself be vulnerable to deterioration, and other methods of dealing with the problem must be employed.

(ii) NEWLATH DAMP-PROOF SHEETING
Newlath is a damp-proof lightweight sheet material made from high-density polyethylene,

0.5 mm thick, formed into a pattern of raised studs linked by reinforcing ribs. The 8 mm high studs face the wall, creating channels which allow air to circulate freely behind the Newlath. A polythene mesh welded on to the other side of the Newlath provides a rot-proof key for a plaster finish. The material is inert and highly resistant to water, alkalis, saline solutions, and organic acids, and is not affected by minerals. It is also resistant to bacteria, fungi and other small organisms. Newlath is particularly suited to rehabilitation and improvement work where rising and penetrating damp is a serious problem in the existing walls. It is supplied in 1.5 metre wide rolls, 10 metres in length and works on the principle of providing a ventilated moisture-proof barrier between the existing wall surface and the new applied finish, as shown in Fig. 4.21.

All damp or crumbling plaster, where it exists, should be removed prior to fixing the Newlath to the wall surface. The material can then be fixed to the background, using 50 mm long polypropylene plugs at not more than 300 mm vertical and horizontal centres. Closer centres should be adopted on uneven or curved surfaces. For fixing to wood or other nailable surfaces, galvanized clout nails can be used. All joints between adjacent sheets should be lapped by not less than 100 mm.

The provision of adequate through ventilation between the Newlath and the damp wall surface is essential, and this is achieved by leaving ventilation gaps at both bottom and top. The bottom edge of the Newlath must be raised 20–25 mm above the floor, and a 2–3 mm gap left at ceiling level. Once the plaster finish has been applied and has dried, the ventilation gaps can be concealed by a wooden skirting and coving as shown in Fig. 4.21.

Newlath will accept virtually any plaster, which should be applied to a thickness of 13 mm to provide the new, damp-proofed wall finish.

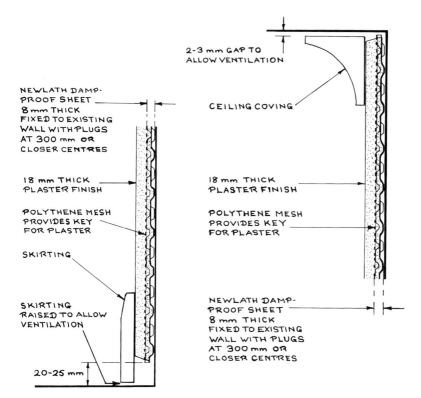

Fig. 4.21 Newlath damp-proof sheeting

In addition to providing a damp-proof base for internal wall finishes, Newlath can be used for ceilings, arches and vaults, and also as a base for external render finishes.

(iii) DAMP-RESISTING COATINGS

A number of proprietary materials have been developed specifically for application by brush or spray to walls suffering from damp penetration. RIW 232 damp-resisting composition and plasterbond is a black, elastic, damp-proof composition formulated for application to interior surfaces of damp external walls above ground level in all types of buildings, to which pre-mixed vermiculite gypsum plaster is applied directly. It ensures thorough and permanent damp-proofing and provides a good bond for the plaster. All holes and voids in the wall surface being treated must be filled with cement mortar prior to brush or spray application of the first coat of the composition, which should be applied to a uniform black finish and allowed to set and dry. The second coat is then applied in the same manner as the first. When this is set and dry, a two-coat plaster finish, minimum thickness 10 mm, is applied to form the new, damp-proofed internal surface.

(b) External treatments

(i) WATER-REPELLENT SOLUTIONS

A number of proprietary water-repellent solutions are available, and these provide a relatively simple and inexpensive means of preventing rainwater penetration through external walls where the problem is not too severe. RIW silicone water-repellent is specifically designed to provide a water-repellent treatment to external building surfaces above ground level. The solution is transparent and does not darken, stain or alter the texture of the surface to which it is applied. After the external surface of the wall has been thoroughly cleaned, the solution is applied in a single 'flooding' brush coat. The solution penetrates from 1.5 to 5.0 mm into the surface of the wall, depending on its porosity, lining the pores with a water-repellent coating which provides excellent protection against rainwater penetration.

(ii) EXTERNAL RENDERS

The application of an external render finish to a building's elevations is a more expensive and time-consuming means of overcoming the problem of rainwater penetration. However, a render finish can also be used to fulfil other upgrading requirements, such as improving the building's appearance, or upgrading the thermal performance of the external walls (see Section 4.4.1(b)). Thus, where upgrading of appearance and/or thermal performance are necessary, in addition to a rainwater penetration problem, it may be convenient and economical to apply a render finish. All of the proprietary exterior thermal insulation systems described in Section 4.4.1(b), in addition to upgrading the thermal properties and appearance of external walls, provide total resistance to rainwater penetration.

(iii) WATERPROOF MASONRY PAINTS

The majority of conventional masonry paints are not capable of providing total resistance to rainwater penetration, and are therefore unsuitable as a means of solving this problem. However, recent developments in paint technology have led to the introduction of exterior coatings that are capable of fully waterproofing external wall surfaces.

Monolastex Smooth, produced by Liquid Plastics Ltd, is a micropolymer elastomeric coating system which, when applied in two coats, will provide full waterproofing to existing wall surfaces for up to ten years. The paint has excellent bonding properties, is permeable to water vapour, allowing underlying moisture to escape without causing flaking or blistering, and is highly elastic, allowing it to accommodate movement. Monolastex Smooth is available in a wide range of colours and can be applied to brickwork, masonry, concrete, render, pebbledash, stucco and tyrolean finished walls by roller, brush or spray. The existing wall surface must be thoroughly cleaned, and localized repairs made where necessary, prior to application. The paint is supplied in 10 and 25 litre containers for application in one or two coats, and it is essential that a two-coat finish is used if full waterproofing of the wall is required.

4.6.2 Preventing rising damp in walls

The penetration of ground moisture, in the form of rising dampness in walls, is a common problem in many old buildings, and it can result from any of the following:

- The lack of a damp-proof course in the original construction
- Deterioration and failure of the existing damp-proof course because of age
- Bridging of the existing damp-proof course.

Bridging of the existing damp-proof course in an external wall by the building up of soil, or by the addition of new paving, to a level above that of the damp-proof course, is a common cause of rising dampness. However, this 'short-circuiting' of the existing damp-proof course can easily be alleviated simply by lowering the adjacent soil or paving level back to 150 mm below that of the damp-proof course. Provided the damp-proof course is in good condition, the problem will not recur once the residual moisture has dried out from the wall. Other common causes of bridging are where a new external render has been applied and taken over the damp-proof course, or where new mortar pointing has been carried out over the outer edge of the damp-proof course. These also have the effect of 'short-circuiting' the damp-proof course by providing a path for rising moisture to pass around it. But the problems can easily be overcome by cutting back the rendering to above the damp-proof course level, or by raking out the offending mortar pointing.

The installation of damp-proof courses was made mandatory by the *Public Health Act 1875,* but in practice their use was not universal immediately. The majority of pre-1900 buildings are, therefore, without damp-proof courses

and, as a result, many of them are found to be suffering from severe rising dampness and its associated problems. In such cases, the only means of overcoming the problem is to install a new damp-proof course to cut off further rising ground moisture from entering the building. The installation of a new damp-proof course will also be essential in those older buildings where a damp-proof course was incorporated initially, but where this has deteriorated and failed with age. Damp-proof course failure is quite common in pre-1920 buildings, where the felts and slates used for damp-proof courses were often of poor durability; although damp-proof course failure is also not uncommon in more recent buildings.

The installation of a new damp-proof course is both time consuming and expensive, but it will be imperative in any building suffering from rising dampness caused by the lack of, or failure of, a damp-proof course.

(a) The installation of new damp-proof courses

New damp-proof courses can be installed using a number of different methods:

(i) The removal of two courses of bricks, a short length at a time, and replacement with two courses of dense engineering bricks. Alternatively, the same bricks can be replaced and a new damp-proof course incorporated during the process.

(ii) Physical insertion of a new damp-proof course by cutting a slot in a suitably located horizontal mortar joint and inserting metal sheet, bitumen felt, dense polythene or other suitable material.

(iii) Pressure injection of a chemical water repellent fluid into the wall at a suitable position to provide a 'band' of masonry which will resist rising damp.

The first two methods described above are only applicable to certain types of wall: method (i) can only be used where the existing walls are of brickwork, and method (ii) can only be used for walls with continuous horizontal mortar joints and is not, therefore, suited to uncoursed masonry.

Until fairly recently, method (ii), the physical insertion of a new damp-proof course into a slot cut into an existing mortar joint, was the most widely used means of installing new damp-proof courses. However, the chemical injection method has now overtaken physical insertion techniques and is almost universally used as a means of overcoming rising dampness in walls.

(b) Pressure-injected chemical damp-proof courses

Pressure-injected damp-proof courses involve the use of silicone resin based water repellents, or aluminium stearate polymeric water repellents. A large number of proprietary injection systems are available from specialist companies which normally provide a full diagnosis and treatment service. Water repellents work on the principle of lining, rather than blocking, the pores within the material being treated. This allows the passage of some water vapour, but prevents the rise of liquid moisture. The procedures used for the injection of a typical chemical damp-proof course are described below and illustrated in Fig. 4.22 and 4.23.

(i) PREPARATION

(1) Expose the walls externally to at least 150 mm below the proposed new damp-proof course level. This may involve digging a trench (see Fig. 4.22).
(2) Remove all skirtings and floorboards adjacent to the walls suffering from rising dampness and check for timber decay.
(3) If timber decay is evident, this should be treated and additional underfloor ventilation provided if necessary.
(4) Cut away the plaster, or other surface rendering, to 450 mm above the last visible signs of dampness. If dampness is not evident, expose 230 mm of wall along the proposed damp-proof course line.

(ii) TREATMENT

(1) Select the course of masonry to be treated. With a timber floor this should ideally be below the timber level and with a solid floor, the course immediately above the floor level (see Fig. 4.22). Avoid engineering bricks or similar dense masonry.
(2) Drill the holes for injection of the damp-proofing solution. If, due to ground conditions, access to this course externally is not possible, the injection should take place 150 mm above ground level, and the section of wall below tanked internally (see Fig. 4.22).
(3) Connect the electric pump, feed lines and injector lances to the pre-drilled holes and seal the mouth of each hole (up to six injector lances can be used at once – see Fig. 4.23).
(4) Open the control valves and commence the pressure injection process. When the section of wall being treated is saturated, move to the next set of drillings.

The 9.5 mm or 12.7 mm diameter injection holes should be drilled horizontally into the wall at the rate of two per stretcher, to a depth of 75 mm, and one per header, to a depth of 190 mm. For solid brick walls between 230 mm and 460 mm thick, and for cavity walls, the injection is carried out in two stages, as illustrated in Fig. 4.22. After the outer zone/skin of the wall has been treated, further drilling takes place and the injector lances are passed through the original holes to treat the inner zone/skin. For stone walls, the drilling and injection procedures are similar to those for brickwork, with injection holes drilled at 120 mm to 150 mm centres to a depth of two-thirds of the thickness of the wall. Thicker walls should be treated in two stages, as for brickwork.

The walls of many older buildings consist of dry loose rubble fill between an outer facing and an inner skin, and in order to achieve an effective damp-proof course, this infill must be treated separately. After injecting the outer facing and

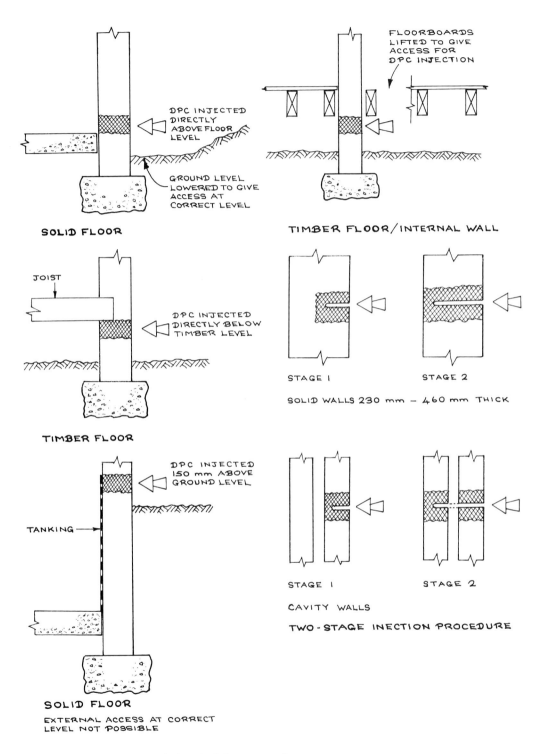

DPC INJECTED
DIRECTLY
ABOVE FLOOR
LEVEL

GROUND LEVEL
LOWERED TO GIVE
ACCESS AT
CORRECT LEVEL

SOLID FLOOR

FLOORBOARDS
LIFTED TO GIVE
ACCESS FOR
DPC INJECTION

TIMBER FLOOR/INTERNAL WALL

JOIST

DPC INJECTED
DIRECTLY BELOW
TIMBER LEVEL

TIMBER FLOOR

STAGE 1   STAGE 2

SOLID WALLS 230 mm – 460 mm THICK

DPC INJECTED
150 mm ABOVE
GROUND LEVEL

TANKING

STAGE 1   STAGE 2

CAVITY WALLS

TWO-STAGE INJECTION PROCEDURE

SOLID FLOOR
EXTERNAL ACCESS AT CORRECT
LEVEL NOT POSSIBLE

Fig. 4.22 Pressure-injected chemical damp-proof courses

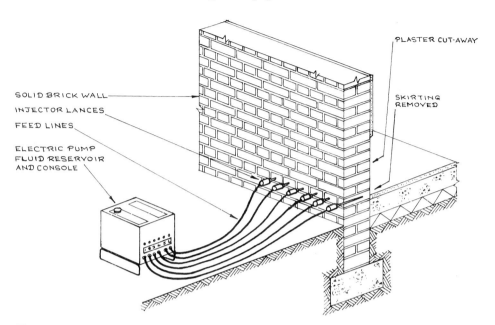

Fig. 4.23 Pressure-injected chemical damp-proof courses

inner skin, separate drillings are made directly through into the rubble, which must be flooded with injection fluid to extend the moisture-resistant band across the full thickness of the wall.

4.6.3 Preventing rising damp in solid ground floors

In pre-1939 construction, solid ground floors were not normally provided with damp-proof membranes, and floors of concrete, stone flags, or quarry tiles in older buildings are, therefore, often found to be suffering from rising damp-ness. Originally, these floors were not usually covered, and the rising dampness was, therefore, allowed to evaporate and not cause problems. However, if, in a rehabilitation scheme, a new covering is applied to such a floor, evaporation of the rising dampness will be prevented, and the covering will rapidly become damp and may ultimately lift and/or deteriorate.

It is therefore essential, firstly to check for rising dampness and, if it is present, to provide a new damp-proof membrane before laying the

new floor covering. An effective method of checking for rising dampness is to lay a piece of roofing felt on the floor: the underside of the felt will become wet within a few days if rising dampness is present.

Mastic asphalt or pitch-mastic are suitable materials for damp proofing solid ground floors. Two 10 mm coats should be applied and the coating set into a 25 mm × 25 mm chase in the wall bonding with the damp-proof course. Provision of the new damp-proof membrane will usually involve removing existing skirting boards together with the wall coverings and plaster and, possibly, some of the floor edge itself in order to expose the damp-proof course in the wall (where one exists), and bond the new membrane to it to completely seal the walls and floors against rising dampness.

4.6.4 Preventing rainwater penetration through roofs

Rainwater penetration through the roof of a building, in addition to causing inconvenience to the occupants, often results in deterioration and decay of the roof structure, thermal insulation, ceilings and internal finishes. It is therefore essential in the rehabilitation of old buildings that existing roofs are thoroughly examined, and, in cases where rainwater leakage is evident, that proper remedial action is taken.

(a) Preventing rainwater penetration through pitched roofs

A vital barrier against rainwater penetration into pitched roofs is the lining of impervious sarking felt provided immediately beneath the tiles or slates. Any rainwater penetrating the roof covering, due to wind pressure or damaged tiles or slates, is effectively drained away by the sarking felt and prevented from entering the roof. However, sarking felt has only been in use since around 1938 and, therefore, the roofs of many older buildings, particularly those whose coverings have deteriorated or been damaged, are often found to be suffering from rainwater penetration and its effects.

The only effective solution, where there is evidence of rainwater penetration through a roof without sarking felt, is to take off the existing covering, add a new lining of sarking felt, and re-cover the roof. Whether or not the original tiles or slates are re-used will depend on their condition. In many older buildings, the tiles or slates will have deteriorated because of frost or chemical attack, or mechanical damage and generally, if more than 10% of the total are in bad condition, an entirely new roof covering will be advisable.

(b) Preventing rainwater penetration through flat roofs

Flat roofs are inherently more susceptible to rainwater penetration because of the much slower rate of run-off. The points most vulnerable to leakage are at flashings, upstands and parapets, at points where openings are formed for soil pipes, flues, etc. and at joints between separate sheets of the roof covering.

Lead was widely used as a flat roof covering until late last century, when it was replaced by zinc, which is lighter and cheaper. The relative lifespans of these materials are 80–100 years, and 40 years respectively and, if they are encountered in rehabilitation work, it is likely that they will be near the end of their useful life and in poor condition. It is therefore recommended, if an old lead or zinc flat roof is found to be leaking, that the covering should be stripped and entirely replaced, since localized repair is likely to give only temporary relief before other faults develop in different parts of the roof.

The flat roofs of more recent buildings are likely to be covered with either asphalt or built-up felt, these materials having lifespans of 20–40 years and 10–15 years respectively. In the event of rainwater leakage, it is possible to carry out localized patch repairs, but these tend to be unsatisfactory and provide only temporary relief. In view of the potentially serious effects of rainwater penetration, it will therefore be advisable, in the majority of cases, to strip the existing roof covering and replace it with a new covering. Alternatively, a new covering can be laid over the existing covering.

Where a roof has suffered from rainwater penetration over a lengthy period, it is likely that associated decay and deterioration of the roof structure and ceilings below will have occurred. It is therefore essential, in addition to repairing or replacing the defective roof covering, that the presence and nature of associated defects is established, and that proper remedial work is carried out.

4.7 PREVENTING CONDENSATION

4.7.1 The causes and effects of condensation

Before considering how to prevent condensation, it is necessary to have some understanding of its causes and effects. Water vapour in varying quantities is always present in the air, and the quantity of water vapour that the air can carry depends upon its temperature; the warmer the air, the greater its vapour carrying capacity. Condensation occurs in a building when warm air, containing water vapour, comes into contact with a cold surface which reduces its temperature and, therefore, its vapour carrying capacity. Any excess water vapour that the air is incapable of carrying because of its reduced temperature is deposited as condensation on the cold surface.

For any given air condition (temperature/water vapour content) there is a corresponding 'dewpoint temperature'. If air containing water vapour comes into contact with surfaces which are at, or below, this dewpoint temperature, it will deposit some of its water vapour as condensation. This usually shows itself as mist, beads of condensation, or damp patches on windows, walls and other surfaces including fabrics, but it will be most obvious on the harder, more impervious surfaces.

Condensation can also occur within a permeable building element, where the dewpoint temperature occurs at some point within its thickness, rather than on its surface. Interstitial condensation is potentially more harmful than surface condensation, since it is not visible, and the resulting dampness may remain undetected until substantial decay and damage has been caused.

The adverse effects that are possible as a result of condensation occurring within a building are as follows:

- Misting up of windows
- Moisture deposited on window frames and sills leading to mould growth and rot
- Moisture deposited on wall, floor and ceiling surfaces (most evident on hard, impervious surfaces)
- Moisture on and within the surface layers of absorbent surfaces (may not be evident until the surface becomes saturated)
- Mould growth on all surfaces affected by condensation
- Internal breakdown of materials and elements where interstitial condensation has occurred
- A general deterioration in the internal en-

vironment due to the occurrence of associated dampness, smells caused by mould growth and rot, and deterioration of the appearance of surface finishes.

4.7.2 Preventive measures

Condensation is a widespread problem, and its adverse effects are capable of leaving a building uninhabitable if preventive measures are not taken. It is therefore essential that the following steps are taken when carrying out rehabilitation work in order to ensure that condensation does not occur:

(a) Check for the presence of condensation in the existing building and, where applicable, eliminate it.
(b) Ensure that the upgrading or replacement of any existing elements does not increase the risk of condensation.
(c) Where a proposed change of use is likely to introduce new conditions that are conducive to condensation, ensure that appropriate measures are taken to prevent its occurrence.

Condensation is caused by a combination of different factors, but is most likely to occur in those buildings where large quantities of water vapour are produced, such as buildings housing certain industrial processes and, particularly, housing where modern living habits create conditions that are conducive to condensation. The risk of condensation occurring in buildings can be significantly reduced by paying attention to three specific factors, as follows.

(a) Ventilation

Ventilation helps to remove air containing water vapour from the building and is particularly important where large quantities of moisture are released, such as areas housing certain industrial processes, kitchens, bathrooms, showers, etc. Good ventilation is best achieved using powered extractor fans, and their installation is recommended in areas where large quantities of water vapour are produced. In areas where water vapour levels are lower, natural, rather than mechanical, ventilation will usually be satisfactory and this can be achieved by means of openable windows or ventilators.

(b) Heating

Adequate heating reduces the risk of condensation in two ways: firstly, it warms room surfaces, keeping them above dewpoint and preventing surface condensation; and secondly, it increases the moisture carrying capacity of the ventilated air. Different heating methods vary considerably in their efficiency at reducing condensation. Short periods of high-level heating with no heating in between are conducive to condensation. While the heat is off, the interior surfaces become cold and may fall below dewpoint. The heating periods usually correspond with a significant increase in water vapour production while the building is occupied and this, in conjunction with the cold interior surfaces, aggravates the problem of condensation.

Leaving some rooms unheated while the remainder of the building is heated, increases the possibility of condensation. The cold interior surfaces of the unheated rooms will be susceptible to condensation as warmer air, with a higher vapour content, migrates to them from heated rooms.

Flueless oil and gas heaters release large quantities of water vapour into the atmosphere and their use significantly increases the possibility of condensation.

Continuous background heating of the whole building, used in conjunction with the main heating periods, is the most effective means of preventing condensation, and, where possible, a system which is capable of economically providing this should be installed.

(c) Thermal insulation and vapour barriers

Thermal insulation of walls, floors and roofs helps to reduce the risk of surface condensation by ensuring that their internal surfaces are kept above dewpoint temperature. However, the provision of thermal insulation, while preventing surface condensation, can increase the risk of interstitial condensation within the building element. This is because the insulation has the effect of moving the position of the dewpoint temperature from the element's surface to a point within its thickness. Water vapour will then diffuse into the insulation and the element until it reaches the position of the dewpoint temperature, where interstitial condensation will occur. To prevent interstitial condensation, the water vapour must be prevented from diffusing into the insulation and the element, and this is achieved by providing a vapour barrier on the 'warm side' of the insulation.

Several materials are resistant to the passage of water vapour, including certain paints, wallpapers, polythene sheeting, plastic and aluminium foils. In rehabilitation work, vapour barriers are often provided pre-bonded to other materials, one of the most common proprietary examples being Gyproc vapour check thermal board. This is similar to Gyproc thermal board, described in Section 4.4.1, and comprises gypsum wallboard, factory bonded to a backing of expanded polystyrene insulation, with a vapour-resistant membrane incorporated between the two. These composite boards are widely used to upgrade the thermal performance of existing walls and roofs (see Section 4.4) and, when fixed, the vapour-resistant membrane is on the warm side of the polystyrene insulation, therefore preventing the passage of water vapour into the insulation and the existing element.

Where existing elements are insulated by other methods (see Section 4.4), but still require a new internal lining, normal plasterboard with a pre-bonded vapour-resistant membrane can be used. Gyproc Duplex wallboard comprises gypsum wallboard, capable of direct decoration, with a metallized polyester film on the inner face which provides resistance to the passage of water vapour.

Ideally, the vapour barrier should be continuous over the whole area of the element, but this is difficult to achieve in practice, especially where the above types of material are used. Joints between the boards and holes around pipes etc. allow some 'leakage' of water vapour, but, in normal circumstances, this should not cause problems. However, in pitched roof spaces with insulated ceilings, and in 'cold' flat roofs with insulated ceilings (see Section 4.4.2), the risks of condensation are much greater and additional precautions are essential. In such cases, the roof void above the insulated ceiling should be properly ventilated in order to remove any water vapour that succeeds in penetrating joints in the vapour barrier or 'leaking' through holes around pipes, badly fitting loft trapdoors, etc.

Part F2 of the Building Regulations, which deals with ventilation in dwellings, requires that "reasonable provision shall be made to prevent excessive condensation in a roof void above an insulated ceiling", and it is essential that this is complied with if condensation within cold roof voids is to be avoided.

4.7.3 Preventing condensation in pitched roof spaces

As stated in Sections 4.4.2 and 4.7.2, the addition of thermal insulation to the ceiling beneath a pitched roof significantly increases the risk of condensation within the roof space. The additional insulation has the effect of lowering the temperature within the roof space and, consequently, increasing the condensation risk as warmer moist air from the building migrates upwards into the roof. The incorporation of a suitable vapour barrier at ceiling level will considerably reduce the amount of water vapour migrating into the roof space, but, in practice, large quantities of vapour will still enter the roof at 'weak points', such as around loft access trapdoors, at ceiling roses, and where service pipework penetrates the ceiling. The water vapour entering the roof will condense on any cold surface, such as the sarking felt, or will be absorbed by the timber components of the roof. Over a period of time, this can lead to serious defects, including:

- Fungal decay of roof timbers
- Deterioration of the roof insulation due to water dripping off the sarking felt and saturating the insulation material
- Short circuiting of electrical wiring

The thermal upgrading of existing elements is now a major feature of building rehabilitation, with roofs receiving particular attention because of the excessive heat loss that can take place through them. With the majority of existing pitched roofs, the additional insulation is provided at ceiling level, and it is therefore essential that special provision is made to reduce the associated increased risk of condensation and its damaging effects.

The most effective means of reducing the condensation risk within pitched roofs is to provide adequate ventilation, which will remove the water vapour from the roof space before it has the opportunity to condense. It is now mandatory for all new buildings to incorporate roof space ventilators and, in order to alleviate the condensation problem in existing buildings, a number of proprietary ventilators have recently been developed.

(a) Soffit ventilators
Glidevale soffit ventilators have been specifically designed for incorporation into existing roofs during rehabilitation work, and two ventilators from the range are described below and illustrated in Figs. 4.24 and 4.25. It should be noted that both types of ventilator should be installed in conjunction with Glidevale roof ventilators to ensure that they do not become blocked by the roof insulation material (see Fig. 4.24).

(i) GLIDEVALE TWIST AND LOCK SOFFIT VENTILATORS
Twist and lock soffit ventilators (see Fig. 4.24) are manufactured from ultraviolet resistant polystyrene with an integral grid supporting a PVC covered glass fibre mesh insect screen. The 70 mm diameter ventilators, available in black, white or brown, are inserted by a simple 'twist

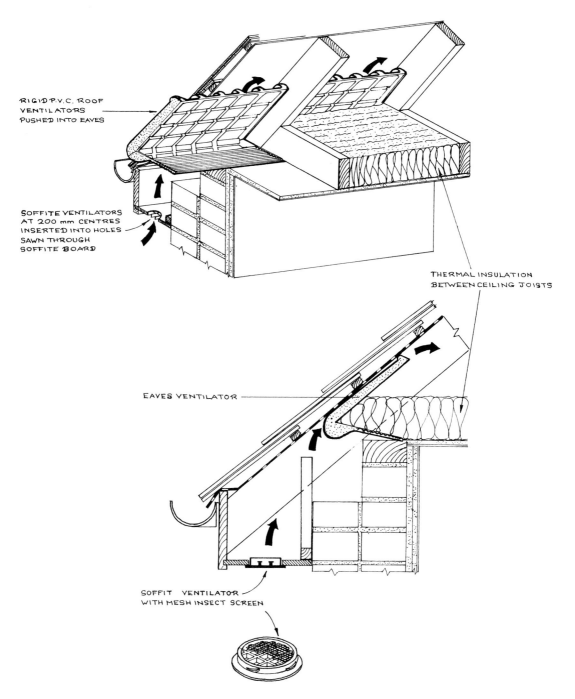

RIGID P.V.C. ROOF
VENTILATORS
PUSHED INTO EAVES

SOFFITE VENTILATORS
AT 200 mm CENTRES
INSERTED INTO HOLES
SAWN THROUGH
SOFFITE BOARD

THERMAL INSULATION
BETWEEN CEILING JOISTS

EAVES VENTILATOR

SOFFIT VENTILATOR
WITH MESH INSECT SCREEN

Fig. 4.24 Glidevale twist and lock soffit ventilator and roof ventilator

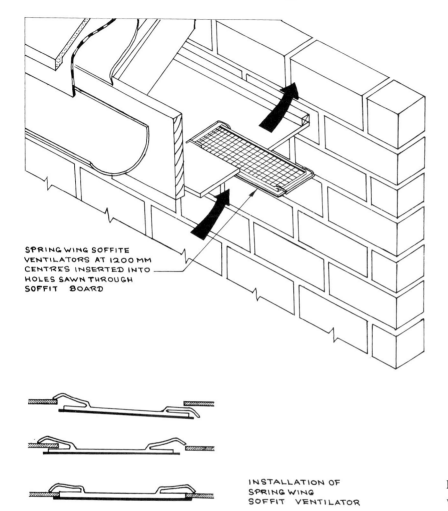

SPRING WING SOFFITE
VENTILATORS AT 1200 MM
CENTRES INSERTED INTO
HOLES SAWN THROUGH
SOFFIT BOARD

INSTALLATION OF
SPRING WING
SOFFIT VENTILATOR

Fig. 4.25 Glidevale spring
wing soffit ventilator

and lock' action into 70 mm diameter holes
formed through the existing soffit board using a
special Glidevale hole saw. The soffit ventilators
should be inserted at 200 mm centres, and, to
ensure fully effective and permanent ventilation,
they should be used in conjunction with Glidevale roof ventilators, described below.

*(ii) GLIDEVALE SPRING WING SOFFIT
VENTILATORS*
Spring wing soffit ventilators (see Fig. 4.25) are
manufactured in polypropylene and comprise
an integral insect grille and spring clips which
enable them to be easily installed into 270 mm

long × 92 mm wide holes sawn through the
existing soffit board. The ventilators should be
inserted at 1200 mm centres, and, to ensure fully
effective permanent ventilation, they should be
used in conjunction with Glidevale roof ventilators described below.

(iii) GLIDEVALE ROOF VENTILATORS
Glidevale roof ventilators (see Fig. 4.24) are
designed for pushing into the eaves to prevent
spillage of roof insulation material into the soffit,
and consequent blocking of the soffit ventilators
(described above). The ventilators, which are
effective with both quilt and granular-fill insula-

tion, are available in two sizes to suit 600 mm and 400 mm rafter spacings. They are manufactured from rigid PVC sheet, formed to provide a series of channels through which air may pass. When pushed into the eaves, the ventilators automatically adjust to the correct roof pitch. The quilt or granular-fill insulation is then laid into the ventilators to complete their installation.

(b) Tile and slate vents

Eaves-to-eaves ventilation of roof spaces is the most preferable method, and should be employed where possible. However, certain types of roof construction do not lend themselves to this solution and it is therefore essential to use some other means of ventilation. A very effective means of providing adequate roof space ventilation, where eaves-to-eaves ventilation is

not practicable, is to employ purpose-made tile and slate vents, fixed at strategic positions over the roof area in place of the normal tiles or slates. Glidevale tile and slate vents are manufactured from polystyron, a robust plastic suitable for external use, and are available in a wide range of sizes, colours, textures and profiles, allowing them to be installed in conjunction with the main tile and slate manufacturers' products. Typical tile and slate vents are shown in Fig. 4.26.

The majority of proprietary tile and slate vents are designed for installation where an entirely new roof covering is being provided, which is not uncommon in rehabilitation work. However, if the building in question does not require re-roofing, it will be necessary to insert tile or slate vents individually into the existing roof.

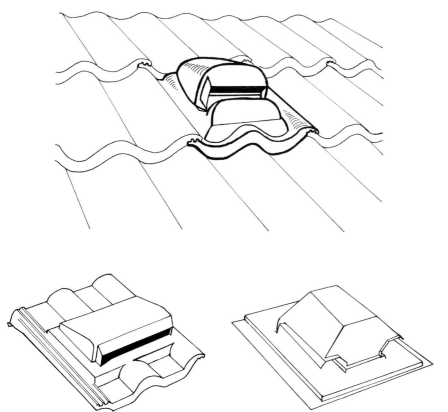

Fig. 4.26 Glidevale tile and slate vents

To install a ventilating tile, one existing tile is removed, the sarking felt is cut and folded in a prescribed way, and the new ventilating tile positioned and secured. To install a ventilating slate, it is necessary to remove a number of slates from the area where the vent is to be positioned.

(c) Air bricks
A relatively simple, inexpensive means of further improving roof space ventilation in buildings where the roof has gable ends, is to insert new air bricks into the gable walls. Air bricks of any standard size can be inserted into the roof's gable ends after carefully cutting out sections of the existing brickwork or masonry, and these will provide an effective means of cross ventilation to supplement that provided by the methods described above.

4.8 ERADICATING TIMBER DECAY

The majority of older buildings contain many more timber components than modern buildings, and it is not unusual to encounter timber decay in rehabilitation work, particularly where the existing building has suffered from neglect and lack of maintenance.

Timber decay can result from fungal attack or insect attack, both of which cause a gradual weakening of the timber, and, if remedial action is not taken, its eventual disintegration.

Where timber decay is evident in a building which is about to be rehabilitated, it is advisable to call in one of the many companies which specialize in its diagnosis and treatment, such as Rentokil, Phoenix or Renofors. A specialist company will carry out a detailed survey and diagnosis of the timber decay, and provide a treatment and eradication package backed by an extensive guarantee, usually for a minimum of 30 years after treatment.

The nature and treatment of the main forms of timber decay are outlined below.

4.8.1 Fungal attack

Fungal attack occurs only where sufficient moisture is present in the timber, and it is usually caused by one of two wood-destroying fungi.

(a) Dry rot
The best known wood-destroying fungus is *Serpula lacrymans* or 'dry rot', and this typically grows on timber remaining moist, rather than very wet, over long periods, resulting from moisture penetration into the building, leaking plumbing, or condensation, often combined with bad ventilation (see Sections 4.6 and 4.7). Dry rot has the unique property of being itself able to produce the moisture it needs for further growth, even when the moisture content of the timber has been reduced to below the level needed to sustain fungal growth (around 20%).

The most vulnerable parts of the building include timber ground floors, joists built into solid external walls, and roof timbers. However, all timber within the building will be vulnerable, particularly in the event of a severe attack. Once established in moist timber, the fungus will readily extend into adjoining dry timbers and will penetrate masonry and plasterwork in order to reach other sound timber which then, in turn, becomes infected. The fungus grows from very fine airborne spores, rusty red in colour, which have alighted on damp timber, and it gradually spreads, either as a silky white sheet or a greyish felted skin. The fungus feeds on the timber, causing it to lose strength, and reduces it to a dry, brittle state. The rotted timber has a pale brown colour and the surface splits into cuboidal or brick-shaped sections formed by a combination of deep, longitudinal and transverse cracks (see Fig. 4.27). The early symptoms may be a characteristic musty, mouldy smell with, later on, the presence of a rusty red powder (the spore dust) and the appearance of flat mushroom-like growths through joints in the timber.

TREATMENT OF DRY ROT FUNGUS
Because dry rot is so prolific, and capable of spreading through other materials and attacking dry timber, its eradication treatment involves not only the replacement of all affected wood

81

Fig. 4.27 Deep cuboidal cracking resulting from dry rot attack (photograph by courtesy of Rentokil Group PLC)

with pre-treated timber, but also the treatment of adjoining timbers, brickwork, plasterwork and adjacent areas well away from the point of decay. All of the following operations must be carried out in order to ensure that the fungus is completely eradicated:

(i) Locate and eliminate the dampness responsible for the original dry rot attack. This may involve providing a new damp-proof course, preventing moisture penetration through walls, repairing leaking roofs and plumbing, eliminating condensation, clearing the bridging of damp-proof courses and improving ventilation, including the provision of additional airbricks etc.

(ii) Cut out, remove from the site, and burn all defective timbers showing cuboidal cracking, pale brown colouration, white fungal mycelium or soft areas when probed. All apparently sound timber within 1 metre of defective timber should also be cut out, removed and burned, together with all debris and loose material within roof voids, sub-floor voids and other areas in the vicinity of the attack.

(iii) Carry out a thorough check of all other

timbers within the building to which the fungus might have spread. This may involve removing skirtings, architraves, wall panels or ceilings, lifting floorboards, etc.

(iv) Strip off all wall plaster which may contain fungal strands to 1 metre beyond the observed limit of growth, and clean down all exposed masonry by wire brushing. Remove all stripped plaster, debris and dust from the site.

(v) Sterilize all masonry within 1 metre beyond the observed limit of fungal growth by firstly applying a blowlamp until the surface is too hot to touch and, secondly by treating the masonry with a proprietary fungicidal solution.

(vi) Replace all timber that has been cut out with new, well-seasoned timber which has been pre-treated with fungicidal preservative by brush, spray or, preferably, full immersion or vacuum treatment.

(vii) Treat all sound timber within 2 metres beyond the observed limit of fungal growth with fungicidal preservative, applied liberally by brush or spray.

(viii) Make good all work that has been disturbed during investigation, treatment and eradication of the dry rot attack, including renewing stripped plasterwork, decorative finishes, etc.

(b) Wet rot

Coniophora puteana or 'wet rot' is the other common wood-destroying fungus, and this requires much wetter timber than dry rot in order to develop. It is therefore more common in exterior joinery exposed to rain, such as windows, fascia boards, timber cladding, etc., although interior timbers that have become wet because of excessive moisture penetration or leaks in plumbing are also vulnerable.

Unlike dry rot, the wet rot fungus is incapable of spreading to, and infecting, dry timber, and outbreaks are therefore confined to the affected wet timber and its immediate vicinity. In an advanced stage, the wet rot fungus produces slender, thread-like, dark brown or black strands, and there are seldom any signs of a fruiting body or of the olive brown spores. The decayed timber is dark in colour, and any cracking is less deep than in timber affected by dry rot (see Fig. 4.28).

TREATMENT OF WET ROT FUNGUS

Because wet rot is not as prolific as dry rot, its outbreaks usually being much more localized, treatment and eradication is simpler, and usually only involves replacement of the affected timber with new pre-treated timber, together with the elimination of the original cause of the wet rot attack.

A wet rot attack can be remedied by cutting out the affected wood well back from the point of decay, and splicing-in new, preservative-treated timber. However, where the attack is widespread, as is often the case with neglected window frames, localized repair is often not justified, and complete replacement with new units will be preferable. Where the existing windows are badly rotted, their replacement with 'maintenance-free' metal or plastic units is advisable, since these will neither rot, nor require the expense of regular painting throughout the life of the rehabilitated building.

Where exterior woodwork has suffered an attack of wet rot, the usual cause is breakdown of the protective paint finish, allowing rainwater to penetrate the timber and create suitable conditions for attack. In the case of internal elements, the cause is usually water penetration through the building envelope, or leaking plumbing, and, in addition to replacing the rotted timber, it is essential that the source of the water or

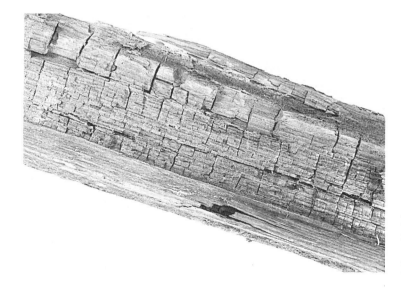

Fig. 4.28 Shallow cracking resulting from wet rot attack (photograph by courtesy of Rentokil Group PLC)

moisture is ascertained and eliminated in order to rule out the risk of further outbreaks.

4.8.2 Insect attack

The symptoms of insect attack are disfigurement of the timber's surface by small circular or oval shaped holes, accompanied by deposits of bore dust, and a gradual reduction in strength. Although insects will attack dry timber, it will be more vulnerable if it is damp, or weakened by fungal decay.

Wood-boring insects lay their eggs in the surface or in crevices in timber and, after the larvae hatch out, they bore into the timber, feeding on it and growing in the process. After a period of between one and several years, the larvae pupate near the surface of the timber, and the beetles emerge, leaving a hole which is characteristic for the particular species of insect. The exit holes are usually clear, sharp edged, and accompanied by bore dust and are thus not easily confused with man-made nail or pin holes.

The most prevalent wood-boring insect is the common furniture beetle (see Figs 4.29 and 4.30), which is responsible for around three-quarters of all cases of insect attack in buildings. The insect's name is misleading, since it attacks all structural timbers, both hardwood and softwood. Its exit holes are circular, and about 1.5 mm in diameter.

Wood-boring weevils, responsible for around 5–6% of all cases of insect attack, usually attack very damp or decayed hardwoods and softwoods, often where fungal decay is also present. The exit holes are oval or slit-shaped with ragged edges and are only $\frac{1}{2}$–1 mm wide.

The death watch beetle (see Figs 4.31 and 4.32), which accounts for about 5% of all cases of insect attack, leaves larger exit holes, approximately 3 mm in diameter, but only attacks hardwoods, and particularly oak. It is therefore usually only found in much older buildings where the use of oak was common.

The *Lyctus* powder post beetle also attacks only hardwoods, including oak, ash and particularly elm. Its exit holes are circular, and 1–2 mm in diameter, and its bore dust is a fine talcum-like powder, distinguishing it from that of the death watch beetle, which produces a much coarser dust.

The house longhorn beetle attacks only softwoods and its area of activity is restricted to only the south of England. The insect causes rapid deterioration of the timber it attacks, leaving very large oval exit holes of approxi-

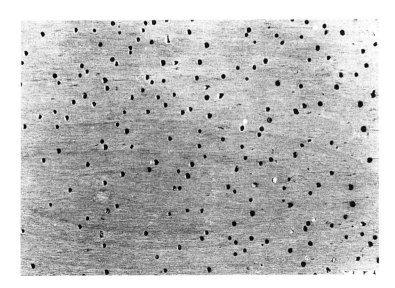

Fig. 4.29 Furniture Beetle exit holes (photograph by courtesy of Rentokil Group PLC)

Fig. 4.30 Furniture Beetle damage (photograph by courtesy of Rentokil Group PLC)

mately 9 mm × 5 mm in size. This insect, and the *Lyctus* powder post beetle, are together responsible for only about 1% of all cases of insect attack.

Treatment of insect attack
Where the extent of the insect attack is not advanced, usually indicated by few and scattered exit holes, causing negligible reduction in the strength of the timber, it is recommended that the timber be treated with either brush or spray-applied insecticide. This will kill any insects that are still active and leave the wood toxic to wood-boring insects, therefore preventing further attack. All apparently unaffected timbers within the building should also be treated with insecticide, on the assumption that insects have emerged and laid eggs elsewhere, the adverse results of which might take several more years to appear. Modern proprietary insecticides are

Fig. 4.31 Death watch beetle larva (photograph by courtesy of Rentokil Group PLC)

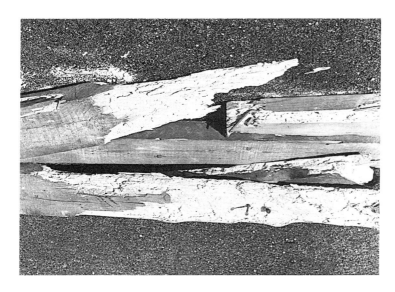

Fig. 4.32 Death watch beetle damage (photograph by courtesy of Rentokil Group PLC)

capable of penetrating timbers deeply, and being retained by the wood for very long periods, irrespective of other causes of deterioration, and, if properly applied, will ensure the timber remains toxic to wood-boring insects for 30 years or more.

Timbers that have been structurally weakened by insect attack must either be treated with insecticide and strengthened, or cut out, burned and completely replaced with new, pre-treated timber. Particular attention should be paid to structural timbers in roofs and floors. In addition, all apparently unaffected timbers within the building should receive full insecticide treatment.

Because many older buildings are likely to have suffered from both insect and fungal attack, it is advisable, when carrying out a programme of treatment and eradication, to use one of the more recently developed 'combination fluids', which contain both insecticide and fungicide. If the treatment is thorough, this should ensure that further timber decay of any description will not occur in the rehabilitated building for at least thirty years, after which re-treatment will be advisable.

4.8.3 In-situ injection techniques for the preservation of timber components

The in-situ injection of preservatives into timbers that have been affected by, or are susceptible to, fungal and insect attack is a relatively recent development. Where fungal or insect attack in timber components is not sufficiently advanced to have caused a significant loss in strength, specially designed plastic nozzles, inserted into the timber, can be used to pressure-inject preservatives much more deeply than can be achieved by surface application. The technique can also be used on components that have not suffered attack, but which are considered vulnerable.

The minimum size of timber that can be treated by in-situ injection is 50 mm × 25 mm, and typical applications include external softwood joinery, such as window and door frames, floor joists, roof timbers, beams and lintels. In the Wykamol timber injection system (see Fig. 4.33), hollow polypropylene injectors (36 mm long × 9.5 mm diameter, or 24 mm long × 6.5 mm diameter) are inserted into pre-drilled

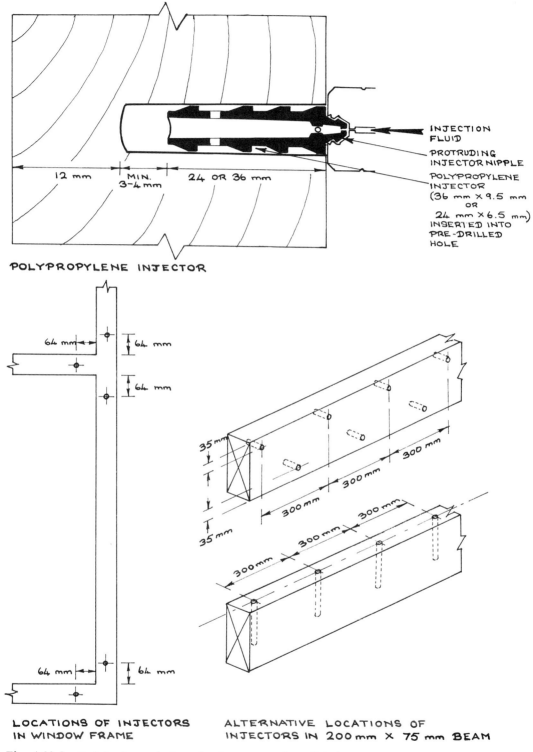

POLYPROPYLENE INJECTOR

INJECTION FLUID

PROTRUDING INJECTOR NIPPLE

POLYPROPYLENE INJECTOR
(36 mm × 9.5 mm
OR
24 mm × 6.5 mm)
INSERTED INTO
PRE-DRILLED
HOLE

12 mm   MIN. 3-4 mm   24 OR 36 mm

64 mm   64 mm

64 mm

35 mm   35 mm

300 mm   300 mm   300 mm

300 mm   300 mm   300 mm

64 mm   64 mm

LOCATIONS OF INJECTORS
IN WINDOW FRAME

ALTERNATIVE LOCATIONS OF
INJECTORS IN 200 mm × 75 mm BEAM

Fig. 4.33 *In situ* injection technique for the preservation of timber components

holes in the timber. The injector holes must penetrate to within 12 mm of the component's far face and be at least 40 mm deep for the larger injector, and 30 mm for the smaller. The outer end of each injector has an injector nipple containing a non-return valve which is left protruding from the face of the timber, and to which the injection line and pump is attached. The organic preservative fluid is then injected under pressure for at least two minutes, or until the timber is seen to be saturated.

The positions and number of polypropylene injectors required will vary according to the type and size of component being treated. For example, a 200 mm × 75 mm beam on edge would require injectors inserted at 300 mm staggered centres in two rows 35 mm from the top and bottom edges of the wide face, or where the upper narrow face is accessible, in one row at 300 mm centres (see Fig. 4.33). Small section external softwood joinery, such as window and door frames, can be treated using the smaller, 24 mm long injectors, which should be inserted from the exterior in areas susceptible to decay, such as the lower and intermediate joints of frames, including sills. They should be inserted into each member at a distance of approximately 64 mm from each side of the joints and, if required, at regular centres between joints.

After the injection procedure has been completed, the injector nipples can be cut off flush with the surface, and the holes sealed with putty and matching paint. Alternatively, the injectors and nipples can be driven fully into the timber and plastic sealing caps inserted. In particularly high risk areas, where appearance is not important, the injector nipples can be left intact, allowing further injections of preservative fluid in the future where this is considered necessary. However, under normal circumstances, this technique of timber preservation should ensure that sections are free from fungal and insect attack for at least ten years after treatment. Ideally, the injection treatment should be combined with normal painting maintenance and repairs to stop further decay in affected areas and protect sound joints from attack. Injection of the organic preservative does not impart strength to rotted wood or render unnecessary the application of normal standards in deciding the extent of repairs and/or replacements, which should always precede the protective injection where necessary.

4.8.4 Localized repair techniques for decayed timber window frames

Timber window frames are highly susceptible to wet-rot attack and subsequent localized decay, and it is not unusual to find extensive damage to window frames in older buildings, particularly where maintenance has been neglected.

Provided the areas of decay are not too extensive, and the larger proportion of timber remains unaffected, it is possible to carry out localized repair to good effect. The Renofors system for localized repair of decayed timber windows is illustrated in Fig. 4.34 and entails the following operations:

(i) Remove all decayed wood completely and drill holes into the sound wood in the vicinity of the removed parts. The holes should be of a sufficient diameter and depth to facilitate thorough penetration of preservative fluid into the timber surrounding the decayed area.

(ii) Thoroughly impregnate the wood in the area of decay with Renofors R1200 preservative fluid, to consolidate and strengthen the timber and arrest decay.

(iii) Replace all removed parts of the wood with Renofors special filler, leaving proud of the original profile.

(iv) Tool back filler to original profile.

These operations should preferably be carried out in conjunction with the complete removal of the existing paint system, which should be renewed after the repairs have been completed.

Where maintenance has been neglected over an extensive period, window frames will not be the only timber elements that are vulnerable to

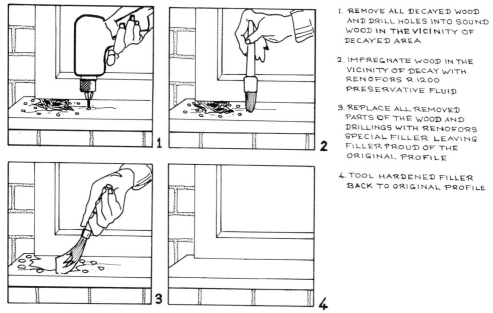

1. REMOVE ALL DECAYED WOOD AND DRILL HOLES INTO SOUND WOOD IN THE VICINITY OF DECAYED AREA

2. IMPREGNATE WOOD IN THE VICINITY OF DECAY WITH RENOFORS R.1200 PRESERVATIVE FLUID

3. REPLACE ALL REMOVED PARTS OF THE WOOD AND DRILLINGS WITH RENOFORS SPECIAL FILLER LEAVING FILLER PROUD OF THE ORIGINAL PROFILE

4. TOOL HARDENED FILLER BACK TO ORIGINAL PROFILE

Fig. 4.34 Localized repair of decayed timber windows

decay, and this technique is equally applicable to the localized repair of other components such as door frames, claddings, fascia boards, etc.

4.8.5 Epoxy-resin based repair and restoration of decayed timbers

The use of synthetic resins for the repair of damaged or defective concrete members has been commonplace for many years, and, more recently, these materials have been successfully applied to timber repair. With timber restoration, the bonding capability of the synthetic resin is not the only criterion in effecting a successful repair: reinforcing rods of glass-fibre or polyester, and steel reinforcing bars and plates also play a major role in the techniques employed. It is essential, where reinforcement is used, that it is set deep into the sound portion of the timber to ensure an effective connection and load transfer, and the epoxy resins used must have good fluidity in order to obtain maximum penetration and impregnation of the wood fibres to obtain a good bond. Epoxy-resin based repair involves highly specialized skills, and the

selection of resin mixes, reinforcement types and the solutions to individual problems requires a thorough understanding of the techniques available. It is therefore essential, where it is considered that this type of repair and restoration might be appropriate in a particular rehabilitation scheme, to call in one of the specialist contractors experienced in such work.

(a) Repair of decayed beam ends

The ends of beams or floor joists that are built into the solid external walls of old buildings often become damp or wet because of rainwater penetration, and they are therefore highly vulnerable to both fungal and insect attack.

Decay in the ends of built-in timbers in this way can clearly have serious structural implications, and in-situ, resin-based repair techniques are now widely used in preference to the traditional repair methods which involve splicing-in new timber and using unsightly steel plates, angles and bolts. Renofors (UK) Ltd is one company specializing in resin-based repairs, and their beam-end repair system is illustrated and described in Fig. 4.35. The work involves

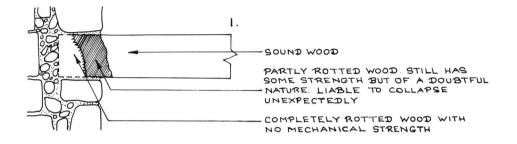

1.

SOUND WOOD

PARTLY ROTTED WOOD. STILL HAS
SOME STRENGTH BUT OF A DOUBTFUL
NATURE. LIABLE TO COLLAPSE
UNEXPECTEDLY

COMPLETELY ROTTED WOOD WITH
NO MECHANICAL STRENGTH

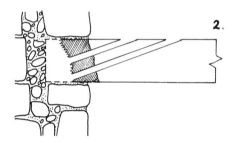

2.

28 mm DIAMETER HOLES DRILLED
FROM TOP OF BEAM AT AN ANGLE
OF 20 DEGREES FROM SIDE OF BEAM.
THE MINIMUM QUANTITY OF MASONRY
IS REMOVED SUFFICIENT TO ENABLE
THE DECAY TO BE REMOVED SO THAT
A CAVITY RESULTS

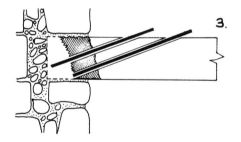

3.

20 mm DIAMETER POLYESTER
REINFORCEMENT BARS INSERTED
INTO HOLES

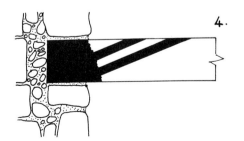

4.

EPOXY MORTAR POURED INTO THE
HOLES TO FILL ALL CAVITIES FORMING
A PLASTIC 'FOOT' IN THE SPACE
FORMERLY OCCUPIED BY ROTTED WOOD.
THE NEW FOOT HAS AN UNBREAKABLE
ADHESIVE CONNECTION INTO THE
SOUND WOOD VIA THE MORTAR-ENCASED
POLYESTER REINFORCEMENT BARS

Fig. 4.35 Resin-based beam end repair system

removing the decayed wood at the beam end and replacing it with a new epoxy-resin 'foot' which is bonded to the sound timber using polyester reinforcement rods embedded in epoxy resin.

(b) Repair of decayed roof truss ends

Another common point at which timber fails in older buildings is at the ends of roof trusses supported on wall plates. Rainwater penetration often occurs at this point because of deterioration and lack of maintenance of the roof covering and guttering. This, combined with poor ventilation at the eaves, often results in timber decay which, if left unattended, can lead to partial or total collapse of the roof.

An effective technique of carrying out structural restoration of decayed roof truss ends, employed by Resin Bonded Repairs Ltd, is described below, and illustrated in Fig. 4.36. Where a roof truss has decayed at the wall plate, a reinforcing plate is introduced into the main tie beam, and the decayed end timber cut out and replaced with epoxy-resin mortar. Additional corner reinforcement in the form of reinforcing bars can be inserted into holes drilled through

the end of the rafter to pass each side of the reinforcing plate in the main tie beam. It is essential that the reinforcing plate and bars are set and fully bonded deep into the sound portion of the timber if a totally effective repair is to be achieved.

(c) Repair of decayed beams between supports

In some buildings which have suffered from neglect over a lengthy period, timber decay may be more widespread, and not merely restricted to those more vulnerable points discussed above. Timber decay may occur in beams and the main ties of roof trusses between their supports, and epoxy-resin repair techniques are effective enough to be capable of repairing beams that have virtually completely rotted through. A repair technique employed for this purpose by Resin Bonded Repairs Ltd, and illustrated in Fig. 4.37, involves inserting steel bar or plate reinforcement into a specially cut slot which extends deeply into the sound timber of the beam on each side of the decayed area. The plate is fully bonded into the slot with epoxy resin,

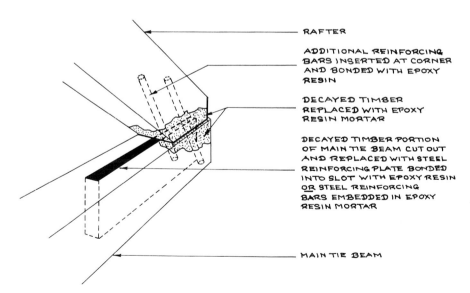

RAFTER

ADDITIONAL REINFORCING BARS INSERTED AT CORNER AND BONDED WITH EPOXY RESIN

DECAYED TIMBER REPLACED WITH EPOXY RESIN MORTAR

DECAYED TIMBER PORTION OF MAIN TIE BEAM CUT OUT AND REPLACED WITH STEEL REINFORCING PLATE BONDED INTO SLOT WITH EPOXY RESIN OR STEEL REINFORCING BARS EMBEDDED IN EPOXY RESIN MORTAR

MAIN TIE BEAM

Fig. 4.36 Resin-based repair of decayed roof truss ends

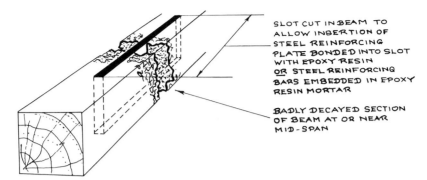

SLOT CUT IN BEAM TO
ALLOW INSERTION OF
STEEL REINFORCING
PLATE BONDED INTO SLOT
WITH EPOXY RESIN
OR STEEL REINFORCING
BARS EMBEDDED IN EPOXY
RESIN MORTAR

BADLY DECAYED SECTION
OF BEAM AT OR NEAR
MID-SPAN

Fig. 4.37 Resin-based repair of decayed beams

and epoxy-resin mortar is used to fill the void left after cutting out the area of decayed timber.

(d) General repairs to decayed timber members

In addition to the repairs described above, epoxy-resin based repair techniques, using various types of reinforcement and epoxy-resin mortars, can also be used to effect permanent repairs to decayed timbers and joints in many other situations where fungal or insect attack has taken place. As stated previously, where this type of repair might be considered appropriate, a specialist contractor should be consulted in the first instance.

4.9 STRENGTHENING OF EXISTING TIMBER FLOORS

In certain rehabilitation schemes, the existing floors may need to be strengthened in order to cater for increased loadings imposed by the proposed new use. The most common examples occur where existing buildings are converted to office use. In such cases, the existing timber floors may not be capable of carrying the excessive localized loads imposed by modern filing and storage systems, office machinery and equipment.

A number of solutions are available where an existing timber floor needs to be strengthened, as follows.

(a) Replacing with new timber or steel sections

The existing floor beams are replaced with new timber or steel sections capable of supporting the increased loads. This solution usually involves major disruption to the existing structure and may necessitate removal and reinstatement of the existing floorboards, joists and ceiling. In view of the considerable expense and inconvenience involved, the method is not, therefore, generally recommended, and an alternative solution should be considered.

(b) Strengthening with new steel channel sections

The existing floor beams are strengthened with new steel channel sections fixed to both sides to cater for the increased floor loadings. This technique is also very disruptive and expensive, requiring the removal of floorboards and ceilings, the cutting back of floor joists and reinstatement of their ends on to the new steel channels. Access holes may also need to be formed through the existing external walls to allow insertion of the steel channels.

(c) Stiffening with steel or timber

The existing floor beams are stiffened with steel or timber fixed to their top or bottom surfaces. Figure 4.38 shows the application of this solution using epoxy-resin bonding and dowelling techniques to increase the depth of a floor beam. The

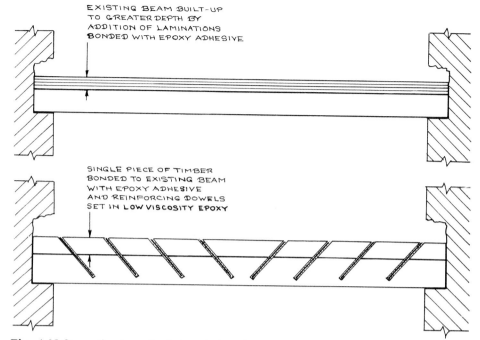

EXISTING BEAM BUILT-UP
TO GREATER DEPTH BY
ADDITION OF LAMINATIONS
BONDED WITH EPOXY ADHESIVE

SINGLE PIECE OF TIMBER
BONDED TO EXISTING BEAM
WITH EPOXY ADHESIVE
AND REINFORCING DOWELS
SET IN LOW VISCOSITY EPOXY

Fig. 4.38 Strengthening of existing timber floors by increasing beam depths

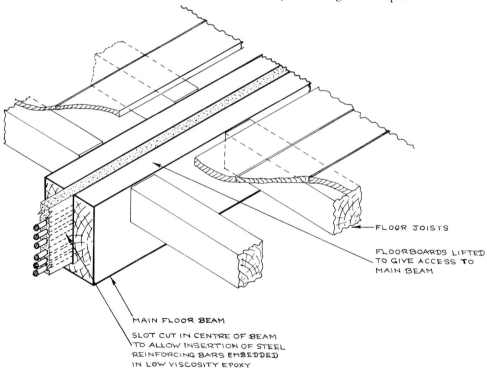

FLOOR JOISTS

FLOORBOARDS LIFTED
TO GIVE ACCESS TO
MAIN BEAM

MAIN FLOOR BEAM

SLOT CUT IN CENTRE OF BEAM
TO ALLOW INSERTION OF STEEL
REINFORCING BARS EMBEDDED
IN LOW VISCOSITY EPOXY

Fig. 4.39 Strengthening of existing timber floors by the insertion of resin-bonded stiffening reinforcement

93

Table 4.6 Index of products and systems referred to in Chapter 4, with manufacturers' addresses

	Product/system	Referred to in section	Manufacturer's address	Telephone No.
1.	Evo-Stik floor level and fill	4.3.3	Evode Ltd, Common Rd, Stafford, ST16 3EH	0785 57755
2.	Expolath	4.4.1	Eglinton Stone Group Ltd, 76 Carlton Place, Glasgow G5 9TE	041 429 2182
3.	Glidevale soffit and roof ventilators	4.7.3	Willan Building Services, 2 Brooklands Rd, Sale, Cheshire M33 3SS	061 973 1234 6262
4.	Glidevale tile and slate vents			
5.	Gyproc Duplex plasterboard	4.7.2		0602 844844
6.	Gyproc MF system	4.3.1	British Gypsum Ltd,	
7.	Gyproc thermal board	4.4.1 4.4.2 4.7.2	Ruddington Hall, Ruddington, Nottingham, NG11 6LX	
8.	Gyproc urethane laminate	4.4.1		
9.	Insulath	4.4.1	Tinsley Building Products Ltd, PO Box 119, Shepcote Lane, Sheffield S9 1TY	0742 430344
10.	Limpet mineral fibre	4.2.2 4.2.3	TAC Construction Materials Ltd, PO Box 22, Trafford Park, Manchester M17 1RU	061 872 2181
11.	Mandolite P20	4.2.3	Mandoval Coatings Ltd, Mark House, The Square, Lightwater, Surrey GU18 5SS	0276 71617
12.	Monolastex Smooth	4.6.1	Liquid Plastics Ltd, PO Box 7, London Road, Preston PR1 4AJ	0772 59781
13.	Newlath	4.6.1	John Newton and Co. Ltd, 157–160 Piccadilly, London W1V OBX	01 409 0414
14.	Nullifire WD	4.2.2	Nullifire Ltd, Lifford Way, Binley, Coventry, West Midlands CV3 2SP	
15.	Nullifire S60	4.2.3		
16.	Renofors timber repair systems	4.8.4 4.8.5	Renofors (UK) Ltd, 116 Darwen Rd, Bromley Cross, Bolton BL7 9BQ	0204 58336
17.	Resin Bonded Repairs timber repair systems	4.8.5	Resin Bonded Repairs Ltd, Windsor House, Wycombe Lane, Wooburn Green, Bucks HP10 0HE	06285 27794
18.	Rickards Timber Treatment floor strengthening system	4.9	Rickards Timber Treatment Ltd, Brooklands Approach, North St, Romford, Essex RM1 1DX	0708 25127 64576

Table 4.6 *contd.*

Product/system	Referred to in section	Manufacturer's address	Telephone No.
19. RIW damp-resisting composition and plasterbond	4.6.1	RIW Protective Products Co. Ltd, Broadway House, Shute End, Wokingham, Berks, RG11 1BR	0734 792566
20. RIW silicone water-repellent solution	4.6.1		
21. Roofmate	4.4.2	DOW Construction Products, St Catherine's Court, 10 Herbert Rd, Solihull West Midlands B91 3RR	021 705 6363
22. Styroliner	4.4.1 4.4.2	Panel Systems Ltd, Units 3–9, Welland Close, Parkwood Industrial Estate, Rutland Rd, Sheffield S3 9QY	0742 752881
23. Supalux	4.2.2	Cape Boards and Panels Ltd, Iver Lane, Uxbridge UB8 2JQ	0895 37111
24. Thermafloor	4.4.3	Thermaliner Insulations Ltd, Unit 7, Buckley Rd. Industrial Estate, Buckley Road, Rochdale, OL12 9DQ	
25. Permoglaze Thermarend	4.4.1	Blundell-Permoglaze Ltd Building Insulation Dept., Sculcoates Lane, Hull HU5 1RU	0482 492241
26. Thistlebond dry lining Thistle renovating plaster	4.3.1 4.3.1	British Gypsum Ltd, Ruddington Hall, Ruddington, Nottingham NG11 6LX	0602 844844
27. Tilcon foamed perlite	4.2.2	Tilcon Special Products Division, Fire Protection Section, Lingerfield, Scotton, Knaresborough, North Yorks, HG5 9JN	0423 864041
28. Vermiculux	4.2.3	Cape Boards and Panels Ltd, Iver Lane, Uxbridge, UB8 2JQ	0895 37111
29. Vicuclad	4.2.2 4.2.3	William Kenyon Vicuclad, Division of TAC Construction Materials Ltd, PO Box 22, Trafford Park, Manchester M17 1RU	061 872 2181
30. Wykamol timber injection system	4.8.3	Cementone-Beaver Ltd, Tingewick Road, Buckingham MK18 1AN	0280 814000

additional depth of timber may be built up in laminations, bonded to the existing, and each other, using epoxy adhesive. Alternatively, a single piece of timber may be added and bonded to the existing beam using epoxy adhesive and reinforcing dowels set in epoxy-resin mortar.

Clearly, this solution will either raise the floor level, or lower the ceiling level, and it will also involve partial disruption of the existing floor or ceiling. In view of these factors, therefore, this form of floor strengthening may not be appropriate in many circumstances.

(d) Stiffening with steel plates

The existing floor beams are stiffened by means of steel plates fixed on both sides. Where supported members (e.g. secondary beams, floor joists) are seated on top of the member being strengthened, this technique will produce an effective and economic method of strengthening. However, where supported members are connected to the sides of the member, the detailing and fixing can be cumbersome, time consuming and expensive.

(e) Strengthening with steel stiffening reinforcement

The existing floor beams are strengthened by inserting steel stiffening reinforcement, embedded in low viscosity epoxy within their thickness.

This technique, developed by Rickards Timber Treatment Ltd, is illustrated in Fig. 4.39 and involves cutting a slot out of the centre of the beam and inserting a number of steel reinforcing bars embedded in, and bonded to the existing timber with low viscosity epoxy. The size of the slot, and the number and diameter of reinforcing bars are designed to suit the particular circumstances, an increase of 50% in load-carrying capacity being possible in the majority of cases. The advantages of this technique over those previously described are as follows:

- Access is only required from above the beam
- Disturbance of the existing floor is minimized
- Disturbance of the existing ceiling is avoided,

a particularly important advantage with valuable, ornate ceilings
- The existing components are fully retained
- Any existing distortion can be accommodated, since the reinforcing bars will bend to the beam's deflected shape, if necessary
- It avoids the need to form holes in existing walls to introduce replacement members
- It obviates the need to manhandle heavy materials
- It does not adversely affect the fire resistance of the existing construction.

FURTHER READING

Benson, J. *et al.* (1980) *Housing Rehabilitation Handbook,* Architectural Press, London.

British Standards Institution (1972) *Fire Tests on Building Materials and Structures: Test Methods and Criteria for the Fire Resistance of Elements of Building Construction,* BS 476, Part 8, 1972, BSI, London.

British Standards Institution (1983) *Fire Precautions in the Design and Construction of Buildings: Code of Practice for Office Buildings,* BS 5588, Part 3, 1983, BSI, London.

British Standards Institution (1984) *Fire Precautions in the Design and Construction of Buildings: Code of Practice for Single-Family Dwelling Houses,* BS 5588, Section 1.1, 1984, BSI, London.

British Standards Institution (1985) *Fire Precautions in the Design and Construction of Buildings: Code of Practice for Shops,* BS 5588, Part 2, 1985, BSI, London.

British Standards Institution (1985) *Guide to Fire Doors,* PD 6512, Part 1, 1985, BSI, London.

Building Research Establishment (1972) *Double Glazing and Double Windows,* Digest 140, HMSO, London.

Building Research Establishment (1982) *Sound Insulation of Party Floors,* Digest 266, HMSO, London.

Building Research Establishment (1982) *Slated or Tiled Pitched Roofs: Ventilation to Outside Air,* Defect Action Sheet 1, BRE, Watford, England.

Further reading

Building Research Establishment (1982) *Slated or Tiled Pitched Roofs: Restricting the Entry of Water Vapour from the House,* Defect Action Sheet 3, BRE, Watford, England.

Building Research Establishment (1982) *Pitched Roofs: Thermal Insulation Near the Eaves,* Defect Action Sheet 4, BRE, Watford, England.

Building Research Establishment (1982) *External Walls: Reducing the Risk from Interstitial Condensation,* Defect Action Sheet 6, BRE, Watford, England.

Building Research Establishment (1983) *Condensation in Insulated Domestic Roofs,* Digest 270, HMSO, London.

Building Research Establishment (1983) *Wood Windows: Arresting Decay,* Defect Action Sheet 13, BRE, Watford, England.

Building Research Establishment (1983) *Wood Windows: Preventing Decay,* Defect Action Sheet 14, BRE, Watford, England.

Building Research Establishment (1983) *Flat Roofs: Built-up Bitumen Felt – Remedying Rain Penetration,* Defect Action Sheet 33, BRE, Watford, England.

Building Research Establishment (1983) *External Walls: Rendering – Resisting Rain Penetration,* Defect Action Sheet 37, BRE, Watford, England.

Building Research Establishment (1984) *Standard U-values,* Digest 108, 2nd edn, revised, HMSO, London.

Building Research Establishment (1984) *Heat Losses Through Ground Floors,* Digest 145, 1st edn, revised, HMSO, London.

Building Research Establishment (1984) *Wood Preservatives Pretreatment Application Methods,* Digest 201, 1st edn, revised, HMSO, London.

Building Research Establishment (1984) *Increasing the Fire Resistance of Existing Timber Floors,* Digest 208, 2nd edn, revised, HMSO, London.

Building Research Establishment (1984) *Cavity Insulation* Digest 236, 1st edn, revised, HMSO, London.

Building Research Establishment (1984) *Intermediate Timber Floors in Converted Dwellings – Sound Insulation,* Defect Action Sheet 45, BRE, Watford, England.

Building Research Establishment (1985) *Rising Damp in Walls: Diagnosis and Treatment,* Digest 245, 1st edn, revised, HMSO, London.

Building Research Establishment (1985) *Improving the Sound Insulation of Separating Walls and Floors,* Digest 293, HMSO, London.

Building Research Establishment (1985) *Surface Condensation and Mould Growth in Traditionally Built Dwellings,* Digest 297, HMSO, London.

Building Research Establishment (1985) *Dry-Rot: Its Recognition and Control,* Digest 299, HMSO, London.

Building Research Establishment (1985) *Preventing Decay in External Joinery,* Digest 304, HMSO, London.

Department of the Environment and Welsh Office (1985) *The Building Regulations 1985,* Statutory Instruments 1985, No. 1065, HMSO, London.

Department of the Environment and Welsh Office (1985) *Manual to the Building Regulations 1985,* HMSO, London.

Department of the Environment and Welsh Office (1985) *Approved Document B: Fire Spread,* HMSO, London.

Department of the Environment and Welsh Office (1985) *Approved Document E: Sound,* HMSO, London.

Department of the Environment and Welsh Office (1985) *Approved Document F: Ventilation,* HMSO, London.

Department of the Environment and Welsh Office (1985) *Approved Document L: Conservation of Fuel and Power,* HMSO, London.

Department of the Environment and Welsh Office (1985) *The Building Regulations 1985: Mandatory Rules for Means of Escape in Case of Fire,* HMSO, London.

Eley, P. and Worthington, J. (1984) *Industrial Rehabilitation: The Use of Redundant Buildings for Small Enterprises,* Architectural Press, London.

Feilden, B.M. (1982) *Conservation of Historic Buildings,* Butterworths, London.

Twiston-Davies, J. (1986) Products in practice: thermal insulation. *Architects' Journal Supplement,* 26 February 1986, Architectural Press, London.

Chapter five

Statutory requirements affecting rehabilitation and re-use

The rehabilitation and re-use of old buildings is, like new construction, subject to statutory constraints, and the need to comply with various forms of legislation can have a significant effect on the viability of schemes. For example, complying with fire safety legislation can involve a considerable amount of work and expense in upgrading the structure, providing means of escape and fulfilling compartmentation requirements, possibly making an otherwise attractive scheme economically prohibitive.

Although the number of statutory constraints that could affect rehabilitation work might appear considerable, in fact only a handful of key provisions will apply to the majority of schemes. These key provisions are as follows:

- The *Town and Country Planning Act 1971*
- Provisions under the *Town and Country Planning Act 1971,* concerning listed buildings and conservation areas
- The Building Regulations
- The *Factories Act 1961*
- The *Offices, Shops and Railway Premises Act 1963*
- The *Fire Precautions Act 1971*

Because of the significant effect that these statutory provisions can have on the rehabilitation and re-use of old buildings, it is vital that all of those involved in such work are thoroughly conversant with them. The effects of the legislation on the design of any scheme under consideration can then be fully understood,

together with the all-important economic implications which, in most cases, will be the factor which decides whether or not the rehabilitation option is chosen.

5.1 THE TOWN AND COUNTRY PLANNING ACT 1971

Under the *Town and Country Planning Act 1971,* planning permission must be obtained in order to carry out "development" (the full meaning of which is described later), and the making of an application for planning permission may require a considerable amount of preparation with several weeks, or even months, elapsing before a decision is given. If, therefore, an application is made in relation to a scheme for which permission is not required, there may be a significant waste of time, effort and money. It is therefore essential for the developer and his professional advisers to be aware of the principles which govern the need for planning permission.

Section 23(1) of the *Town and Country Planning Act 1971* states that "... planning permission is required for the carrying out of any development of land". The meaning of "development" is defined in Section 22(1) of the Act as "... the carrying out of building, engineering, mining or other operations in, on, over or under land, or the making of any material change in the use of any buildings or other land". "Development", therefore, consists of two basic elements:

- The carrying out of certain operations
- The making of any material change of use.

Section 290(1) of the Act provides further definitions which assist in the interpretation of Section 22(1), and the relevant ones are as follows:

- "building": ". . . includes any structure or erection, and any part of a building, as so defined, but does not include plant or machinery comprised in a building"
- "building operations": "includes rebuilding operations, structural alterations of or additions to buildings, and other operations normally undertaken by a person carrying on business as a builder"
- "engineering operations": "includes the formation or laying out of means of access to highways"

It is clear that the rehabilitation and re-use of old buildings will, in the vast majority of cases, include "building operations" as defined by the Act, and that planning permission will therefore be required. However, certain building operations are exempted from the need to obtain planning permission, either because they are specifically excluded from the Act's definition of "development", or because they are classed as "permitted development"

5.1.1 Building operations not requiring planning permission

Section 22(2) of the Act lists operations and uses which are specifically excluded from the meaning of "development", and which therefore do not require planning permission. The two most notable exclusions from the meaning of "development" are:

- "the carrying out of works for the maintenance, improvement or other alteration of any building, being works which affect only the interior of the building or which do not materially affect the exterior of the building . . ."

Many rehabilitation schemes fall into this category and do not, therefore, require planning permission, provided no material change of use is involved (see later)

- "in the case of buildings . . . which are used for a purpose of any class specified in an order made by the Secretary of State under this section, the use thereof for any other purpose of the same class".

This exclusion relates to *The Town and Country Planning (Use Classes) Order 1972* which categorizes buildings into Use Classes, according to the activities for which they are used. The effect of the exclusion is that any change in the use of a building will not constitute "development", provided the old and new uses fall within the same Use Class. The Use Class Order and its effects are given detailed consideration in Section 5.1.2.

The *Town and Country Planning General Development Order 1977* (GDO) automatically confers planning permission on various categories of "permitted development", and these are detailed in Schedule 1 of the GDO. Those that might relate to the rehabilitation of existing buildings are summarized below.

(a) The enlargement, improvement or other alteration of a dwellinghouse is permitted provided that its cubic content is not exceeded by more than:
  - In the case of a terraced house, 50 cubic metres or 10%, whichever is the greater, or;
  - In any other case, 70 cubic metres or 15%, whichever is the greater.

Both cases are subject to a maximum of 115 cubic metres. The following qualifications apply:
  - The limits must be applied to the original building, i.e. as existing on 1 July 1948, or, if built later, as first built; and thus the right to extend is a "once and for all' right
  - The height of the altered building must not exceed that of the highest part of the roof of the original building

99

- No part of the altered building may project beyond the forward-most part of any wall of the original dwellinghouse which fronts on a highway
- The erection of a garage, stable, loose box or coach house within the curtilage of the dwellinghouse is treated for all purposes as an enlargement of the dwellinghouse.

(b) Other development within the curtilage of a dwellinghouse is permitted as follows:

- The construction of a porch outside any external door of a dwellinghouse, so long as it does not exceed two square metres in area, and three metres in height, and is not less than two metres from any boundary of the site that fronts on a highway
- The construction, alteration, etc. of any building or enclosure required for a purpose incidental to the enjoyment of the dwellinghouse, so long as it does not project beyond the forward-most point of any wall of the original dwellinghouse which fronts on a highway, so long as the height does not exceed three metres (four metres in the case of a ridged roof), and (ignoring the dwellinghouse itself and the land on which it stands) so long as the development does not result in more than half the area of the curtilage being covered by buildings
- The construction of a hardstanding for vehicles for a purpose incidental to the enjoyment of the dwellinghouse
- The erection or placing of an oil storage tank for domestic heating so long as it does not project beyond the forward-most part of any wall of the original dwellinghouse which fronts on a highway, and so long as the capacity does not exceed 3500 litres and the tank does not project more than three metres above ground level.

(c) Sundry minor operations to all types of property as follows:

- The erection of walls, fences, gates, etc. subject to a maximum height of one metre where abutting a highway or two metres otherwise
- The provision of a means of access to a highway other than a classified or trunk road, if required for the purposes of any other development permitted by the GDO
- The painting of the exterior of any building except for the purpose of advertisement, announcement or direction

(d) Change of use from Use Class IV (a general industrial building used for any purpose) to Use Class III (a light industrial building used for any purpose).

(e) Change of use from any of the shop uses excluded from Use Class I (i.e. a shop for the sale of hot food, a tripe shop, a pet shop, a cats' meat shop, a shop for the sale of motor vehicles) to any other shop use.

(f) The enlargement of industrial buildings by up to 20% of the original cubic content, provided the floor area of the extension does not exceed 750 square metres, and the height of the original building is not exceeded.

(g) The rebuilding, restoration or replacement of war damaged buildings, so long as the cubic content of the original building is not increased (except as permitted under (a) and (f) above), and there is no material variation from the external appearance of the original building.

It should be pointed out that the above is a summary only of the categories of permitted development that might relate to rehabilitation schemes, and for full details, the GDO itself should be consulted.

5.1.2 Material change of use

As stated earlier, under the *Town and Country Planning Act 1971,* "development" includes the making of any material change of use, and this relates to *The Town and Country Planning (Use Classes) Order 1972.* The Order categorizes buildings into Use Classes according to the activities for which they are used, and these are summarized below. (For full details of the Use Classes, together with specific definitions of the terms used, reference should be made to the Use Classes Order itself.)

Class I: Use as a shop for any purpose except as a shop for the sale of hot food, a tripe shop, a pet shop, a cats' meat shop, a shop for the sale of motor vehicles.

Class II: Use as an office for any purpose.

Class III: Use as a light industrial building for any purpose.

Class IV: Use as a general industrial building for any purpose.

Classes V–IX: These are "Special Industrial" classes, and cover various categories of heavy, dangerous or obnoxious industry which are specifically itemized.

Class X: Use as a wholesale warehouse or repository for any purpose.

Class XI: Use as a boarding or guest house, or an hotel providing sleeping accommodation.

Class XII: Use as a residential or boarding school or a residential college.

Class XIII: Use as a building for public worship or religious instruction or for the social or recreational activities of the religious bodies using the building.

Class XIV: Use as a home or institution providing for the boarding, care and maintenance of children, old people or persons under disability, a convalescent home, a nursing home, a sanatorium or a hospital.

Class XV: Use (other than residentially) as a health centre, a school treatment centre, a clinic, a creche, a day nursery or a dispensary, or use as a consulting room or surgery unattached to the residence of the consultant or practitioner.

Class XVI: Use as an art gallery (other than for business purposes), a museum, a public library or reading room, a public hall or an exhibition hall.

Class XVII: Use as a theatre, cinema, music hall or concert hall.

Class XVIII: Use as a dance hall, skating rink, swimming bath, Turkish or other vapour or foam bath, or as a gymnasium or sports hall.

The term "material" in the context of material change of use is not defined in the *Town and Country Planning Act 1971,* but in the majority of cases any change of use from one Use Class to another will be deemed to be a material change, therefore bringing it within the definition of "development" and, in turn, meaning that planning permission will be required.

Any change of use *within* the same Use Class, however, is specifically excluded (by both the Use Class Order and the *Town and Country Planning Act 1971*) from the meaning of "development" and, therefore, will not require planning permission provided it also falls within the criteria outlined in Section 5.1.1. Thus, the rehabilitation of an estate agency office to provide premises for a building society (both are within Use Class II), which affects only the interior of the building and does not materially affect its exterior, will not require planning permission.

5.1.3 Summary

The preceding paragraphs explain the situations where planning permission may or may not be required for rehabilitation schemes, and these are briefly summarized below:

(a) Planning permission IS required for work involving building operations, with the following exceptions – (b) and (c):
(b) Planning permission IS NOT required for maintenance, improvement or other alteration work which affects only the interior of

a building, or which does not materially affect its exterior.

(c) Planning permission IS NOT required for "permitted development" as specified in the *Town and Country Planning General Development Order 1977*. The principal types of permitted development are:

- The enlargement of a dwellinghouse by, in the case of a terraced house, up to 50 cubic metres, or 10%, whichever is the greater; and in any other case, 70 cubic metres or 15%, whichever is the greater. (Both cases are subject to a maximum of 115 cubic metres)

- The enlargement of industrial buildings by up to 20% of the original cubic content, provided the floor area of the extension does not exceed 750 square metres, and the height of the original building is not exceeded.

(d) Planning permission IS NOT required for a change in the use of a building, provided the old and new uses fall within the same Use Class, as defined in the *Town and Country Planning (Use Classes) Order 1972*. However, if building operations are required which materially affect the original building's exterior, and which are not classed as "permitted development" (see (b) and (c) above), then planning permission will be required.

(e) Planning permission IS required (regardless of (b) and (c) above) where a material change of use is made to a building. See the *Town and Country Planning (Use Classes) Order 1972*.

5.1.4 Applications to determine whether planning permission is required

Under Section 53 of the *Town and Country Planning Act 1971*, any person proposing to carry out operations on land, or to change the use of land, may apply to the local planning authority for a determination as to whether or not the proposal constitutes development, and, if so, whether, having regard to the provisions of the GDO, planning permission is required.

Where there is doubt regarding the need for planning permission for a rehabilitation scheme, this procedure may prove a useful means of avoiding an unnecessary application, thereby saving time and expense. However, it should be borne in mind that the planning authority may require detailed information about the proposal in order to make a determination which, with larger schemes, might not be reached too quickly. It is advisable, in the first instance, that the Development Control Officer within the planning authority is contacted informally in order to gain some idea of the amount of detail required, and the length of time a determination might take.

5.2 LISTED BUILDING AND CONSERVATION AREA LEGISLATION

5.2.1 Listed buildings

Section 54 of the *Town and Country Planning Act 1971* requires the Secretary of State for the Environment to compile lists of buildings of special architectural or historic interest in order that such buildings can be protected from demolition or insensitive alteration and, therefore, preserved for the enjoyment of present and future generations. When a building has been included in the list of buildings of special architectural or historic interest, it is an offence, under Section 55 of the Act, to carry out works of complete or partial demolition, alteration or extension in any manner which would affect its character without first having obtained listed building consent from the local planning authority. In considering whether or not to grant listed building consent, the local planning authority must consult specified national conservation bodies, and take into account any representations made by interested parties including local conservation groups, together with its own internal professional conservation officers. In addition, the Secretary of State must be consulted to enable him to decide whether or not to call in the application for his own decision.

The detailed requirements with regard to listed buildings are contained in the *Town and Country Planning (Listed Buildings and Buildings in Conservation Areas) Regulations 1977,* and comprehensive guidance is given in Department of the Environment Circular 23/77: *Historic Buildings and Conservation Areas – Policy and Procedure.* Further guidance is also given in Circular 12/81: *Historic Buildings and Conservation Areas* (Details contained in *Further Reading* at the end of the chapter).

The number of listed buildings in Great Britain at present is in excess of 300 000 and it is estimated that after the new listing (currently in progress) the figure will be nearer half a million. It is quite likely, therefore, especially in our older towns and cities, that a 'developable' building might be listed, and this will almost certainly rule out the possibility of total demolition which is only very rarely permitted.

However, it is possible in the majority of cases, to carry out sensitive rehabilitation and alteration (including partial demolition and extension) of listed buildings, provided those features for which the building was listed, are retained. The extent of the alteration permitted will depend on the Grade of Listing; for example, the majority of listed buildings are Grade II and these often only possess external features worthy of retention, such as a main street facade, or possibly the entire external envelope of an isolated building. In such cases it may be possible to go as far as replacing the entire interior with a new structure, with only the external elevation(s) that led to the building's listing being retained. On the other hand, if the building is a Grade I listed building (these represent only 1% of the total) any possible alterations will be severely limited since Grade I buildings are of "exceptional" interest and

usually possess both interior and exterior features worthy of retention.

It is clear, therefore, where a listed building is the subject of a proposed development, that the developer will be restricted to the rehabilitation option within the constraints imposed by its listing, although, as has been stated, in many cases it may be possible to carry out a considerable amount of reconstruction behind the retained external elevations. On the other hand, if the design constraints imposed by the building's listing are too great, the developer will be left with no choice but to find a different site, or another building.

It should be pointed out that, where a developer intends to rehabilitate a listed building, in addition to obtaining listed building consent, which is only concerned with aspects of preservation, full planning permission must also be obtained before the development can proceed.

5.2.2 Buildings in conservation areas

Section 277 of the *Town and Country Planning Act 1971* requires every local planning authority to determine which parts of its area are areas of special architectural or historic interest, the character or appearance of which it is desirable to preserve or enhance, and to designate those areas as conservation areas. Local planning authorities must then pay special attention to the desirability of preserving or enhancing the character or appearance of conservation areas within their jurisdiction.

Detailed guidance regarding conservation areas is given in Department of the Environment Circular 23/77: *Historic Buildings and Conservation Areas – Policy and Procedure* which explains that conservation areas ". . . may be large or small, from whole town centres to squares, terraces and smaller groups of buildings (Details contained in *Further Reading* at the end of the chapter) They will often be centred on listed buildings, but not always. Pleasant groups of other buildings, open spaces, trees, an historic street pattern . . . may also contribute to the special character of an area. Areas appropriate for designation as conservation areas will be found in almost every town and many villages. It is the character of areas, rather than individual buildings, that Section 277 of the 1971 Act seeks to preserve or enhance".

Section 277A of the Act requires anyone wishing to demolish an unlisted building within a conservation area to apply for listed building consent, which must be obtained before demolition (or partial demolition) can be carried out.

It is clear, therefore, that in executing its responsibilities of preserving or enhancing the character or appearance of conservation areas, the local planning authority may impose strict constraints on the proposed development of all buildings within conservation areas whether or not they have been listed. In most cases, this will rule out the possibility of total demolition and redevelopment, and it is also unlikely that any alterations to a building will be permitted if they are likely to detract from the character or appearance of the conservation area.

Many 'developable' buildings, while they may not be listed, stand in conservation areas and, as has been stated, if such a building forms an essential part of the conservation area's character or appearance, the development possibilities will be limited. It is therefore essential that the developer, or the developer's agent, establishes what design constraints are likely to be imposed on any rehabilitation scheme as early as possible, since these may well be a key factor in determining whether or not it is worth while going any further in examining the feasibility of the scheme. Generally, however, it will usually be possible to go further in partially demolishing, altering or extending an unlisted building in a conservation area than would be possible with any listed building where the design constraints tend to be much more severe.

5.3 THE BUILDING REGULATIONS 1985

5.3.1 Format of the Building Regulations

Most new and rehabilitated buildings, including those that are extended, altered, or put to a different use, must comply with *The Building Regulations 1985*. The Regulations, which came into operation on 11 November 1985, apply in England and Wales (including Inner London). Scotland has its own separate regulations – *The Building Standards (Scotland) Regulations 1981* – but it is intended that these will be simplified and brought into harmony with the England and Wales Regulations in due course.

Before considering the effect that the Regulations have on the rehabilitation of existing buildings, it is necessary to know something of their format and content.

The Building Regulations 1985 were made under *The Building Act 1984,* and comprise the following parts and schedules:

Part I: General
Part II: Control of building work
            This part describes the categories of work that come within the scope and control of the Regulations and the statutory requirements that must be complied with.
Part III: Relaxation of requirements
            This part states that the relevant local authority has the power to dispense with or relax any requirement contained in the Regulations in certain circumstances.
Part IV: Notices and plans
            This part describes the formal procedures that must be complied with when applying for Building Regulations approval and when carrying out the work.
Part V: Miscellaneous
Note: Parts I to V contain Regulations 1 to 20,

The Building Regulations 1985

which are numbered consecutively through from Part I to Part V.

Schedule 1 Requirements

Schedule 1 contains the main technical requirements of the Regulations. These technical requirements can be met either by using the practical guidance contained in the "Approved Documents" (see later) or by devising acceptable alternative solutions. Schedule 1 consists of the following parts:

Part A Structure
Part B Fire
Part C Site preparation and resistance to moisture
Part D Toxic substances
Part E Resistance to the passage of sound
Part F Ventilation
Part G Hygiene
Part H Drainage and waste disposal
Part J Heat producing appliances
Part K Stairways, ramps and guards
Part L Conservation of fuel and power

Note: All of the "Requirements" contained in Parts A to L of Schedule 1 do not necessarily apply fully to every type of building. For example, Part B1 (Means of escape) applies only to offices, shops and certain dwellings. These "limits on application" are shown in the Regulations alongside the relevant Parts.

Schedule 2 Facilities for disabled people

Schedule 2 also contains technical requirements. These concern the provision of access and facilities for disabled people in wheelchairs, and are only applicable to new buildings.

Schedule 3 Exempt buildings and work

Schedule 3 lists those buildings (including certain extensions of limited size) that are totally exempted from the requirements of the Regulations.

Schedule 4 Revocations

Schedule 4 lists the Regulations that have been revoked, and superseded by *The Building Regulations 1985*.

Approved Documents

Approved Documents give practical guidance on meeting some of the requirements of the Regulations, and there is an Approved Document covering each of the requirements of Schedule 1. There is also an Approved Document which gives guidance on meeting Regulation 7 (Materials and workmanship). Regulation B1 (Means of escape) has a set of Mandatory rules for means of escape in case of fire, rather than an Approved Document.

The designer of the building can choose whether or not to use the Approved Documents in meeting the requirements of the Regulations. As an alternative, designers have the option of devising their own solution, and this is acceptable, provided the chosen solution is adequate to meet the requirements of the Regulations.

The eleven Approved Documents relating to Schedule 1 are given the notations A to L to correspond directly with Parts A to L of the Schedule itself. The Approved Documents may give guidance on meeting the requirements of the Regulations in more than one form. They may describe specific methods of construction (Technical Solutions), make reference to other publications, such as British Standards (Alternative Approaches), or give Acceptable Levels of Performance.

Currently, there is only one set of Approved Documents produced by the Department of the Environment. However, it is possible that, in due course, other documents produced by other bodies may be accepted as Approved Documents.

105

5.3.2 Work to which the Building Regulations apply

The Building Regulations apply in England and Wales to:

- *"Building work"* and
- The *"Material change of use"* of existing buildings.

"Building work" is defined in Regulation 3 as:

(a) The erection or extension of a building;
(b) The material alteration of a building;
(c) The provision, extension or material alteration of a controlled service or fitting in, or in connection with, a building;
(d) Work required by Regulation 6, i.e. when a "material change of use" takes place.

Certain small buildings and extensions, along with buildings used for special purposes, are totally exempt from the Regulations, and these exemptions are listed in Schedule 3 to the Regulations. Schedule 3 lists seven classes of exempt buildings. Classes I to VI cover a wide range of buildings for certain specialized uses, temporary buildings, and small detached buildings (of total floor area not exceeding 30 m^2) with no sleeping accommodation. Class VII gives exemption to the extension of a building by the addition at ground level of a greenhouse, conservatory, porch, covered yard or covered way, or a carport open on at least two sides (where the total floor area does not exceed 30 m^2).

When "building work" takes place, it must be carried out so that it complies with Schedule 1 of the Regulations, which contains specific technical requirements; and Schedule 2, which contains requirements to provide facilities in new buildings for disabled people in wheelchairs (see Regulation 4).

"Material change of use" of an existing building is defined in Regulation 5, and is deemed to have taken place if there is a change in the purpose for which the building is used which falls within one of five specific categories of change laid down in Regulation 5(a) to (e) (see Section 5.3.6). Any other change cannot be classed as a material change of use.

Regulation 6 requires that when a material change of use of either the whole (or part) of an existing building takes place, the work must be carried out so that the whole (or part) of the building complies with certain specified Parts of Schedule 1 to the Regulations (see Section 5.3.6).

It can be seen, therefore, that most categories of rehabilitation, including extensions, alterations and changes of use will come wholly or partly within the scope of the Building Regulations and their statutory requirements. Section 5.3.2, above, has outlined the categories of work that must comply with the Regulations, and those associated with the rehabilitation and re-use of old buildings will now be considered in more detail.

5.3.3 The extension of existing buildings

The rehabilitation and re-use of existing buildings often incorporates the addition of extensions to provide increased floorspace, and extensions are brought within the scope of *The Building Regulations 1985* by Regulations 3 and 4: Regulation 4(1)(a) states that "Building work (which is defined by Regulation 3(1)(a) as including the extension of a building) shall be carried out so that it complies with the relevant requirements contained in Schedules 1 and 2 . . .".

Thus, if a building is extended, *the extension* must comply with Schedule 1 as if it were a newly erected building. However, extensions to existing buildings do not have to comply with Schedule 2 (Facilities for disabled people). This is indirectly stated in paragraph 2 of Schedule 2, which states that its requirements apply to the *erection* of certain buildings; any reference to extension being specifically excluded. (Note that

Regulation 3(a), in defining building work, separates the terms "erection" and "extension").

In addition to bringing extensions within the scope of the Regulations, Regulation 4 introduces certain requirements relating to existing buildings affected by extensions. Regulation 4(2)(a) states that "Building work shall be carried out so that, after it has been completed, no building which is extended . . . is "*adversely affected*" in relation to compliance with any relevant requirement contained in Schedule 1". The term "adversely affected" is defined in Regulation 2(4), and further reference is made to it in Regulation 2(5). These references are rather complex, and are clarified in the explanatory notes contained in the *Manual to the Building Regulations 1985* (Details contained in *Further Reading* at the end of the chapter):

"Where work is done to an existing building, service or fitting, the work itself must comply with all the relevant requirements of Schedule 1, but the existing building must not be adversely affected. This means that while it will not usually be necessary to bring the (existing) building up to the standards of the Regulations, it should not be made worse as measured by the standards of the relevant requirements in Schedule 1. The exception is where the work to be carried out will bring the whole building within the ambit of a requirement which previously did not apply. For example, if a four storey building is extended to five storeys, the whole building will need to comply with A3".
(Regulation A3 applies only to buildings with five or more storeys, and public buildings where the structure incorporates a clear span exceeding nine metres.)

Therefore, in the majority of cases, when an existing building is extended, only the extension itself need comply with Schedule 1 of the Regulations, with the proviso that the existing building must not in any way be made worse.

5.3.4 The material alteration of existing buildings

The "material alteration" of existing buildings is brought within the scope of *The Building Regulations 1985* by Regulations 3 and 4. Regulation 4(1)(a) states that "Building work (which is defined by Regulation 3(1)(b) as including the material alteration of a building) shall be carried out so that it complies with the relevant requirements contained in Schedules 1 and 2 . . .".

The meaning of "material alteration" is clarified in the explanatory notes contained in the *Manual to the Building Regulations 1985* which states that: "If an alteration to a building, or any part of the work involved, would "adversely affect" (i.e. make worse) the existing building as regards Part A (Structure); B1 (Means of escape in case of fire); B3 (Internal fire spread – structure) or B4 (External fire spread) *unless other work were done,* it is a "material alteration" subject to control. Examples of such alterations are:

- Removing part of a loadbearing wall which consequently requires the insertion of a beam to carry the load
- Altering a three storey house in such a way that additional work is necessary to maintain the means of escape from the third storey
- Removing part of a wall which is non-loadbearing, but is necessary for fire resistance.

Therefore, any part of a building that is adversely affected with regard to Parts A, B1, B3 or B4 during rehabilitation or alteration work must be made to comply fully with the requirements of those Parts of the Regulations.

In addition to the above, the insertion of cavity fill insulation into an existing wall, and the underpinning of existing buildings, are defined as material alterations. Where cavity fill insulation is inserted, the work must comply with Part C4 (Resistance of walls to passage of moisture) and D1 (Toxic substances).

5.3.5 The provision, extension or material alteration of building services

The provision, extension or material alteration of building services is brought within the scope of *The Building Regulations 1985* by Regulations 3 and 4. Regulation 4(1)(a) states that "Building work (which is defined by Regulation 3(1)(c) as including 'the provision extension or material alteration of a controlled service or fitting in or in connection with a building') shall be carried out so that it complies with the relevant requirements contained in Schedules 1 and 2 . . .".

The term "controlled service or fitting" is defined by Regulation 3(3) as meaning a service or fitting in relation to which paragraph G2, G3 or G4, Part H or J, or paragraph L4 or L5 of Schedule 1 imposes a requirement. (These Parts of the Regulations deal with bathrooms, hot water storage, sanitary conveniences, drainage and waste disposal, heat producing appliances, heating system controls and insulation of heating services.)

Therefore, if any of the above services, or related fittings, are installed, extended or adversely affected (i.e. made worse) during the rehabilitation, alteration or extension of an existing building, the work must comply fully with the relevant Parts of Schedule 1 of the Regulations (i.e. G2, G3, G4, H, J, L4 or L5).

5.3.6 The material change of use of existing buildings

The "material change of use" of existing buildings is defined and brought within the scope of *The Building Regulations 1985* by Regulation 5, which gives the meaning of material change of use, and Regulation 6, which specifies the requirements relating to material change of use.

A material change of use of an existing building occurs when there is a change in the purpose for which the building is used, if, after that change:

(a) The building is used for the purposes of a dwelling, where previously it was not
(b) The building contains a flat, where previously it did not
(c) The building is used as a hotel or institution, where previously it was not
(d) The building is a public building, where previously it was not
(e) The building is not a building described in Classes I to VI in Schedule 3, where previously it was.

Any other change cannot be classed as a material change of use.

Typical examples of material changes of use would therefore include the rehabilitation and conversion of:

- A redundant church into flats or maisonettes
- An existing office building into a hotel
- A disused barn or stable into a house
- A redundant warehouse into a community centre

Regulation 6(1) requires that, where there is a material change of use of *the whole* of an existing building, the work must be carried out so that *the whole* building complies with the relevant requirements of the following paragraphs of Schedule 1:

(a) In all cases: B1 (Means of escape)
B2 (Internal fire spread – surfaces)
B3 (Internal fire spread – structure)
B4(2) (External fire spread – roofs)
F1 and F2 (Ventilation)
G1 (Food storage)
G2 (Bathrooms)
G4 (Sanitary conveniences)
H4 (Solid waste storage)
J1 to J3 (Heat producing appliances)
(b) In the case of a material change of use described in (e) above:
A1 to A3 (structure); and
(c) In the case of a building exceeding fifteen metres in height:
B4(1) (external fire spread – walls)

Regulation 6(2) requires that, where there is a material change of use of *part only* of an existing building, the work must be carried out so that *the affected part* (and not the whole building) complies with the requirements of (a) and (b) above.

However, where there is a material change of use of *part only* of an existing building exceeding fifteen metres in height, the *whole building* (and not merely the affected part) must comply with the requirements of (c) above.

5.3.7 Relaxation of Building Regulations requirements

Part III of *The Building Regulations 1985* (Regulation 10) gives the local authority the power to dispense with or relax any requirement of the Regulations. All applications for dispensation or relaxation of any requirement must be made to the relevant local authority, and if an application is refused, the applicant may appeal to the Secretary of State for the Environment.

Dispensation is agreement by the local authority that a particular requirement of the Regulations need not be complied with at all.

Relaxation is agreement by the local authority that, because of special circumstances, all aspects of a requirement need not be fully met.

The *Manual to the Building Regulations 1985* states that, because most of the technical requirements in Schedule 1 are "functional" and ask for something to be provided at an "adequate" level, they cannot be relaxed. This is because, to provide something less than adequate is to fail to comply with the Regulations. In such cases, however, while relaxation is not possible, it might be reasonable to dispense with the requirement. Relaxation *can* be considered where requirements are "specific", i.e. Regulations B1 (Means of escape in case of fire), L2 and L3 (Resistance to the passage of heat), and Schedule 2 (Access for disabled people).

If an application is made to the local authority for a dispensation or relaxation, the applicant must explain why the particular requirement is unreasonable in the circumstances.

The rehabilitation of existing buildings often creates circumstances where the dispensation or relaxation of certain requirements of the Regulations can be advantageous, or even essential, if the scheme is to be viable. For example, if an existing staircase, which is to be retained and used as a means of escape *almost* complies with Regulation B1 (Means of escape) as it stands, and to make it comply fully would involve excessive expenditure, the designer would be well advised to apply for a dispensation or relaxation, particularly if the expenditure threatened the viability of the scheme.

In many cases, before a requirement of the Regulations can be relaxed, it will be necessary to carry out some additional work, particularly where the item for which relaxation is required falls well below the relevant requirement. The extent of the additional work necessary to bring the item nearer to compliance and therefore to obtain relaxation will be a matter for negotiation with the enforcing authority.

5.3.8 The Building Regulations Package

The previous sections give an insight into the various aspects of building rehabilitation and re-use that are controlled by *The Building Regulations 1985,* and it is essential that the full Building Regulations Package be consulted in order to establish the specific detailed requirements. The Package, published by HMSO, consists of fourteen documents:

- The *Manual to the Building Regulations 1985,* which includes: (i) an explanation of which types of work are controlled by the Regulations; (ii) detailed information on the two alternative systems of building control; (local authority, or private approved inspector); (iii) an explanation of the various means of complying with the Regulations, including the use of Approved Documents etc.; (iv) the

ons and Schedules 1–4 (see Section
-, accompanied by useful explanatory
notes to aid interpretation.
- Eleven Approved Documents which give
  detailed practical guidance on meeting the
  requirements of the Regulations contained in
  Schedule 1
- A further Approved Document giving guidance on meeting the requirements of Regulation 7: (Materials and workmanship)
- A set of "Mandatory rules for means of escape
  in case of fire".

Proper reference to the Manual and its
supporting documents should enable the
designer of a rehabilitation scheme to interpret,
and comply with, the Building Regulations
without difficulty. If, however, the designer
does meet with uncertainties, it is advisable to
consult and seek the guidance of a local authority
building control officer, or a private approved
inspector, at an early stage so as to avoid the risk
of submitting plans that might be rejected or
need amendment.

5.4 THE FACTORIES ACT 1961

The *Factories Act 1961* lays down various
minimum standards which must be complied
with in all factories, whether newly constructed
or converted. The detailed requirements are
given in the Act itself and comprehensive
guidance on compliance is given in various
published guides and advisory leaflets, all of
which should be referred to in detail at the
design stage. Some of the more important
requirements of the Act that will affect the
design and cost of any building rehabilitated for
use as a factory are outlined below.

5.4.1 Space standards

In order to prevent overcrowding, minimum
space standards are laid down. At least 400 cubic
feet per person is required, and, in calculating the
space in any room, no space more than 14 feet
above floor level may be taken into account.

5.4.2 Temperature

In any workroom where most of the work is
done sitting, and no serious physical effort is
involved, a temperature of not less than 60°F
must be maintained after the first hour. However, it is possible to vary this "reasonable
temperature" according to the particular nature
of the activities or operations being undertaken.

5.4.3 Ventilation

Effective and suitable provision must be made
for adequate ventilation by the circulation of
fresh air, in order to render harmless all fumes,
dust and other impurities generated by the work
being undertaken.

5.4.4 Lighting

Sufficient and suitable lighting, either natural or
artificial, must be provided in every part of a
factory in which persons are working or passing.
The Act does not refer to any specific standards
for lighting, and, generally, the design of
lighting should be based on British Standard
Code of Practice CP 3, Chapter 1, and the
Illuminating Engineering Society Code of Practice.

5.4.5 Sanitary conveniences

Sufficient and suitable sanitary conveniences
must be provided, and effective provision must
be made for lighting them. Where persons of
both sexes are to be employed, separate male and
female sanitary accommodation must be provided.

Currently, the detailed requirements regarding sanitary conveniences in factories are contained in the *Sanitary Accommodation Regulations
1938,* which lay down the following minimum
standards:

- Females: 1 w.c. for every 25 females
- Males: 1 w.c. for every 25 males. Where the
  number of males exceeds 100 and sufficient

urinals are also provided, there must be 1 w.c. per 25 persons up to the first 100, and 1 w.c. per 40 persons thereafter

- The sanitary accommodation must be properly ventilated, not entered from the working area except by means of a ventilated lobby, and protected from the weather. It should be private, urinal fittings must be screened, so as not to be visible from the outside, and the interiors of enclosures must not be visible when the door is open from any place where persons of the opposite sex have to work or pass.

5.4.6 Washing facilities

Adequate and suitable facilities for washing must be provided. These must include a supply of clean running hot and cold or warm water, soap and clean towels or other suitable means of cleaning and drying.

5.4.7 Fire precautions

The *Factories Act 1961* requires that all buildings within its scope shall have:

- Means of escape in case of fire as may reasonably be necessary in the particular premises
- Appropriate firefighting equipment, properly maintained and readily available for use
- An effective fire alarm system capable of being operated without exposing anyone to undue risk.

In addition, factories where more than a given number of persons are employed, or where explosive or highly flammable materials are used or stored, are required to have a Fire Certificate, issued by a fire authority, which states that the building is provided "with such means of escape in case of fire for the persons employed in the factory as may reasonably be required in the circumstances of the case".

Although many existing factories comply with these requirements, and have valid Fire Certificates issued under the *Factories Act 1961*, all of the fire precautions clauses of this Act have now been superseded by the *Fire Precautions Act 1971*. However, because of the means by which various building types are brought under the control of the *Fire Precautions Act 1971*, the fire precautions clauses of the 1961 Act were not in fact superseded until 1 January 1977, as explained in Section 5.6. Thus any new factory building, and any building that is rehabilitated for factory use, must now comply not with the fire clauses of the *Factories Act 1961*, but with the *Fire Precautions Act 1971*, the requirements of which are virtually identical. The 1971 Act is given more detailed consideration in Section 5.6.

5.5 THE OFFICES, SHOPS AND RAILWAY PREMISES ACT 1963

The *Offices, Shops and Railway Premises Act 1963* lays down various minimum standards which must be complied with in all offices, shops, and most railway buildings where people are employed. The detailed requirements are given in the Act and, as with the Factories Act, various guides and advisory leaflets have been published which give extensive guidance on compliance in a more comprehensible manner than the legal jargon contained in the Act itself. The provisions of the Act apply to rehabilitated buildings as well as to new buildings, and some of the more important requirements that will affect rehabilitation schemes are outlined below.

5.5.1 Space standards

Minimum space standards are specified in order to prevent overcrowding. Any room in which people work must be of such a size that there is 40 square feet of floor space per person, or, where the ceiling is lower than 10 feet, 400 cubic feet per person. For this purpose, regard must be paid not only to the number of persons in the room, but also to the amount of space occupied by furniture, fittings, machinery, etc.

5.5.2 Temperature

In any room where people work, and where a substantial proportion of the work does not involve severe physical effort, a "reasonable temperature" of 16°C (60.8°F) must be maintained after the first hour.

The minimum standard is not required in offices used by the public where its maintenance is not reasonably practicable, or in rooms in shops where its maintenance is not reasonably practicable or would cause deterioration of goods.

5.5.3 Ventilation

In all workrooms there must be effective and suitable means of ventilation by the circulation of adequate supplies of either fresh, or artificially purified air.

5.5.4 Lighting

Sufficient and suitable lighting, either natural or artificial, must be provided in every part of the premises in which people work or pass. As with lighting in factories, reference should be made to British Standard Code of Practice CP 3, Chapter 1 for guidance.

5.5.5 Sanitary conveniences

Sufficient and suitable sanitary conveniences must be provided with effective provision for lighting and ventilating them. Where persons of both sexes are employed, proper separate sanitary accommodation for each sex must be provided. For the purposes of the Act, the provision of sanitary conveniences must be in compliance with the *Sanitary Conveniences Regulations 1964*, the main requirements of which are as follows:

(1) One w.c. is sufficient where either the number of people employed does not regularly exceed five, or each of the regular employees works in the premises for only two hours or less per day

(2) In all other cases the following provisions apply:

(a) *For females and males (except where urinals are provided)*

Nos. regularly employed at any one time	Nos. of w.c.s to be provided
1–15	1
16–30	2
31–50	3
51–75	4
76–100	5
over 100	5 plus 1 additional w.c. for every 25 persons in excess of 100

(b) *For males where urinals are provided in addition to w.c.s*

No. of males regularly employed at any one time	No. of w.c.'s to be provided	No. of urinal stalls to be provided (or 600 mm space of slab urinal)
1–15	1	—
16–20	1	1
21–30	2	1
31–45	2	2
46–60	3	2
61–75	3	3
76–90	4	3
91–100	4	4
over 100	4	4 plus 1 w.c. for every 25 persons (or fraction of 25) in excess of 100.

Every fourth additional w.c. may be replaced by a urinal as follows:

101–125	5	4
126–150	6	4
151–175	7	4
176–200	7	5

(3) In premises where more than ten people are regularly employed at the same time, and the conveniences which they use are also made available for general use by customers, an extra w.c. must be provided (one for each sex if both are employed) in addition to the numbers given in the schedules above

(4) No sanitary convenience may be situated in a workroom, and there must always be a space with means of ventilation between sanitary accommodation and any work-room

(5) All sanitary conveniences must be protected from the weather.

5.5.6 Washing facilities

Suitable and sufficient washing facilities must be provided, including a supply of clean, running hot and cold or warm water and, in addition, soap and clean towels or other suitable means of cleaning or drying. For the purposes of the Act, provision of washing facilities must be in accordance with the *Washing Facilities Regulations 1964*. The number of wash basins required under the Regulations is identical to the number of w.c.s required in female sanitary accommodation or male sanitary accommodation where no urinals are provided (i.e. as Section 5.5.5(a)).

The requirements regarding ventilation, protection from the weather, provision of additional facilities where they are used by customers and the separation of male and female accommodation are all similar to those applying to sanitary accommodation (see Section 5.5.5).

5.5.7 Fire precautions

The fire precautions requirements of the *Offices, Shops and Railway Premises Act 1963* are very

similar to those of the *Factories Act 1961*, and have, in the same way, been superseded by the *Fire Precautions Act 1971*, as explained in Section 5.4.7. Since 1 January 1977, any new office, shop or railway premises, and any building rehabilitated for such use, must comply, not with the fire clauses of the 1963 Act, but with the *Fire Precautions Act 1971* which is considered more fully in Section 5.6.

5.6 THE FIRE PRECAUTIONS ACT 1971

The *Fire Precautions Act 1971* was the first Act to deal exclusively with fire and is described as "an Act to make further provision for the protection of persons from fire risks, and for purposes connected therewith".

The Act stipulates that a Fire Certificate, issued by the fire authority, is required for all premises covered by the Act. Various building types are brought under the Act's control by means of "designating orders" and, to date, designating orders have been made for the following:

- Hotels and boarding houses where sleeping accommodation is provided for more than 6 persons (including staff)
- Factories, offices, shops and railway premises in which more than 20 persons are employed at any one time, or more than 10 persons are employed other than on the ground floor
- Buildings containing two or more factory, office, shop or railway premises where the aggregate number of persons exceeds 20, or 10 other than on the ground floor
- Factory premises where explosive or highly flammable materials are stored in such quantity as to constitute a serious additional risk in case of fire.

The designating orders for factories, offices, shops and railway premises came into force on 1 January 1977 and, until that date, these buildings were required to comply with the fire precautions requirements of the *Factories Act 1961*, and the *Offices, Shops and Railway Premises Act*

1963 respectively. However, since 1 January 1977, the fire precautions requirements of the 1961 and 1963 Acts have been superseded by the *Fire Precautions Act 1971*. The requirements of the 1971 Act are virtually identical to those concerning fire precautions in the 1961 and 1963 Acts, and any Fire Certificate issued under those Acts (i.e. before 1 January 1977) continues in force and is "deemed to be a certificate validly issued under the 1971 Act" for the premises while they are still being put to the use to which the certificate relates and, of course, while they remain unaltered.

The *Fire Precautions Act 1971* requires that:

- Means of escape and their safe and effective use
- Means of firefighting
- Means of giving warning in case of fire

should attain a reasonable standard, and the fire authority's Fire Officer must be satisfied that this is the case before issuing a Fire Certificate. The Act applies to both new and altered buildings, and its requirements must therefore be taken into account in the design of rehabilitation schemes. Detailed guidance on the requirements for the various building types covered by the Act is contained in the following *Guides to the Fire Precautions Act 1971* published by the Home Office (Details contained in *Further Reading* at the end of the chapter):

- No. 1: Hotels and Boarding Houses
- No. 2: Factories
- No. 3: Offices, Shops and Railway Premises

Where it is necessary to obtain a Fire Certificate, the extent of the fire precautions provisions will normally be at the discretion of the Fire Officer issuing the certificate, since the Act itself uses the term "reasonable standard" which clearly is open to interpretation. Even in the three guides to the Act, referred to above, which do give detailed guidance, it is made clear that they have "no statutory force" and that they are "issued without prejudice to the statutory responsibility of the fire authorities for enforcing

the Act and in particular for satisfying themselves that the means of escape in case of fire and other related fire precautions are such as may *reasonably be required in the circumstances of each case*".

The fire precautions provisions required under the Act, particularly means of escape which can have a significant effect on the design of a rehabilitation scheme, are best decided upon as early as possible in the design process by negotiation with the Fire Officer who will be responsible for issuing the Fire Certificate, since this will save having to make amendments at a later stage. Generally, in deciding the means of escape provisions that are required in rehabilitation schemes, the Fire Officer will be flexible and take into account the additional problems and expense associated with carrying out extensive alterations to existing layouts, and it may be possible to obtain relaxations if negotiations are sensibly pursued.

The three guides to the *Fire Precautions Act 1971* contain comprehensive guidance on requirements regarding means of escape, fire alarm systems and firefighting, and all of these aspects will affect the design and cost of any rehabilitation scheme. However, the means of escape requirements will have the most significant design and cost implications and they will therefore be the main focus of attention. Some of the more important aspects with which the means of escape requirements are concerned include the following:

- Travel distances from within rooms to room exits
- Travel distances from room exits to protected stairways or final exits
- Escape routes in alternative directions
- Width of escape routes
- Number of protected stairways
- Width of stairways
- External fire escapes

Probably the single most important factor with regard to means of escape is the number of escape stairways required, since additional protected stairways will involve extensive structural alterations, and their required locations will have a major effect on the layout of the building.

5.7 RULES OF THE FIRE OFFICES COMMITTEE

Insurance companies have their own criteria for assessing the fire risks of buildings, and rules that are used as a basis for insuring property have been drawn up by the Fire Offices Committee (FOC) which is made up of most of the major fire insurance companies in the United Kingdom. These rules differ from the requirements contained in *The Building Regulations 1985* and *The Fire Precautions Act 1971* and, even though they have no statutory force, they represent a major constraint on the design of new and rehabilitated buildings. Compliance with the FOC Rules is essential if the building owner wishes to pay realistic fire insurance premiums, and the Rules also contain provision for substantial premium reductions if the building's construction and firefighting provisions are considered to significantly reduce the degree of risk from fire. It is therefore essential to consult the building owner's insurance company at an early stage in the design process so that specialist advice can be obtained on the fire protection provisions that will be necessary in order to avoid paying high annual insurance premiums. In assessing the degree of risk from fire, and, therefore, the insurance premiums payable, insurance companies are concerned with the following aspects:

- The construction of the building (materials, combustibility, internal subdivision, etc.)
- Provision of fire detection and alarm systems
- Provision of firefighting systems.

Generally, the building owner will have the following choices with regard to fire insurance premiums:

- Paying basic premiums if the building satisfies the FOC's basic requirements

- Paying increased premiums if the building does not satisfy these requirements
- Paying reduced premiums if the building is superior to the FOC's basic requirements.

Increased insurance premiums may result from:

- Inadequate fire-resisting separation between different parts of the premises
- Insufficient internal subdivision into fire-resisting compartments, resulting in excessive floor areas throughout which fire can spread unrestricted
- Construction that does not comply with the FOC's basic construction standards
- Other construction features such as combustible linings, ceilings and partitions
- Openings connecting different floor levels, unless they are protected by fire-resisting enclosures
- Hazardous plant which is not segregated by fire-resisting construction
- Hazardous processes, materials and machinery, depending on the particular trade or occupation.

Reduced premiums may result from:

- Construction superior to that to which a basic rate normally applies
- Fire-resisting separation between different parts of the premises, and segregation of hazardous sections
- Fire detection and firefighting equipment including automatic fire detection and alarm systems, automatic sprinkler systems, fire-extinguishing equipment including hydrants, hose reels and portable extinguishers.

Insurance discounts varying from 5% to as much as 80% are available for the incorporation of suitable fire detection and firefighting equipment in buildings other than those of low hazard and low insurance rating. Some of the most favourable discounts are for the incorporation of automatic sprinkler systems which must be of a type approved by the FOC, and installed and maintained in accordance with their requirements. Other types of firefighting equipment, together with automatic alarm systems, also qualify for premium reductions.

As stated earlier, the FOC's requirements have no statutory force, but they have been outlined in this chapter because it would clearly be unrealistic not to take them into account in the design of rehabilitation schemes. To ignore the FOC's requirements could result in either the need to carry out costly alterations to the completed scheme, or the client having to pay unnecessarily high annual insurance premiums throughout the building's life. It is vital, therefore, that the insurers are consulted as early as possible in the design of any rehabilitation scheme so that the most economic balance between fire protection provisions and the cost of insurance premiums can be achieved.

Some of the more important publications issued by the Fire Offices Committee are listed below (Details contained in *Further Reading* at the end of the chapter):

- Rules for the Construction of Buildings, Grades 1 and 2
- Rules for Standards I to V Construction
- Rules for the Construction and Installation of Fireproof Doors, Lobbies and Shutters
- Rules for Automatic Sprinkler Installations
- Rules for Automatic Fire Alarm Systems.

FURTHER READING

British Standards Institution (1972) *Fire Tests on Building Materials and Structures: Test Methods and Criteria for the Fire Resistance of Elements of Building Construction,* BS 476, Part 8, 1972, BSI, London.
British Standards Institution (1983) *Fire Precautions in the Design and Construction of Buildings: Code of Practice for Office Buildings,* BS 5588, Part 3, 1983, BSI, London.
British Standards Institution (1984) *Fire Precautions in the Design and Construction of Buildings: Code of Practice for Single-Family Dwelling Houses,* BS 5588, Section 1.1, 1984, BSI, London.
British Standards Institution (1985) *Fire Precautions in the Design and Construction of Buildings: Code of Practice for Shops,* BS 5588, Part 2, 1985, BSI, London.
British Standards Institution (1985) *Guide to Fire Doors,* PD 6512, Part 1, 1985, BSI, London.
Building Research Establishment (1981) *Office Lighting for Good Visual Task Conditions,* Digest 256, HMSO, London.
Chartered Institution of Building Services (1984) *Code of Practice for Interior Lighting,* CIBS, London.
Department of Employment (1971) *The Offices, Shops and Railway Premises Act 1963: A General Guide,* 2nd edn, HMSO, London.
Department of Employment (1973) *Means of Escape in Case of Fire in Offices, Shops and Railway Premises,* Health and Safety at Work booklet No. 40, HMSO, London.
Department of the Environment (1977) *Historic Buildings and Conservation Areas – Policy and Procedure,* Circular 23/77, HMSO, London.
Department of the Environment (1981) *Historic Buildings and Conservation Areas,* Circular 12/81, HMSO, London.
Department of the Environment and Welsh Office (1985) *The Building Regulations 1985,* Statutory Instruments 1985, No. 1065, HMSO, London.
Department of the Environment and Welsh Office (1985) *Manual to the Building Regulations 1985,* HMSO, London.
Department of the Environment and Welsh Office (1985) *Approved Documents A to L,* HMSO, London.
Department of the Environment and Welsh Office (1985) *Approved Document to Support Regulation 7: Materials and Workmanship,* HMSO, London.
Department of the Environment and Welsh Office (1985) *The Building Regulations 1985: Mandatory Rules for Means of Escape in Case of Fire,* HMSO, London.
Fire Offices' Committee and Fire Offices' Com-

mittee of Ireland (1964) *Rules for the Construction and Fixing of Fireproof Doors, Compartments and Shutters,* FOC, London.

Fire Offices' Committee and Fire Offices' Committee of Ireland (1973) *Rules for Automatic Sprinkler Installations,* FOC, London.

Fire Offices' Committee and Fire Offices' Committee of Ireland (1979) *Rules for the Construction of Buildings Standards I to V,* FOC, London.

Fire Offices' Committee and Fire Offices' Committee of Ireland (1983) *Rules for Automatic Fire Alarm Systems,* FOC, London.

Fire Offices' Committee and Fire Offices' Committee of Ireland (1984) *Rules for the Construction of Buildings, Grades 1 and 2,* FOC, London.

Great Britain (1961) *Factories Act 1961,* ch. 34, HMSO, London.

Great Britain (1963) *Offices, Shops and Railway Premises Act 1963,* ch. 41, HMSO, London.

Great Britain (1971) *Fire Precautions Act 1971,* ch. 40, HMSO, London.

Great Britain (1972) *Town and Country Planning Act 1971,* ch. 78, HMSO, London.

Great Britain (1972) *Town and Country Planning (Amendment) Act 1972,* ch. 42, HMSO, London.

Great Britain (1972) *Town and Country Planning (Scotland) Act 1972,* ch. 52, HMSO, London.

Great Britain (1974) *Town and Country Amenities Act 1974,* ch. 32, HMSO, London.

Great Britain (1975) *Town and Country Planning (Listed Buildings and Buildings in Conservation Areas) (Scotland) Regulations 1975,* Statutory Instruments, 1975 No. 2069, HMSO, London.

Great Britain (1977) *Town and Country Planning (Listed Buildings and Buildings in Conservation Areas) Regulations 1977,* Statutory Instruments, 1977 No. 228, HMSO, London.

Health and Safety Executive (1976) *The Factories Act 1961: A Short Guide,* 2nd edn, HMSO, London.

Home Office (1971) *Guides to the Fire Precautions Act 1971,* 1, Hotels and Boarding Houses, HMSO, London.

Home Office (1977) *Guides to the Fire Precautions Act 1971,* 2, Factories, HMSO, London.

Home Office (1977) *Guides to the Fire Precautions Act 1971,* 3, Offices, Shops and Railway Premises, HMSO, London.

Howell James, D.E. (ed.) *et al. Notes on the Need for Planning Permission,* 3rd edn, Oyez Longman, London.

Ministry of Housing and Local Government and Welsh Office (1968) *Town and Country Planning Act 1968 – Part V. Historic Buildings and Conservation,* Joint Circular 61/68 and 57/68, HMSO, London.

Chapter six

Financial aid for building rehabilitation

6.1 GENERAL

Financial aid for the rehabilitation, repair and maintenance of buildings is available in the form of loans and grants from a large number of different bodies. Sources of finance range from public funds, provided by central government and local authorities, to private funds from banks, insurance companies, building societies, etc. The main categories of financial aid are as follows.

6.1.1 Loans

A loan is a sum of money lent to the recipient which must be repaid to the lender over an agreed period, at an agreed rate of interest. The rate of interest charged for a normal loan will be at current commercial rates.

6.1.2 Soft loans

A soft loan is similar in principle to a normal loan, with the important exception that the rate of interest charged will be *below* current commercial rates.

6.1.3 Grants

A grant is a sum of money awarded towards the cost of a scheme which the recipient is not required to repay.

Many sources of financial aid are subjected to specific conditions and restrictions with which the recipient must comply. These vary considerably, and details should be obtained from the various awarding bodies. However, the following points apply to many of the loans and grants that are available:

(a) The award of a loan or grant will normally only be made if the scheme is viable.

(b) Awards are often restricted to schemes that would be unable to proceed without the receipt of financial aid.

(c) Awards for a specific aspect of the work may not be duplicated where more than one source of funding is available.

(d) Awards are normally made on completion of the work, unless it is a large scheme, in which case the award may be made in instalments.

(e) Generally, awards must be applied for and approved before the scheme commences, although it will normally be necessary to have obtained planning permission.

(f) The majority of awards are discretionary.

(g) Loans and grants normally provide only a part of the total funding necessary for rehabilitation schemes, and only rarely are awards of 100% made. Thus, for the majority of schemes, every one pound provided in the form of an award will have to be matched by *at least* one other pound provided by the recipient.

(h) The funds available for financial aid are strictly limited in the majority of cases, with demand exceeding supply.

Generally, awards are made on a 'first come, first served' basis or by the use of specific priority criteria.

6.2 SOURCES OF FINANCIAL AID

This section itemizes the main sources of financial aid available for the rehabilitation of existing buildings. For each source, the information has been restricted to the basic details, since the conditions and constraints are generally far too complex to be contained in a single chapter. However, should the reader wish to obtain full and detailed information on any particular source of financial aid, the addresses of the bodies administering the various awards are also provided.

It will be seen that certain sources of financial aid are concerned with only the repair or maintenance of historic buildings, or buildings in conservation areas. However, the rehabilitation of any historic building will usually involve an element of repair or maintenance, and these sources of finance can therefore provide a useful contribution towards the cost of relevant schemes.

It should also be noted that most sources of financial aid described in this chapter apply to newly constructed buildings as well as rehabilitated buildings, and there may therefore be considerable competition for the limited funds available. However, where a rehabilitation scheme does fulfil the criteria which make it eligible for financial aid, the developer would be well advised to apply, since the award of a grant or loan could significantly increase its viability.

It will be seen that specific figures have been quoted as part of the essential information on grants and loans, and these were current as at the second half of 1985. Clearly, the figures will be updated from time to time, and it is inevitable that certain sources of funding may change or cease to exist in the future. It is essential, therefore, that the following sections are used for guidance only, and that detailed current information is obtained direct from the various bodies administering the financial aid.

6.2.1 Grants for outstanding buildings

Grants are available, under Section 4 of the *Historic Buildings and Ancient Monuments Act 1953,* for the repair of buildings of *outstanding* architectural or historic interest. Examples of works attracting grants include dry-rot eradication, re-roofing and other structural repairs. Grants are not made for works other than structural repairs and do not, therefore, cover alterations, improvements, re-decoration (except as a consequence of structural repairs), minor repairs or maintenance. Grants may be up to 40% of the cost of eligible repairs, and building owners must show that they would be unable to carry out the work without financial aid.

Grants are not normally offered for any property purchased within the two years preceding the grant application, since it is considered that the purchase price should have reflected the cost of repairs required. Generally, the repair works must cost in excess of £4000 to be eligible for a grant, which is paid after the work has been completed, and in instalments if necessary. Grants are made on the condition that the public are given access to the building on at least 30 days during the summer months, and that the arrangements are given adequate publicity.

It is a standard condition of grant that if the recipient sells the building within ten years of the date the grant was offered, all or part of the grant may be reclaimed.

Further information:

Historic Buildings and Monuments
Commission for England
25 Savile Row, London W1X 2BT
Tel: 01–734–6010

Similar schemes apply in Scotland, Wales and Northern Ireland.

.~uer information:
Scottish Development Department
Historic Buildings Branch
25 Drumsheugh Gardens
Edinburgh EH3 7RN
Tel: 031–226–3611, ext. 293

Welsh Office, Conservation and Land
Division
New Crown Building, Cathays Park
Cardiff DF1 3NQ
Tel: 0222–825111

Department of the Environment for
Northern Ireland
Historic Monuments and Buildings
Branch
1 Connsbrook Avenue, Belfast BT4 1EH
Tel: 0232–653251

6.2.2 Historic buildings grants

Local authorities are able to make grants for the repair, maintenance and restoration of buildings of architectural or historic interest under powers contained in the *Local Authorities (Historic Buildings) Act 1962*. Eligible buildings may be listed, have notable architectural or historic features, or contribute to the character of a conservation area. Not all local authorities have funds for historic buildings grants, and rules for eligibility vary.

Further information: Conservation Officer, local authority Planning Department.

6.2.3 Conservation area grants

Grants may be made, under Section 10 of the *Town and Country Planning (Amendment) Act 1972*, where the expenditure to be incurred will make a significant contribution towards preserving or enhancing the character or appearance of a conservation area. Grants are normally up to 25% of the cost of eligible repair and restoration work to the main external structure. Normal maintenance work is not eligible. Eligible items include structural repairs to the fabric of the building using natural or traditional materials (e.g. natural slate roofs, stonework, cast iron rainwater goods), and restoration of features of architectural or historical interest (e.g. door cases, windows, cornices and balconies).

Conservation area grants are available to local authorities, housing associations, amenity societies, preservation trusts and private owners. To receive a grant, the cost of the eligible items of conservation work must normally exceed £2000, and the applicant must show that the work could not be carried out without financial aid. As with grants for outstanding buildings (see Section 6.2.1), conservation area grants are not normally available for properties purchased within the two years preceding the grant application. If a property is sold within a stated period after receiving a grant, the recipient may be required to repay all or part of the grant.

Further information: as Section 6.2.1.

6.2.4 Town scheme grants

These grants are made under the provisions of Section 10B of the *Town and Country Planning (Amendment) Act 1972*. Under the town scheme grant system, the Historic Buildings and Monuments Commission and the respective local authority agree to allocate equal sums of money towards the cost of repairing buildings which are included in the list of designated town schemes.

The grants are awarded for the preservation and enhancement of buildings which may either be outstanding in themselves, or contribute to an outstanding group of buildings. Grants are made toward the costs of work to exteriors, although interior work may also be considered when it is viewable by the public. Grants are generally awarded to a maximum of 50% of the costs of eligible works, the percentage being made up as follows:

County Council	$12\frac{1}{2}\%$
District Council	$12\frac{1}{2}\%$
Historic Buildings and Monuments Commission	25%

Further information: Conservation Officer, local authority Planning Department

6.2.5 The Architectural Heritage Fund: soft loans

The Architectural Heritage Fund, administered by the Civic Trust, provides short-term, low-interest loans to assist local buildings preservation trusts (see Section 3.3.1) and other appropriate charitable bodies to acquire and rehabilitate any buildings which merit conservation. Interest is charged at a rate of 5% per annum, and loans are normally made for a period of not more than two years. The fund does not normally lend more than 50% of the gross cost of acquisition and restoration, any balance of working capital required having to be found by the local trust from its own capital, bank borrowing or other sources. Applicants are also expected, wherever possible, to seek official grant aid such as a local authority home improvement grant (see Section 6.2.15) or an Historic Buildings Commission grant (see Section 6.2.1).

Loans so far made range in size from £2000 to £250 000, reflecting the wide variety of schemes supported by the fund.

Further information:

The Architectural Heritage Fund
Civic Trust
17 Carlton House Terrace
London SW1Y 5AW
Tel: 01–930–0914

6.2.6 Regional development grants

Regional development grants are available for approved projects, but only in those parts of Great Britain that have been designated by the Department of Trade and Industry as 'Development Areas'. Grants may be made in respect of capital expenditure on plant, machinery, buildings (new or rehabilitated), or works; or in respect of the number of new jobs created.

The actual grant is payable at either:

(a) 15% of approved capital expenditure on the project (subject, where applicable, to a limit related to the number of new jobs created);

or
(b) £3000 for each net new job created

The grant is calculated on whichever basis is the more favourable to the applicant.

Four criteria must be satisfied in order for a project to be eligible:

(a) The project must be carried out by an eligible 'person', including a limited company, a partnership or a sole trader
(b) The project must provide assets and/or create jobs in a Development Area
(c) The project must create new, or expand existing, capacity to *produce goods* or *provide a service*
(d) The project must relate to specified qualifying activities: over 200 industrial/manufacturing activities are specified, together with numerous 'commercial' activities including banking, finance, insurance, business services, etc. Thus, office development, as well as industrial development may be eligible for regional development grant aid. There is no minimum or maximum limit on the cost of a project.

Eligible capital expenditure can include the cost of adapting or rehabilitating an existing building. To be eligible for grant aid, the adaptation must involve substantial work to the building fabric to make it fit for a given purpose or improve it, e.g.:

(a) Structural alterations
(b) Provision of service installations, such as sprinkler or central heating systems
(c) Restoring or otherwise making fit for use a building which has been purchased or leased.

Normal repair and maintenance is not classed as adaptation for the purposes of grant calculation.

Application for a regional development grant can be made before, during or after completion of a project. Grants become repayable if either the grant-aided assets cease to be available for use within a period of 36 months after their provision; or, where grant aid is dependent on job creation, the jobs cease to exist within a period of 18 months after their provision.

Further information:

Department of Trade and Industry
Kingsgate House
66 Victoria Street
London SW1E 6SJ
Tel: 01–212–7676

6.2.7 Regional selective assistance

Grants are available under Section 7 of the *Industrial Development Act 1982* for approved projects in the manufacturing and service sectors, but only in those parts of Great Britain that have been designated by the Department of Trade and Industry as 'Assisted Areas'. (There are more than twice as many Assisted Areas in Great Britain as Development Areas, referred to in Section 6.2.6).

The value of grant aid under this scheme is based on the capital expenditure costs of the project, and on the number of jobs to be created or maintained. All sectors of industry and commerce, both manufacturing and service, are eligible to receive grant aid.

The following conditions and criteria apply to regional selective assistance:

(a) The project should have good prospects of achieving viability
(b) The applicant must be able to demonstrate that assistance is necessary in order to go ahead with the project (e.g. a grant may enable the applicant to go ahead with a project which would otherwise not be undertaken)
(c) The project must bring an identifiable regional and national benefit
(d) The project should either create new employment, or safeguard existing employment
(e) The project must make a net contribution to the regional and national economy
(f) The amount of assistance granted will be the minimum necessary for a project to go

ahead, and applicants will normally be expected to find most of the required finance from their own resources, or other private sector sources
(g) The project must be located in an Assisted Area
(h) A grant application must be made, and an offer received *before* the applicant becomes committed to a project. (It takes an average of 9 weeks to process applications.)

Further information: as Section 6.2.6.

6.2.8 National selective assistance

Grants are available, under Section 8 of the *Industrial Development Act 1982,* to manufacturing industries for major projects involving new investments of at least £500 000. To qualify for assistance, projects must substantially improve performance, introduce a substantial new contribution to UK output, or introduce a significant degree of innovation. The grant awarded will be the minimum necessary for the project to proceed, and it must be shown that the project could not go ahead without financial aid.

Further information: as Section 6.2.6.

6.2.9 Urban programme grants

Grants are available to provide assistance on projects which improve the quality of life, overcome economic decline, or overcome physical decay in certain designated inner city areas. To qualify for a grant under this scheme, the project must fulfil social, economic or environmental needs, and the grants are made available to local authorities for their own projects, and any voluntary or other bodies (public or private) that they choose to support.

All applications, from voluntary or other bodies, must be made initially to the local authority which, if it chooses to support the project, makes a 'bid' for funding to the Department of the Environment. The grant from Government is normally 75% of the cost of an approved project, the remaining 25% being provided by the local authority.

A typical example of the type of scheme that might be awarded an urban programme grant would be the rehabilitation of an existing building, such as a redundant chapel or church, to provide a local community centre.

Further information: local authority Planning Department.

6.2.10 Inner Urban Areas Act 1978: grants and loans

Grants and 'soft' loans are made available under various sections of the *Inner Urban Areas Act 1978,* to encourage projects which would help inner city areas, and which would not be able to proceed without financial aid.

Section 4 of the Act provides for the designation of Industrial and Commercial Improvement Areas (which, in turn, can only be located within 'Partnership' or 'Programme' Authorities), and projects within these areas are eligible for financial aid. Any Industrial or Commercial Improvement Area must initially be nominated by the relevant local authority, and then approved by the Secretary of State for the Environment. Generally, they are only small pockets of cities which have become run down and are in need of social, economic or environmental regeneration.

Section 5 of the Act provides for the award of loans and grants of up to 50% for improving the environment or amenities (e.g. landscaping and planting, construction of car parks and access roads, etc.).

Under Section 6 of the Act, loans and grants of up to 50% of the project costs can be awarded for the conversion, extension, improvement or modification of industrial or commercial buildings.

As with urban programme grants (Section 6.2.9), the initial application for financial aid must be made to the local authority, which must support the scheme if an award is to be made.

Further information: local authority Planning Department.

6.2.11 Urban development grants (UDG)

The UDG scheme is intended to create opportunities for the private sector to carry out projects in the inner cities that would not go ahead without financial aid, and to encourage local authorities to take an active part in encouraging and developing such projects. The primary aim is to promote the economic and physical regeneration of inner urban areas by 'levering' private investment into such areas. There are no formal restrictions on the type or size of project for which a UDG may be sought, but the private sector contribution to a project is expected to be significant in relation to total project costs, and the public sector contribution should be the minimum necessary to allow the project to go ahead. The private sector contribution is normally several times that of the public sector, and, overall, the ratio of private to public sector contributions in approved UDG projects has been in the region of 4:1. However, in some projects, this ratio has been as high as 2:1.

To be eligible for a UDG, the project must be within an urban area that has been designated under the *Inner Urban Areas Act 1978,* and it must contribute directly to the alleviation of special social needs, and to economic or physical regeneration.

The following factors are also considered when determining the eligibility of a project:

(a) The acuteness of the special social needs of the inner urban area concerned
(b) The extent to which the project will help fulfil those needs
(c) Whether the project creates new permanent jobs, or safeguards existing jobs
(d) Whether the project provides public sector housing
(e) Whether the project provides additional social or environmental benefits

(f) The cost to the public sector of supporting the project by providing a UDG, and whether it represents good value for money

(g) Whether the project would proceed if a UDG were not awarded

(h) The viability of the project

(i) The commitment of, and risk being taken by, the private sector

(j) The profit being taken by the private sector

The UDG takes the form of a contribution to a project by the relevant local authority. Application must therefore be made direct to the local authority, which is then responsible for carrying out an initial appraisal before deciding whether or not the payment of a grant is desirable. If the authority is satisfied that financial assistance is desirable, it may apply to the Department of the Environment (DOE) for approval of the payment of a UDG, and for Exchequer assistance towards its contribution. If the DOE approves the application, the local authority receives the necessary approval to give financial assistance to the project. The DOE then reimburses a proportion (normally 75%) of the local authority's expenditure in paying the grant.

The types of project that are eligible for UDG include the construction of new industrial buildings, warehousing, shops, offices, hotels, recreation, leisure and community facilities, together with the following categories of building rehabilitation:

(a) Refurbishment or conversion of existing factories, warehouses or other buildings to provide industrial units, housing, shops, warehousing or offices

(b) Provision of private sector housing by rehabilitation

(c) Improvement for sale of 'difficult-to-let' council estates

(d) Hotel refurbishment.

The housing rehabilitation case study at Newcastle upon Tyne, described in Section 7.7.1, was made viable by the award of a UDG of £938 000 which, at the time, was the largest ever grant of this type.

Further information:

> Local authority or Department of the Environment
> 2 Marsham Street
> London SW1P 3EB
> Tel: 01–212–8416

A similar scheme applies in Scotland.

Further information:

> Scottish Development Agency
> 120 Bothwell Street
> Glasgow G2 7JP
> Tel: 041–248–2700

6.2.12 Development Commission grants

The Development Commission is responsible for promoting the economic and social life of rural areas in England, mainly by building small factories and workshops, providing assistance to small businesses, supporting rural services and encouraging community activity and self-help. The bulk of the Commission's financial resources (about £21 million in 1984/85) are concentrated in those areas designated by Government as Rural Development Areas. The Commission has four main agencies through which it operates:

• The Council for Small Industries in Rural Areas (CoSIRA), which is wholly funded by the Commission to provide a wide range of services for small firms throughout the whole of rural England

• English Estates, which designs, builds and manages the Commission's 100% Funded Factory/Workshop Programme

• The National Council for Voluntary Organizations (NCVO), which acts as a resource centre for voluntary organizations, providing them with specialist advice and expertise

• Rural Community Councils (RCCs), which are independent voluntary organizations, receiving substantial funding from the Commission towards their activities in stimulating community development in rural areas, and improving the social fabric of rural life.

The various categories of financial aid provided by the Development Commission through these agencies are as follows:

(a) Factories and workshops: 100% funded schemes

Workshops and small factories, ranging in size from 1500 sq. ft to 5000 sq. ft, are designed, built and managed by English Estates for letting or selling to small manufacturing firms. These schemes are only available in Rural Development Areas and locations are decided in consultation with the relevant local authority and CoSIRA. Proposals for schemes should be submitted by the local authority. Wherever possible, the conversion of existing buildings is encouraged.

(b) 50/50 partnership schemes with local authorities

This scheme encourages local authorities to look closely at projects in their remoter rural areas. Under the scheme, the Commission contributes 50% of the cost of providing workshops, either new buildings or conversions, which are built and managed by local authorities. The remaining 50% of the cost is the responsibility of the relevant local authority. This scheme is available inside and outside Rural Development Areas.

(c) Grants to enable the wider use of village halls

The Development Commission makes grant aid available for communities who are prepared to adapt or extend an existing village hall, or other building such as a redundant school, for a wider general use. Examples include the conversion or extension of existing village halls for such purposes as doctors' surgeries, clinics, libraries, playgroups and sub-post offices.

Grant aid is restricted to the conversion or extension of existing buildings within Rural Development Areas. The amount of aid is limited to 25% of the total cost of a project, up to a maximum of £20 000 grant per project, contingent upon at least a comparable amount of assistance being forthcoming from the relevant local authorities.

Application for grant aid under this scheme must be forwarded through the appropriate local Rural Community Council, which is required to comment upon the project and indicate whether it is considered eligible, and what degree of priority should be given to it. If a grant is approved, it is paid in instalments subject to evidence that expenditure has been, or is about to be, incurred.

(d) Grants for the conversion of redundant buildings

Grants are available to individuals, partnerships, co-operatives and companies for the refurbishment and conversion of redundant buildings for new businesses that will provide job opportunities within Rural Development Areas. Suitable buildings include derelict barns, redundant chapels, disused dairies, unwanted schools, old railway stations, obsolete mills and factories, and typical new uses include craft workshops, research laboratories, factories for light manufacturing, or premises for service industries.

The scheme is administered for the Development Commission by CoSIRA, and converted buildings can be intended for use by the applicants themselves, or for leasing to others. Grant aid normally covers 25% of the actual costs of conversion works and professional fees, and minimum eligible expenditure is £1000; maximum usually £50 000. Approved projects may also qualify for Regional Development Grants (see Section 6.2.6).

Any application for grant must be made and approved before work commences, and if the property is sold, or its use is changed within five years, CoSIRA can reclaim a proportion of the grant.

Further information (a), (b), (c) and (d):

The Development Commission
11 Cowley Street
London SW1P 3NA
Tel: 01–222–9134

6.2.13 Housing Corporation/ Department of the Environment: loans and grants

Considerable financial aid is provided to Housing Associations to fund the provision of homes for rent and for sale, either by new construction or the rehabilitation of existing buildings. Rehabilitation projects eligible for financial aid are not restricted to existing houses in need of improvement, but can also include the adaptation and conversion of other building types, such as redundant mills, warehouses and churches to provide flats or maisonettes (see St Luke's Church, Harrogate: Section 7.6.1).

Individual Housing Associations have to make 'bids' for money to the Housing Corporation annually, following which the latter makes a financial allocation, a typical figure for a medium-sized Housing Association being £$3\frac{1}{2}$ million. This allocation is then used to provide 'soft' loans to the Housing Association for the purchase of land (for new construction projects) or buildings (for rehabilitation projects), and for the actual construction work, professional fees and other costs.

The Housing Corporation provides a loan to cover the total cost of each project, the loan being drawn by the Housing Association in stages as and when costs are incurred. Interest is also paid on the loan from the date that the first stage is drawn. Thus, at the end of each project, the Housing Association will have an outstanding loan, plus accrued interest.

The Housing Association then applies to the Department of the Environment, through the Housing Corporation, for a Housing Association Grant to pay off the loan and the accrued interest. However, this grant will normally only be for a proportion of the outstanding loan, since the remainder can be paid off by the Housing

Association itself, using its income from either the rent or sale of the property, whichever is applicable. Generally, the Housing Association Grant is between 95% and 100% of the total costs for rehabilitation-for-rent projects, approximately 50% for rehabilitation-for-sale projects, and between 75% and 80% of the total costs for new construction projects. The remaining part of the loan, not covered by the Housing Association Grant, is paid off over a period equal to the anticipated life of the dwelling, and this ranges from 15 years for certain rehabilitation projects to 60 years for new construction.

It is currently estimated that between 30% and 40% of all homes provided by Housing Associations are provided by the rehabilitation and conversion of existing buildings. During the financial year 1983/84, a total of 30 294 new homes (including those produced by rehabilitation) were approved for financial aid under this scheme in Great Britain by the Housing Corporation.

Further information:

The Housing Corporation
149 Tottenham Court Road
London W1P 0BN
Tel: 01–387–9466

6.2.14 Department of the Environment: 'Improvement for Sale'

Improvement for Sale is a Government-initiated low-cost home-ownership scheme enabling local authorities and Housing Associations to improve or repair sub-standard houses and then sell them, claiming an Exchequer contribution or Housing Association Grant towards the net cost.

To be eligible for financial aid under this scheme, dwellings must be in need of substantial repair or improvement, and projects may range from 1 or 2 dwellings to in excess of 50. If the total cost of improving a dwelling (including acquisition cost, cost of improvement work, professional fees, interest charges, etc.) exceeds the market value of the dwelling after completion, the difference will be paid by the Exchequer (i.e. the grant covers the net loss on a project). This, therefore, encourages local authorities and Housing Associations to take the financial risk of improving sub-standard houses by guaranteeing to cover them against any net loss if this is incurred. However, the grant per dwelling is limited as follows:

(a) Local authorities:
(i) Outside London: 75% of first £6000 loss; 25% of next £1500 loss; Maximum Exchequer contribution: £4875
(ii) Inside London: 75% of first £8000 loss; 25% of next £2000 loss; Maximum Exchequer contribution: £6500
(b) Housing Associations:
(i) Outside London: Housing Association grant to a maximum of £7500
(ii) Inside London: Housing Association grant to a maximum of £10 000

Clearly by no means all projects make a loss and, indeed, many make a substantial profit, therefore requiring no financial aid from the Exchequer.

Further information:

Department of the Environment
2 Marsham Street
London SW1P 3EB
Tel: 01–212–4261, 01–212–3434

The Housing Corporation
149 Tottenham Court Road
London W1P 0BN
Tel: 01–387–9466

6.2.15 Home improvement grants

Various types of home improvement grant are made by local authorities to enable existing houses to be modernized, repaired or converted. Four types of grant are currently available, as follows.

(a) Improvement grants

Improvement grants are for major improvements, plus associated repairs and replacements, or for conversions. They are intended to help improve homes to a good standard, or to provide additional homes through the conversion of houses of three storeys or more into flats.

A typical example of improvement under this type of grant would be the provision of a built-on extension to a terraced house to provide a bathroom/kitchen where the existing facilities are inadequate or unfit, and where there is insufficient space within the existing house for internal provision.

(b) Intermediate grants

Intermediate grants are for the installation of missing standard amenities which may include some or all of the following: inside toilet, bath, sink, wash basin, hot and cold water supplies to the appliances installed. The grant can also include the cost of associated repairs and replacements.

(c) Special grants

Special grants are for the installation of standard amenities (see intermediate grants), and means of escape from fire in houses in multiple occupation, and for associated repairs and replacements.

(d) Repairs grants

Repairs grants are for substantial and structural repairs to pre-1919 houses. Examples of work attracting repairs grants include major repairs to roofs, walls, floors and foundations.

Intermediate grants are mandatory, which means that the local authority cannot refuse to make a grant, provided the applicant and the building qualify. The other types of grant are normally made at the discretion of the local authority.

The amount of grant payable to the applicant is normally a fixed percentage of the cost of the improvement work, and ranges from 50% to 90%, depending on the individual circumstances. There is also an upper limit to the grant payable, above which the applicant pays 100% of the improvement costs. This upper limit is known as the 'eligible expense limit', and it varies according to the type of grant.

In order to be considered for any of the home improvement grants previously described, the house in question must comply with various criteria. For example, to qualify for an improvement or intermediate grant, the property must have been built or converted before 1961. To qualify for a repairs grant, the property must have been built before 1919. In most cases, the rateable value of the property must not exceed a certain figure. Detailed information about these, and other qualifying criteria, the different types of grant and their respective eligible expense limits, are contained in the booklet *Home Improvement Grants – A guide for home owners, landlords and tenants*, published by HMSO (Details contained in *Further Reading* at the end of the chapter). The booklet is available from local authorities, who are responsible for administering the home improvement grants scheme, and from whom further advice is available.

Further information: Local authority.

6.2.16 Home improvement grants for disabled persons

Local authorities make improvement grants and intermediate grants towards the adaptation of houses occupied by registered disabled persons. The work must be for the accommodation, welfare or employment of a disabled occupant, and typical examples include:

(a) The provision of additional amenities (e.g. wash basin, w.c., bath) of a suitable design, and in a position easily accessible to a disabled person.
(b) Adaptation of existing amenities to suit the particular disability, such as widening doorways for wheelchair access, provision of handrails, ramps, etc.
(c) The provision of additional ground floor sleeping accommodation.

Where a grant is required for a disabled occupant, the age limits and rateable value limits referred to in Section 6.2.15 do not apply, and the eligible expense limit and percentage rate of grant are set at a higher level.

Further information: Local authority.

6.2.17 Grants for adapting buildings for use by disabled persons

The Manpower Services Commission can make grants of up to £6000 to help employers with the cost of adapting their premises to meet the needs of a specific disabled employee, or to enable them to recruit new disabled employees. Typical examples of adaptations attracting grant aid include:

- The installation or modification of ramps for wheelchair users
- The installation of wheelchair lifts, hoists and stair lifts
- Modifications to toilets, e.g. widening doors and installing new w.c.'s and grab rails.

If the adaptation will benefit the business, the employer will normally be required to contribute part of the cost. Grants cannot normally be made to enable employers to meet requirements of the *Chronically Sick and Disabled Persons (Amendment) Act 1976*.

Further information:

Manpower Services Commission
Moorfoot
Sheffield S1 4PQ
Tel: 0742–753275/704531

6.2.18 Tourism Development Grants

The English Tourist Board is empowered, under Section 4 of the *Development of Tourism Act 1969*, to make grants towards the capital cost of tourism development, encompassing a broad range of investment in visitor attractions, leisure and recreational facilities, all types of holiday accommodation and information services. Grant aid is available for the development of these facilities whether provided by the construction of new buildings, or the rehabilitation and alteration of existing buildings. Typical examples of schemes attracting grants include:

(a) Conversion of redundant farm buildings (e.g. barns, houses, outbuildings, etc.) to provide self-catering holiday accommodation

(b) Structural alteration and/or extension of existing self-catering and bed-and-breakfast accommodation, guest houses and hotels in order to enlarge and improve facilities

(c) Alteration and adaptation of existing buildings to provide low-cost hostel accommodation for young people

(d) Alteration and adaptation of existing buildings to provide 'visitor attractions', which project the character of their area, such as heritage centres, museums, craft centres, etc.

For projects whose total capital cost falls between £5000 and £100 000, grant is provided through a faster, simplified procedure known as 'Streamlined Aid'. This grant is limited to a maximum of 25% of the eligible capital cost, and is paid in a single lump sum when the work has been completed.

For projects with a total cost of between £100 000 and £1 million (which account for most of the Tourist Board aid), the grant is calculated as a proportion of the total eligible capital cost, and is usually paid in stages as the project proceeds. In exceptional circumstances, loans for a period of up to 20 years can be made, or grants to relieve the burden of interest on a project. The type and mix of financial aid, and its level, are at the Tourist Board's discretion, and are assessed on the basis of individual need and circumstances. Most grants are between 20% and 30%, and these may be supplemented by grants from other bodies such as the Historic Buildings and Monuments Commission, or other Government schemes. However, the total assistance for a single project from public sector funds will not normally be permitted to exceed 50%.

All grants are made at the discretion of the Tourist Board, and applications are considered selectively on a first come, first served basis. Grants are only made to projects that need the money to get started at all and that, having started, will then be viable.

Similar financial aid to that provided by the English Tourist Board is also available from the Scottish, Welsh and Northern Ireland Tourist Boards.

Further information:

> The English Tourist Board
> 4 Grosvenor Gardens
> London SW1W 0DU
> Tel: 01–730–3400
>
> Scottish Tourist Board
> 23 Ravelston Terrace
> Edinburgh EH4 3EU
> Tel: 031–332–2433
>
> Wales Tourist Board
> Brunel House
> 2 Fitzalan Road
> Cardiff CF2 1UY
> Tel: 0222–499909
>
> Northern Ireland Tourist Board
> River House
> 48 High Street
> Belfast BT1 2DS
> Tel: 0232–231221

6.2.19 Countryside Commission grants

Grants are available for projects that develop or improve amenities and conserve or enhance the countryside. Projects that may be eligible include the rehabilitation of existing buildings to provide information and visitor centres (e.g. wildlife and heritage centres) and hostel-type accommodation.

Areas of the country qualifying for Countryside Commission grants are designated by the Secretary of State for the Environment, priority being given to projects within National Parks. Grants are normally offered as a lump sum, and not as a percentage of costs.

The Countryside Commission also makes similar grants available to local authorities and other public bodies for projects that develop or improve amenities, and conserve or enhance the countryside.

Further information:

The Countryside Commission
John Dower House
Crescent Place
Cheltenham
Glos. GL50 3RA
Tel: 0242–23638

The Countryside Commission for
Scotland
Battleby
Redgorton
Perth PH1 3EW
Tel: 0738–27921

6.2.20 Sports Council grants for statutory bodies and commercial organizations

Grants are available to local authorities, public bodies and commercial organizations in England for the provision of local facilities for sport and recreation which will help alleviate social deprivation in areas of special need. Eligible projects include the provision of new indoor sports facilities, by either newbuild or the adaptation of existing buildings.

The Sports Council's grant contribution is individually assessed for each project, but does not normally exceed 50% of the approved cost of the project (except in areas of special need, where the limit is 75%). Several conditions are applied if a grant is awarded, including the need for the project to be viable, and the requirement that an appropriate proportion of the grant be repaid if the grant-aided facility is disposed of or ceases to be used for sports purposes.

Further information:

The Sports Council
16 Upper Woburn Place
London WC1H 0QP
Tel: 01–388–1277

6.2.21 Sports Council grants and loans for voluntary organizations

Grants and interest-free loans are available to voluntary organizations (not operated for profit) towards the capital cost of providing facilities for those taking an active part in sport. Priority is given to projects which will increase participation in sport, improve performance or help alleviate social or recreational deprivation in areas of special need. Eligible projects include the provision of indoor sports facilities such as sports halls, ancillary halls, and their associated changing facilities. Provision of social accommodation to complement an existing sports facility may also be eligible for financial aid (loan only).

The Sports Council's contribution, in the form of grant and/or loan, is individually assessed for each project, subject to the following limits:

- A grant will not normally exceed 50% of the approved cost of the project (except in areas of special need, where the limit is 75%). The minimum grant is £750.
- A loan will not exceed 50% of the approved cost of the project, the minimum loan being £1000 and the maximum £10 000.
- Loans are interest free, repayable in ten equal half-yearly instalments over five years
- Where both grant and loan are given, the combined total will not exceed 75% of the approved project cost.

As with other forms of financial aid, the applicants and the project itself must comply with several specific conditions if a grant or loan is to be awarded.

Further information: as Section 6.2.20.

6.2.22 Highlands and Islands Development Board: grants and loans

A variety of grants and soft loans (with interest at around 3% below prevailing commercial rates) are available to companies, individuals and other bodies undertaking new developments, or expanding existing businesses, in certain designated areas of Scotland. The financial aid applies to the extension, alteration or improvement (including services and fire precaution work) of existing buildings, as well as the construction of new buildings.

To be eligible for financial aid, a project must contribute to the economic or social development of the area and may fall within any one of a number of categories, including agricultural, tourism, commercial, industrial or fisheries. In most cases, the applicant is expected to contribute at least 50% of the total project cost.

Further information:

> Highlands and Islands Development
> Board
> Bridge House
> Bank Street
> Inverness IV1 1QR
> Tel: 0463–234171

6.2.23 Scottish Development Agency: grants and loans

Grants are available towards the cost of setting up, repairing or renovating craft workshops, and loans are available for a much wider range of projects that improve the economy, maintain or increase job opportunities, or increase exports. Priority is given to projects in areas of high unemployment and depopulated rural areas. Eligible projects include those involving the construction of new buildings, and the rehabilitation or extension of existing buildings.

Loans are only available where a project has failed to obtain all of the finance required from the private sector, and full commercial interest rates and conditions apply to these loans (see Section 6.1.1).

Further information:

> Scottish Development Agency
> 120 Bothwell Street
> Glasgow G2 7JP
> Tel: 041–248–2700

6.2.24 Independent charities

A large number of charitable trusts throughout the United Kingdom make grants available for a wide variety of schemes, including the rehabilitation and re-use of old buildings.

Further information:

> Refer to "The Directory of Grant Making
> Trusts" available from:
> The Charities Aid Foundation,
> 48 Pembury Road
> Tunbridge Wells
> Kent

6.2.25 Banks

Banks offer a wide variety of loans to support both new construction and building rehabilitation. Most of the major commercial clearing banks will consider providing short term loan finance for the rehabilitation and re-use of older buildings, but their terms vary widely, and the individual banks should be approached for detailed information.

Merchant banks provide short and medium term loans for developers, and many of them have their own property investment departments which will arrange financing to suit each developer's individual needs.

6.2.26 Building societies

The building societies are the principal source of finance for new residential development. They also provide loans for the extension of existing residential property, for the improvement and rehabilitation of existing housing, and for homes produced by rehabilitating other building types.

The most common type of funding provided by building societies is the agreed allocation of a quota of mortgage funds to a particular housing scheme. Two of the case studies described in Chapter 7 were funded in this way: The Abbey National Building Society guaranteed to provide mortgages to all buyers at St Luke's Church, Harrogate (see Section 7.6), and at the Bellway Urban Renewal Scheme, Newcastle upon Tyne (see Section 7.7).

Other forms of funding are provided by building societies including the provision of mortgage funds to individual owners for extension, alteration or improvement of existing homes. The nature and terms of financial support vary between the different societies, which should be approached individually for detailed information.

6.2.27 Insurance companies

Insurance companies invest in both new development and in rehabilitation schemes. The type and nature of eligible projects is severely constrained owing to the insurance companies' insistence on specific standards of building design, construction and performance. Additional constraints are also applied with regard to acceptable locations and letting arrangements.

Generally, the insurance companies are only interested in providing financial support for substantial projects with values in excess of £1 million.

6.2.28 Pension funds

Pension funds, like insurance companies, are generally only interested in large-scale projects, and they provide considerable investment in prime developments involving both newbuild and rehabilitation.

Further information on the above and other sources of private funding: Refer to "Money for Business", available from

The Bulletin Group
Bank of England
Threadneedle Street
London EC2R 8AH
Tel: 01–601–4444

and "Official Sources of Finance and Aid in the UK", available from

The National Westminster Bank PLC
Commercial Information Section
National House
14 Moorgate
London EC2R 6BS
Tel: 01–606–6060

The latter publication deals with all sources of Government financial aid and is updated and re-published annually.

FURTHER READING

Civic Trust for the North East (1980) *Guide to Grants and Loans for Conservation*, Civic Trust for N.E.

Department of the Environment and Welsh Office (1984) *Home Improvement Grants: A Guide for Home-Owners, Landlords and Tenants*, HMSO, London.

Ellis, C. *et al.* (1984) Funding for construction. *Architects' Journal*, **180** (34 and 35), 22 and 29 August 1984, 32–92.

Chapter seven

Rehabilitation case-studies

7.1 GENERAL

An entire book could easily be devoted to an examination of case-studies and still fail to cover the almost limitless variety of building types that have been successfully rehabilitated, and the extensive range of design and technical solutions used. For this reason, only six case-studies have been selected for inclusion in this chapter, four of them involving office development and two involving housing, these sectors accounting for the vast majority of the rehabilitation market. The case-studies show examples of low-key rehabilitation, and the much more drastic solutions, involving extensive demolition and major structural 'surgery', at the other end of the scale of redevelopment options (see Chapter 3). Three of the case-studies involve changes of use, while the remainder involve continuation of their existing uses. It was stated in Chapter 1 that almost one thousand churches have been declared redundant during the past fifteen years, and these often provide an ideal basis for a wide range of new uses, including sports halls, community centres, offices and housing. Two of the case-studies describe the sensitive and imaginative re-use of redundant church buildings. Finally, and in order to maximize the value of this short chapter, the case-studies were selected to show, not only the normal 'run of the mill' types of building rehabilitation, but also the more unusual, and possibly controversial, solutions used in the recycling of our old buildings.

The case-study descriptions deal principally with the practicalities of the schemes, the aims being to show typical technical problems and the means used to solve them and, more generally, to illustrate what can be done with our old buildings, provided they are basically structurally sound. Where cost comments have been made, they are only general ones, since detailed costings rapidly become out of date and would therefore be of limited use to the reader.

7.2 PARK HOUSE, PARK SQUARE, LEEDS

7.2.1 The existing building

Park House, which stands in one of Leeds' best preserved Georgian squares, was built at the turn of the century as a cloth warehouse. This use continued until 1939, when it became one of the many public distribution centres used for the allocation of ration books, petrol coupons, gas masks, etc. during and subsequent to the Second World War. Following this, the building was adapted to provide offices for a number of government departments and by the end of the 1970s, the standard of the office accommodation, which had evolved within Park House by changing uses and piecemeal alterations, fell far short of the standards generally demanded. The building, although unlisted, is quite elegant in its proportions, making a positive architectural contribution to the Park Square conservation area, and this was one factor which led its new owners, a property company, to opt for rehabilitation in order to fulfil its aim of providing top-quality speculative office accommodation on the site. The rehabilitation scheme commenced in 1980 and took a year to complete.

The existing five-storey building, 'L'-shaped on plan and approximately ten metres in depth, comprised brick loadbearing external walls, with a simple unobtrusive internal arrangement of cast iron columns and beams supporting timber-joisted floors. This structure, together with the slated, pitched roof, was both substantial and structurally sound, and provided an ideal basis for rehabilitation. On the other hand, several aspects of Park House left much to be desired. The interior finishes were spartan, the brick walls being unplastered, but painted, and the floors lined on their underside with painted plasterboard sheets. Staircase arrangements, toilet accommodation, heating, lighting, fire protection and standards of thermal insulation were all totally inadequate when compared with modern requirements.

7.2.2 The rehabilitation

This was very much a low-key rehabilitation scheme, its purpose being to create a viable, functional and attractive environment with the least possible disturbance to the existing sound and stable structure, and to take advantage of those special features inherent in a building designed for a quite different purpose almost a century before. Plans and cross-sections of Park House after its rehabilitation are shown in Figs 7.1–7.4, and Figs 7.5 and 7.6 show the exterior and interior of the completed building. The details of the rehabilitation work are itemized below.

(a) Demolition

- Existing non-structural internal partitions, lift shaft and two timber staircases removed.
- Part of existing rear wall demolished to allow

for new staircase extension (see Figs 7.1 and 7.2).

(b) Structural work

- Erection of brick extension at rear for new reinforced concrete staircase.
- Construction of two new reinforced concrete staircases and associated fire-resisting enclosures.
- Construction of new brick lift shaft.
- New recessed main entrance formed at ground level in place of existing windows.
- New recessed french windows with balcony formed at first floor level in place of existing windows directly above new main entrance.
- New sound insulated, timber stud partitions finished with plasterboard and skim, constructed to form independent toilet accommodation at each floor level.
- Proprietary w.c. cubicles erected to provide internal division within toilet accommodation.

(c) External envelope

- Brickwork and stonework to all elevations cleaned with mild acid cleaner and washed down with pressurized water lance.
- Stone sills, window heads and string course repaired where necessary using resin/sand mixture built up in layers to match existing.
- Brickwork to rear elevation treated with Mural Plas protective paint finish after cleaning.
- Existing cast iron guttering and downpipes to rear elevation repaired or replaced as necessary.
- Existing cast iron guttering and downpipes to front elevation removed. New concealed plywood box gutter formed at eaves with rafters cut back to enable new downpipes to be taken down inside building.
- New stone-coloured moulded GRP cornice fixed at eaves level (front elevation only).
- Existing industrial-type windows removed and replaced with new aluminium sliding

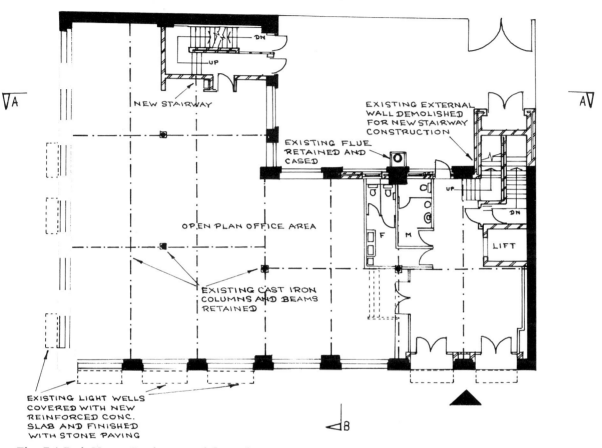

Fig. 7.1 Park House, Leeds: ground floor plan

sashes inserted into original timber sub-frames.

- Topmost window panes at ground to third floor levels in dark tinted glass to conceal new suspended ceiling spaces which extended below the window heads.

(d) Roof

- Chimneys removed and roof made good using slates taken from eaves.
- Lead flashings repaired.
- Valley gutter replaced.
- Minor structural repairs to roof timbers as necessary.

(e) Internal finishes

- All external walls lined on interior face with 25 mm thick Gyproc thermal board (see Section 4.4.1(a)), fixed by adhesive dabs, and finished with 5 mm plaster skim.
- New acoustically absorbent suspended ceiling system (tracked for lighting), with Class 'O' surface spread of flame, provided to all floors.
- All floors overlaid with 9.5 mm plywood sheeting and finished with heavy-duty carpeting.
- All circular cast iron columns framed and boxed in with painted plywood.

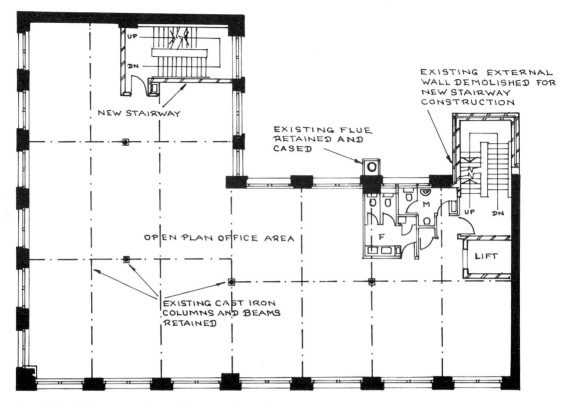

Fig. 7.2 Park House, Leeds: typical upper floor plan

(f) Services

- Existing electrical installation and wiring stripped out and replaced. New wiring at each floor level distributed through trunking integral with new suspended ceiling grids for lighting, and through skirting trunking for power.
- All existing radiators, pipework and plumbing removed.
- Existing boilers and domestic hot water calorifier retained, repaired and reinstated.
- New hot water central heating system installed from existing boiler, using pressed steel radiators.
- New plumbing and sanitary fittings provided to toilet accommodation.
- Existing lift dismantled, lift shaft demolished and new larger brick lift shaft constructed in similar position.

- Existing lift pit enlarged and new ten person hydraulic lift installed.

Architects: John Madin Design Group, Birmingham
Main Contractor: Robert R. Roberts Ltd, Leeds

7.3 37–40 YORK PLACE, LEEDS

7.3.1 The existing building

37–40 York Place is an unlisted building standing close to Leeds city centre in an area where many of the original buildings were constructed around the turn of the century as textile factories and warehouses. The demise of the textile industry, and the more recent increase in demand for commercial and office accommodation, has resulted in a change of focus in the

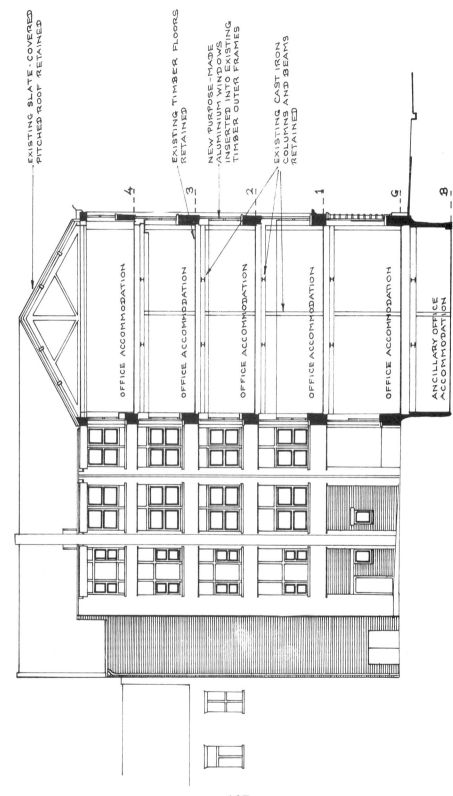

EXISTING SLATE-COVERED PITCHED ROOF RETAINED

EXISTING TIMBER FLOORS RETAINED

NEW PURPOSE-MADE ALUMINIUM WINDOWS INSERTED INTO EXISTING TIMBER OUTER FRAMES

EXISTING CAST IRON COLUMNS AND BEAMS RETAINED

OFFICE ACCOMMODATION

OFFICE ACCOMMODATION

OFFICE ACCOMMODATION

OFFICE ACCOMMODATION

OFFICE ACCOMMODATION

ANCILLARY OFFICE ACCOMMODATION

Fig. 7.3 Park House, Leeds: section/elevation A–A

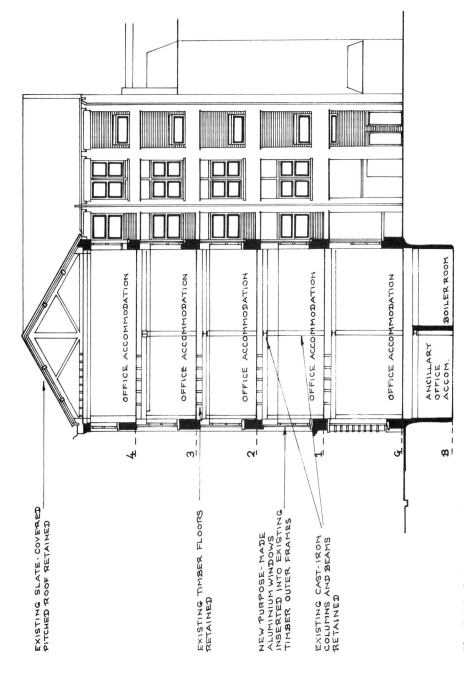

EXISTING SLATE-COVERED PITCHED ROOF RETAINED

EXISTING TIMBER FLOORS RETAINED

NEW PURPOSE-MADE ALUMINIUM WINDOWS INSERTED INTO EXISTING TIMBER OUTER FRAMES

EXISTING CAST-IRON COLUMNS AND BEAMS RETAINED

OFFICE ACCOMMODATION

OFFICE ACCOMMODATION

OFFICE ACCOMMODATION

OFFICE ACCOMMODATION

OFFICE ACCOMMODATION

ANCILLARY OFFICE ACCOM.

BOILER ROOM

Fig. 7.4 Park House, Leeds: section/elevation B–B

138

Fig. 7.5 Park House, Leeds: exterior view after rehabilitation

Fig. 7.6 Park House, Leeds: interior view after rehabilitation

area away from industrial use, in favour of office and showroom type development.

Prior to its rehabilitation in 1979/80, 37–40 York Place had been empty for some eighteen months, and its badly leaking roof had resulted in significant damage to its interior.

The existing four-storey building, the topmost storey of which was added in the late 1950s, was rectangular on plan, with the ground floor divided into two separate sections by a vehicular access from the front of the building through to its rear yard. The existing structure comprised loadbearing brick external walls, with internal brick cross-walls supporting timber floor beams and 8 inch × 3 inch plain-edged floorboards. A small number of timber encased steel columns provided additional support to the floors. The existing roof structure, which was part pitched and part flat, had fallen into disrepair and was leaking badly, allowing rainwater to penetrate throughout the building's interior. The basement walls and floor were also suffering from damp penetration, and the interior finishes, heating, lighting, sanitary accommodation, standards of fire protection, and staircase arrangements were all inadequate and in need of replacement or upgrading. However, despite the building's obsolescence and poor state of repair, it was structurally sound and this, together with the attractiveness of its highly ornate brick facade, resulted in the decision to rehabilitate it to provide modern speculative commercial accommodation.

7.3.2 The rehabilitation

This scheme was one step further up the scale of redevelopment options (see Chapter 3) than the previous case-study in that it involved more extensive structural alterations and additions. The original intention was to have each floor level fully open-plan, but this was ruled out by the greater costs and structural problems that would have resulted from demolition of the existing internal loadbearing walls. (An estimated £16 000 was saved by the decision to retain the existing internal walls.) In addition to upgrading the existing accommodation, extra accommodation was provided at top floor level by converting the existing pitched roof void. Use of the existing basement to provide upgraded accommodation was adjudged by the detailed cost appraisal as not financially viable, and it was therefore only used to house the boiler plant, lift pit and additional toilet accommodation and storage facilities for the ground floor tenant.

The client required the rehabilitated accommodation to be sufficiently flexible in design to allow a range of different uses, including showroom and office. By widening the range of possible uses in this way, the client hoped to increase the building's lettability, in comparison with a less flexible design restricted to one particular use. This is clearly one further means of increasing the viability of rehabilitation schemes, and is well worth considering at design stage.

A further requirement was that the scheme should be completed quickly to enable the building to be let as soon as possible, therefore helping to ensure its financial viability. To fulfil this constraint, the contractor was required to complete the works within 23 weeks. Plans and cross-sections of 37–40 York Place are shown in Figs 7.7–7.12, and Figs 7.13–7.15 show the building before, during and after completion of the work. The details of the rehabilitation are itemized below.

(a) Demolition

- Existing external metal fire escape at rear of building dismantled and removed.
- Existing roof lantern removed and void made good to line with existing flat roof using 175 × 50 mm softwood joists and chipboard decking.
- All existing internal timber framed partitions removed.
- Existing timber staircase and stair partition

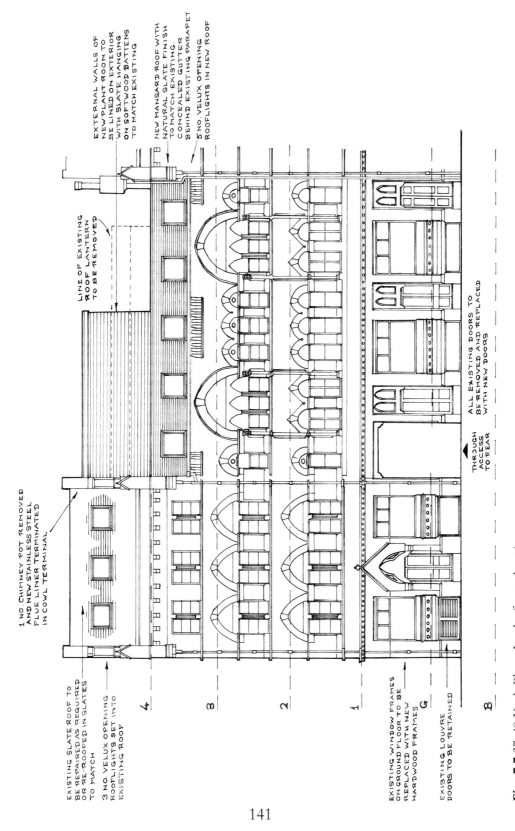

1 NO CHIMNEY POT REMOVED AND NEW STAINLESS STEEL FLUE LINER TERMINATED IN COWL TERMINAL

EXTERNAL WALLS OF NEW PLANT ROOM TO BE LINED ON EXTERIOR WITH SLATE HANGING ON SOFTWOOD BATTENS TO MATCH EXISTING

NEW MANSARD ROOF WITH NATURAL SLATE FINISH TO MATCH EXISTING. CONCEALED GUTTER BEHIND EXISTING PARAPET

5 NO. VELUX OPENING ROOFLIGHTS IN NEW ROOF

LINE OF EXISTING ROOF LANTERN TO BE REMOVED

EXISTING SLATE ROOF TO BE REPAIRED AS REQUIRED OR RE-ROOFED IN SLATES TO MATCH

3 NO VELUX OPENING ROOFLIGHTS SET INTO EXISTING ROOF

ALL EXISTING DOORS TO BE REMOVED AND REPLACED WITH NEW DOORS

THROUGH ACCESS TO REAR

EXISTING WINDOW FRAMES ON GROUND FLOOR TO BE REPLACED WITH NEW HARDWOOD FRAMES

EXISTING LOUVRE DOORS TO BE RETAINED

4

3

2

1

G

B

Fig. 7.7 37–40 York Place, Leeds: front elevation

141

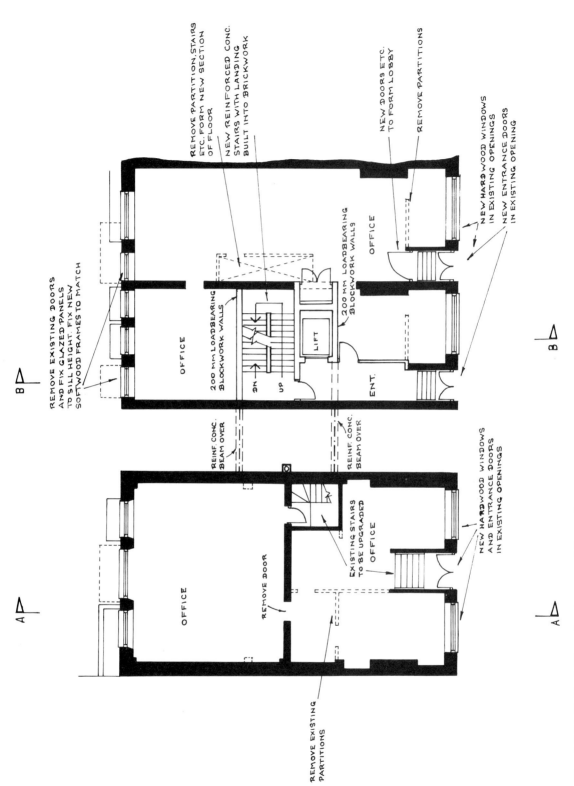

REMOVE PARTITION, STAIRS ETC. FORM NEW SECTION OF FLOOR

NEW REINFORCED CONC. STAIRS WITH LANDING BUILT INTO BRICKWORK

NEW DOORS ETC. TO FORM LOBBY

REMOVE PARTITIONS

NEW HARDWOOD WINDOWS IN EXISTING OPENINGS

NEW ENTRANCE DOORS IN EXISTING OPENING

REMOVE EXISTING DOORS AND FIX GLAZED PANELS TO SILL HEIGHT. FIX NEW SOFTWOOD FRAMES TO MATCH

OFFICE

200 MM LOADBEARING BLOCKWORK WALLS

200 MM LOADBEARING BLOCKWORK WALLS

OFFICE

LIFT

DN

UP

ENT.

B ▷

B ▷

REINF. CONC. BEAM OVER

REINF. CONC. BEAM OVER

OFFICE

REMOVE DOOR

EXISTING STAIRS TO BE UPGRADED

OFFICE

NEW HARDWOOD WINDOWS AND ENTRANCE DOORS IN EXISTING OPENINGS

A ▷

A ▷

REMOVE EXISTING PARTITIONS

Fig. 7.8 37–40 York Place, Leeds: ground floor plan

142

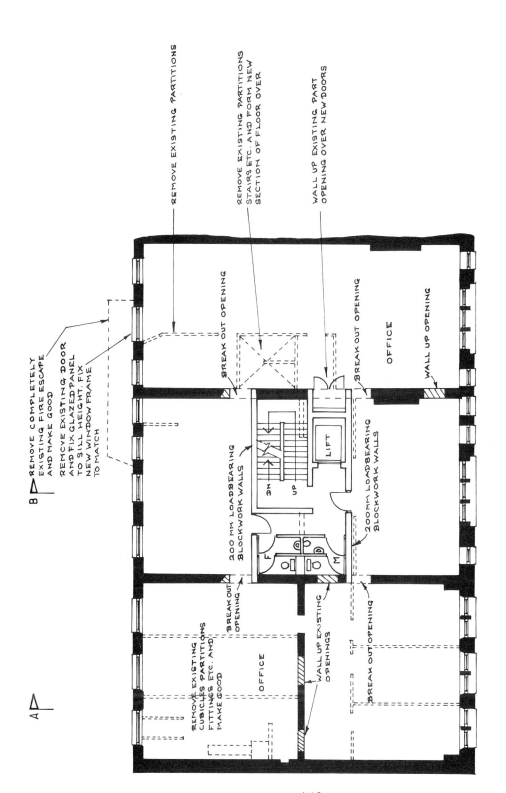

Fig. 7.9 37–40 York Place, Leeds: second floor plan

REMOVE EXISTING PARTITIONS

REMOVE EXISTING PARTITIONS STAIRS ETC. AND FORM NEW SECTION OF FLOOR OVER

WALL UP EXISTING PART OPENING OVER NEW DOORS

BREAK OUT OPENING

BREAK OUT OPENING

WALL UP OPENING

OFFICE

REMOVE COMPLETELY EXISTING FIRE ESCAPE AND MAKE GOOD

REMOVE EXISTING DOOR AND FIX GLAZED PANEL TO SILL HEIGHT. FIX NEW WINDOW FRAME TO MATCH

200 MM LOADBEARING BLOCKWORK WALLS

200MM LOADBEARING BLOCKWORK WALLS

UP

DN

LIFT

F

M

REMOVE EXISTING CUBICLES PARTITIONS FITTINGS ETC. AND MAKE GOOD

OFFICE

BREAK OUT OPENING

WALL UP EXISTING OPENINGS

BREAK OUT OPENING

A

B

A

B

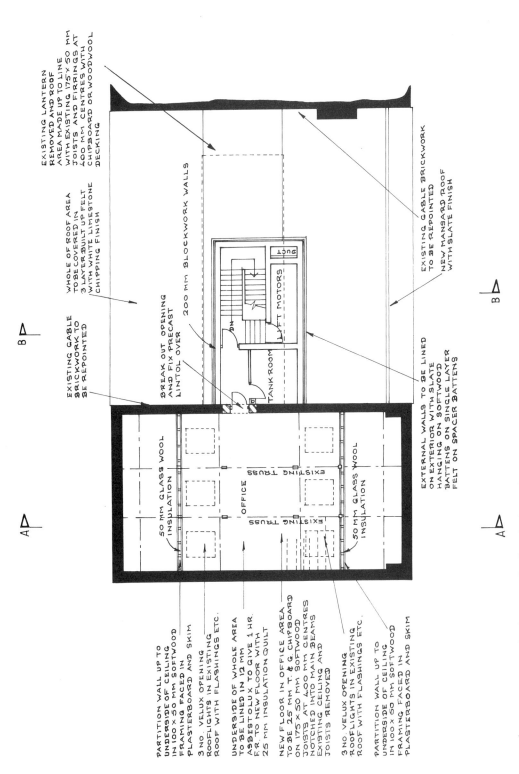

EXISTING LANTERN REMOVED AND ROOF AREA MADE UP TO LINE WITH EXISTING 175 X 50 MM JOISTS AND FIRRINGS AT 400 MM CENTRES WITH CHIPBOARD OR WOODWOOL DECKING

WHOLE OF ROOF AREA TO BE COVERED IN 3 LAYER BUILT UP FELT WITH WHITE LIMESTONE CHIPPING FINISH

EXISTING GABLE BRICKWORK TO BE REPOINTED

200 MM BLOCKWORK WALLS

EXISTING GABLE BRICKWORK TO BE REPOINTED

NEW MANSARD ROOF WITH SLATE FINISH

BREAK OUT OPENING AND FIX PRECAST LINTOL OVER

LIFT MOTORS

TANK ROOM

DN

DUCT

B ▷

B ▷

A ▷

A ▷

OFFICE

EXISTING TRUSS

EXISTING TRUSS

50 MM GLASS WOOL INSULATION

50 MM GLASS WOOL INSULATION

EXTERNAL WALLS TO BE LINED ON EXTERIOR WITH SLATE HANGING ON SOFTWOOD BATTENS ON SINGLE LAYER FELT ON SPACER BATTENS

PARTITION WALL UP TO UNDERSIDE OF CEILING IN 100 X 50 MM SOFTWOOD FRAMING FACED IN PLASTERBOARD AND SKIM

3 NO. VELUX OPENING ROOFLIGHTS IN EXISTING ROOF WITH FLASHINGS ETC.

UNDERSIDE OF WHOLE AREA TO BE LINED IN 12 MM ASBESTOLUX TO GIVE 1 HR. F.R. TO NEW FLOOR WITH 25 MM INSULATION QUILT

NEW FLOOR IN OFFICE AREA TO BE 25 MM T. & G. CHIPBOARD ON 175 X 50 MM SOFTWOOD JOISTS AT 400 MM CENTRES NOTCHED INTO MAIN BEAMS EXISTING CEILING AND JOISTS REMOVED

3 NO. VELUX OPENING ROOFLIGHTS IN EXISTING ROOF WITH FLASHINGS ETC.

PARTITION WALL UP TO UNDERSIDE OF CEILING IN 100 X 50 MM SOFTWOOD FRAMING FACED IN PLASTERBOARD AND SKIM

Fig. 7.10 37–40 York Place, Leeds: fourth floor plan

144

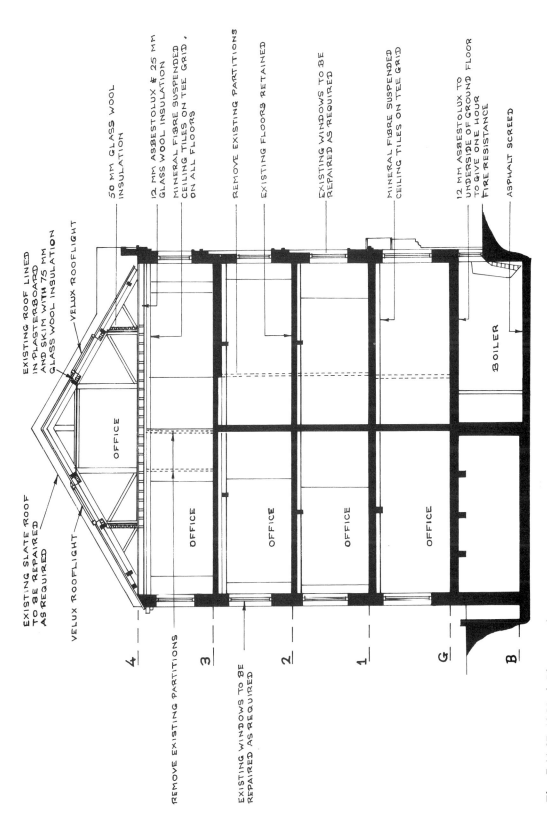

50 MM GLASS WOOL INSULATION

12 MM ASBESTOLUX & 25 MM GLASS WOOL INSULATION

MINERAL FIBRE SUSPENDED CEILING TILES ON TEE GRID, ON ALL FLOORS

REMOVE EXISTING PARTITIONS

EXISTING FLOORS RETAINED

EXISTING WINDOWS TO BE REPAIRED AS REQUIRED

MINERAL FIBRE SUSPENDED CEILING TILES ON TEE GRID

12 MM ASBESTOLUX TO UNDERSIDE OF GROUND FLOOR TO GIVE ONE HOUR FIRE RESISTANCE

ASPHALT SCREED

EXISTING ROOF LINED IN PLASTERBOARD AND SKIM WITH 75 MM GLASS WOOL INSULATION

VELUX ROOFLIGHT

EXISTING SLATE ROOF TO BE REPAIRED AS REQUIRED

VELUX ROOFLIGHT

OFFICE

OFFICE

OFFICE

OFFICE

OFFICE

OFFICE

BOILER

4

3

2

1

G

B

REMOVE EXISTING PARTITIONS

EXISTING WINDOWS TO BE REPAIRED AS REQUIRED

Fig. 7.11 37–40 York Place, Leeds: section A–A

145

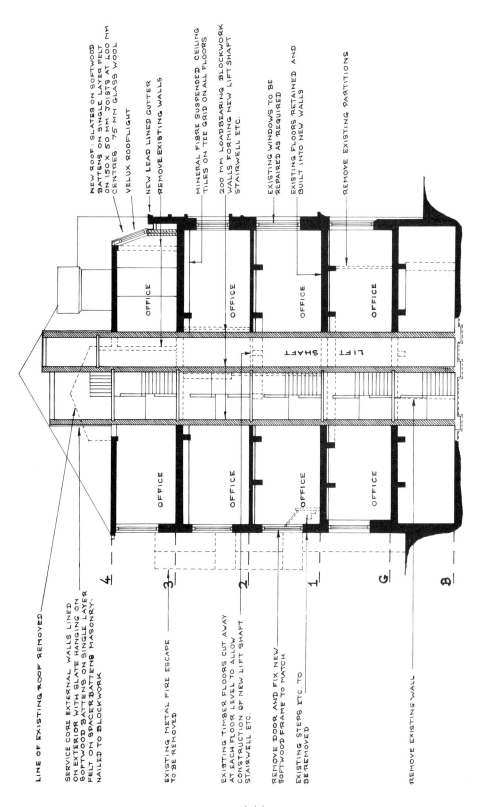

LINE OF EXISTING ROOF REMOVED

SERVICE CORE EXTERNAL WALLS LINED ON EXTERIOR WITH SLATE HANGING ON SOFTWOOD BATTENS ON SINGLE LAYER FELT ON SPACER BATTENS MASONRY NAILED TO BLOCKWORK

EXISTING METAL FIRE ESCAPE TO BE REMOVED

EXISTING TIMBER FLOORS CUT AWAY AT EACH FLOOR LEVEL TO ALLOW CONSTRUCTION OF NEW LIFT SHAFT STAIRWELL ETC.

REMOVE DOOR AND FIX NEW SOFTWOOD FRAME TO MATCH

EXISTING STEPS ETC. TO BE REMOVED

REMOVE EXISTING WALL

NEW ROOF: SLATES ON SOFTWOOD BATTENS ON SINGLE LAYER FELT ON 150 x 50 MM JOISTS AT 400 MM CENTRES. 75 MM GLASS WOOL

VELUX ROOFLIGHT

NEW LEAD LINED GUTTER

REMOVE EXISTING WALLS

MINERAL FIBRE SUSPENDED CEILING TILES ON TEE GRID ON ALL FLOORS

200 MM LOADBEARING BLOCKWORK WALLS FORMING NEW LIFT SHAFT STAIRWELL ETC.

EXISTING WINDOWS TO BE REPAIRED AS REQUIRED

EXISTING FLOORS RETAINED AND BUILT INTO NEW WALLS

REMOVE EXISTING PARTITIONS

OFFICE
OFFICE
OFFICE
OFFICE

LIFT SHAFT

OFFICE
OFFICE
OFFICE
OFFICE

4
3
2
1
G
B

Fig. 7.12 37–40 York Place, Leeds: section B–B

146

Fig. 7.13 37–40 York Place, Leeds: part front elevation before rehabilitation

demolished and removed. New sections of floor inserted to match existing.

- Existing toilet cubicles and sanitary fittings removed.

(b) Structural work

- New blockwork service core constructed through full height of building, including in-situ reinforced concrete stair, lift shaft and sanitary accommodation on each floor. Service core structure (see Figs 7.9, 7.12 and 7.14) erected in stages as follows:
  - (i) Blockwork walls built up from new strip foundations in basement, to underside of existing ground floor until supporting timber floor beams.
  - (ii) Existing timber floor beams and floorboards cut away from within service core zone.
  - (iii) Blockwork service core walls continued up to underside of existing first floor until supporting timber floor beams.
  - (iv) Existing timber floor beams and floorboards cut away from within service core zone. This process was repeated upwards through the building until the new service core structure was completed.

- Two new structural beams inserted over vehicle access passage at first floor level to support section of service core above (see Fig. 7.8).

Fig. 7.14 37–40 York Place, Leeds: interior view during rehabilitation showing construction of new service core at third floor level

- Existing timber stair and enclosure upgraded to comply with fire regulations.
- Openings formed through existing loadbearing brick internal walls at first to fourth floor levels to provide access within building (see Fig. 7.9).
- New office space formed within existing pitched roof void as follows (see Figs 7.10 and 7.11):
  (i) Removal of existing ceiling below roof and replacement with new office floor comprising 25 mm tongued and grooved chipboard on 175 × 50 mm softwood joists at 400 mm centres.
    New floor supported by 4 new steel beams spanning between existing loadbearing brick walls.
  (ii) Construction of new insulated timber stud walling faced with plasterboard to enclose new office space.
  (iii) Provision of new plasterboard lining and insulation to ceiling of new office space.

  (iv) Insertion of 6 Velux rooflights in existing pitched roof.
- New toilet partitions erected to provide self-contained sanitary accommodation at each floor level.
- Part of existing wall to front elevation (level 3 to roof) demolished and replaced with new slated mansard incorporating 5 Velux rooflights (see Figs 7.7 and 7.12).

(c) External envelope

- All brickwork elevations cleaned by sand-blasting and water spray, and re-pointed where necessary.
- Existing asphalt gutter to front elevation replaced with lead-lined gutter along front of new mansard.
- Existing cast-iron rainwater goods, timber gutters, etc. repaired or replaced as necessary.
- All existing windows to ground floor front

Fig. 7.15 37–40 York Place, Leeds: exterior view after rehabilitation

elevation removed and replaced with new hardwood frames.

- All remaining windows repaired, re-glazed and provided with new ironmongcry as required.
- New hardwood frames and entrance doors installed in front elevation to replace existing.
- Fire escape doors to rear elevation removed and replaced by new glazed panels to sill height, and softwood window frames to match existing.

(d) Roof

- Existing slate pitched roof repaired as required.

- Existing flat roof re-covered in 3-layer built-up felt with white limestone chippings.
- Minor structural repairs to roof timbers as necessary.

(e) Internal finishes

- All internal wall surfaces repaired and replastered as required.
- New mineral fibre suspended ceilings, rated Class 1 surface spread of flame, on exposed tee grid provided to all floors.
- Existing timber floors levelled up and covered with hardboard sheeting to receive carpet finish.
- All wall and ceiling surfaces to circulation

areas and main staircase finished to have Class O surface spread of flame.

- Existing steel columns encased in Cape Universal Fireclad hollow encasement.

(f) Services

- New lighting, plumbing and electrical installations provided throughout building.
- New low pressure hot water radiator heating system installed.
- Mechanical extract ventilation installed to toilet areas and lobbies.
- New sanitary fittings installed in toilet accommodation at each floor level.
- New 8 person passenger lift installed.

(g) Treatment of damp penetration and associated work

- Groundwater penetration into basement treated by application of asphalt screed to floor, and Tilcon waterproof plaster finish to walls.
- Rising dampness in walls treated by insertion of new silicone-resin pressure-injected damp-proof course.
- Dry and wet rot in timber floors, roof, etc. treated using fungicidal solution, or by replacement of badly rotted timbers where necessary.
- All masonry in vicinity of dry rot outbreaks sterilized with fungicidal solution.

Architects: William Gower and Partners, Leeds
Main Contractor: Wharfedale Construction, Wakefield

7.4 HEADINGLEY HILL CHURCH, LEEDS

7.4.1 The existing building

Headingley Hill Church, which is situated some two miles from the centre of Leeds, was built in 1866, having been designed by Cuthbert Brod-

rick, the architect of several other outstanding buildings in the city.

The existing stone building, shown in Figs 7.16 and 7.17, was rectangular on plan with a basement, main church hall at ground level, and a tiered balcony at the west end, providing additional seating for the congregation. The east end of the church was subdivided into a number of small rooms, including a vestry, with an organ gallery above. The massive timber roof structure was supported internally by two rows of ornate cast-iron columns, some of which also supported the tiered balcony.

The general state of repair of the building was good, and a detailed survey found it to be structurally sound, although the roof had spread by 150 mm, requiring appropriate remedial work to be carried out.

The church became redundant in 1975 and remained empty until 1980, when the Gillinson Partnership architectural practice, which was then based in a modern building in the city centre, purchased it for conversion to provide itself with new, self-contained premises. The church had been listed Grade II and any proposed development would therefore almost certainly have been constrained to preserving the entire envelope and as many of the interior features as possible.

7.4.2 The rehabilitation

As previously stated, the scheme was carried out to provide premises for an architectural practice. The principal requirements, therefore, were to provide drawing office space, partners' offices and ancillary accommodation; and the nature of the existing building enabled this to be done with the minimum amount of disruption and alteration. This satisfied the conservation constraints imposed by the building's Grade II listing, and allowed a highly cost-effective, low-key scheme to be successfully completed. Plans and cross-sections of Headingley Hill Church, both before and after its rehabilitation, are shown in Figs 7.16–7.20, and Figs 7.21–7.23

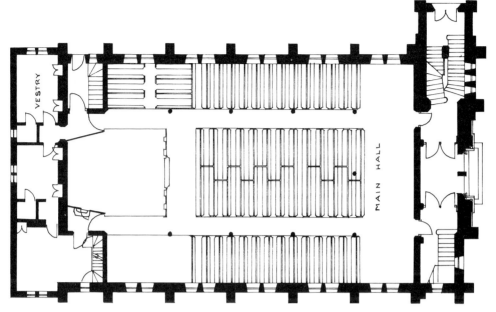

Fig. 7.17 Headingley Hill Church, Leeds: ground floor plan before rehabilitation

VESTRY

MAIN HALL

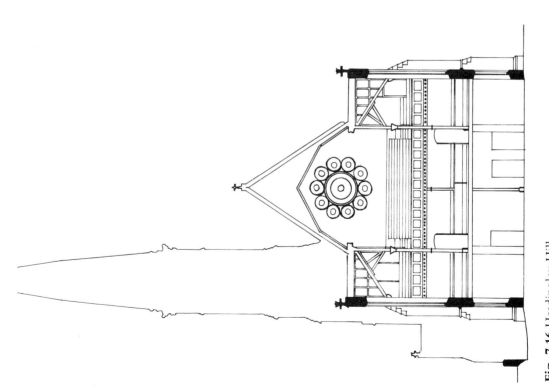

Fig. 7.16 Headingley Hill Church, Leeds: cross-section before rehabilitation

151

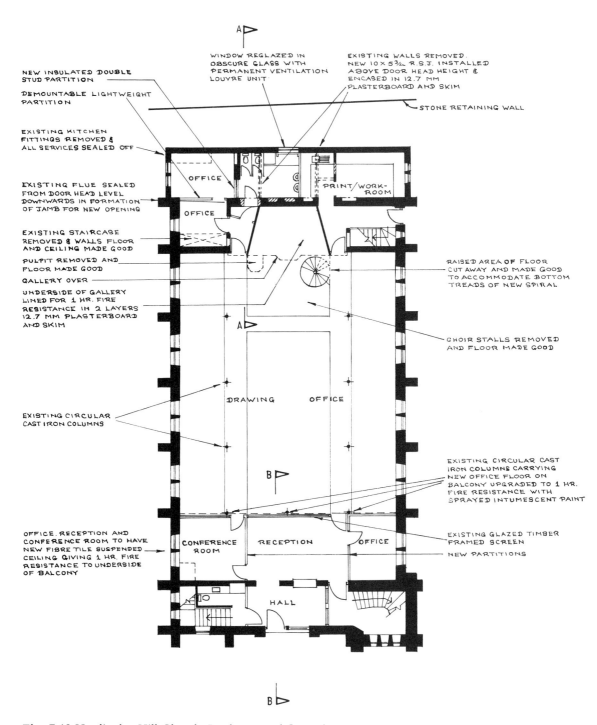

A

WINDOW REGLAZED IN
OBSCURE GLASS WITH
PERMANENT VENTILATION
LOUVRE UNIT

EXISTING WALLS REMOVED.
NEW 10 × 5¾ R.S.J. INSTALLED
ABOVE DOOR HEAD HEIGHT &
ENCASED IN 12.7 MM
PLASTERBOARD AND SKIM

NEW INSULATED DOUBLE
STUD PARTITION

DEMOUNTABLE LIGHTWEIGHT
PARTITION

STONE RETAINING WALL

EXISTING KITCHEN
FITTINGS REMOVED &
ALL SERVICES SEALED OFF

OFFICE

PRINT/WORK-
ROOM

EXISTING FLUE SEALED
FROM DOOR HEAD LEVEL
DOWNWARDS IN FORMATION
OF JAMB FOR NEW OPENING

OFFICE

EXISTING STAIRCASE
REMOVED & WALLS FLOOR
AND CEILING MADE GOOD

RAISED AREA OF FLOOR
CUT AWAY AND MADE GOOD
TO ACCOMMODATE BOTTOM
TREADS OF NEW SPIRAL

PULPIT REMOVED AND
FLOOR MADE GOOD

GALLERY OVER

UNDERSIDE OF GALLERY
LINED FOR 1 HR. FIRE
RESISTANCE IN 2 LAYERS
12.7 MM PLASTERBOARD
AND SKIM

A

CHOIR STALLS REMOVED
AND FLOOR MADE GOOD

DRAWING   OFFICE

EXISTING CIRCULAR
CAST IRON COLUMNS

B

EXISTING CIRCULAR CAST
IRON COLUMNS CARRYING
NEW OFFICE FLOOR ON
BALCONY UPGRADED TO 1 HR.
FIRE RESISTANCE WITH
SPRAYED INTUMESCENT PAINT

OFFICE, RECEPTION AND
CONFERENCE ROOM TO HAVE
NEW FIBRE TILE SUSPENDED
CEILING GIVING 1 HR. FIRE
RESISTANCE TO UNDERSIDE
OF BALCONY

CONFERENCE
ROOM

RECEPTION

OFFICE

EXISTING GLAZED TIMBER
FRAMED SCREEN

NEW PARTITIONS

HALL

B

Fig. 7.18 Headingley Hill Church, Leeds: ground floor plan

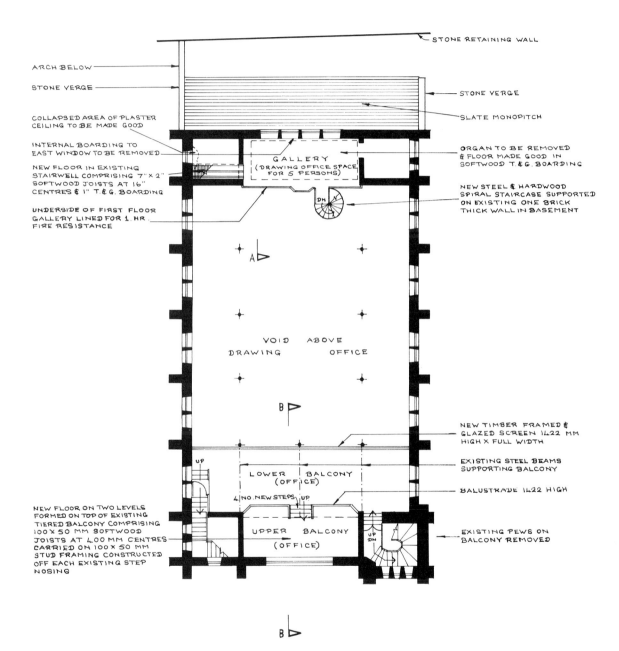

Fig. 7.19 Headingley Hill Church, Leeds: first floor plan

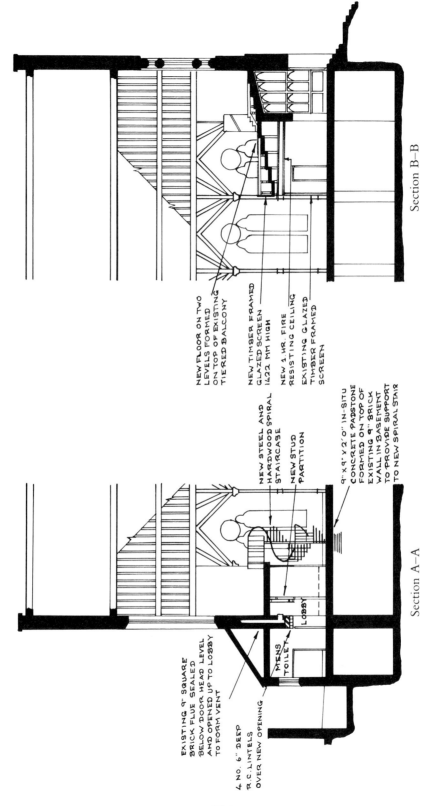

NEW FLOOR ON TWO
LEVELS FORMED
ON TOP OF EXISTING
TIERED BALCONY

NEW TIMBER FRAMED
GLAZED SCREEN
1422 MM HIGH

NEW 1 HR. FIRE
RESISTING EXISTING CEILING

EXISTING GLAZED
TIMBER FRAMED
SCREEN

Section B–B

NEW STEEL AND
HARDWOOD SPIRAL
STAIRCASE

NEW STUD
PARTITION

9"×9"×2'0" IN-SITU
CONCRETE PADSTONE
FORMED ON TOP OF
EXISTING 9" BRICK
WALL IN BASEMENT
TO PROVIDE SUPPORT
TO NEW SPIRAL STAIR

EXISTING 9" SQUARE
BRICK FLUE SEALED
BELOW DOOR HEAD LEVEL
AND OPENED UP TO LOBBY
TO FORM VENT

4 NO. 6" DEEP
R.C. LINTELS
OVER NEW OPENING

MENS
TOILET

LOBBY

Section A–A

Fig. 7.20 Headingley Hill Church, Leeds: section A–A and section B–B

154

Fig. 7.21 Headingley Hill Church, Leeds: interior view after rehabilitation

Fig. 7.22 Headingley Hill Church, Leeds: interior view after rehabilitation

155

Fig. 7.23 Headingley Hill Church, Leeds: exterior view after rehabilitation

show the building after completion of the work.

The main rehabilitation operations are itemized below.

(a) Demolition

- Existing loadbearing internal walls demolished in proposed printroom, toilet and reception areas (see Fig. 7.18).
- Existing staircase at east end of church demolished and floor made good using 7 inch × 2 inch softwood joists at 16 inch centres, and 1 inch tongued and grooved boarding.
- Church organ dismantled and removed and gallery floor made good in 1 inch tongued and grooved boarding.
- Pulpit dismantled and removed and floor made good.

- Pews and choir stalls dismantled and removed from main hall and balcony, and flooring made good.
- Existing kitchen fittings dismantled and removed, and plumbing services sealed off.

(b) Structural work

- New internal partitions erected to form offices, toilet accommodation, print room, entrance hall and reception area (see Fig. 7.18).
- New split level office floor with connecting steps formed on top of existing tiered balcony, comprising 100 × 50 mm softwood joists at 400 mm centres on 100 × 50 mm stud framing constructed of existing steps (see Figs 7.19 and 7.20).

156

- New timber framed and glazed screen 1422 mm high, constructed at front of existing tiered balcony.
- New low-level partition, 1422 mm high, constructed between upper and lower balcony offices.
- New timber framed and panelled screen, 1422 mm high, constructed at front of existing organ gallery (converted to five person drawing office).
- New steel and hardwood spiral stair erected to provide access between main drawing office on ground floor and upper drawing office on former organ gallery.
- 150 mm roof spread arrested by installation of post-tensioned steel tie bars taken through holes drilled in existing beams, and secured with steel backplates (see Figs 7.21 and 7.22).

(c) External envelope/roof

- Minor repairs to stone elevations, roof and rainwater goods as required.
- Internal boarding-up to east window removed.

(d) Internal finishes

- Collapsed area of plaster ceiling over proposed ground floor office in N.W. corner, repaired and made good (see Fig. 7.19).
- New mineral fibre tile suspended ceiling in concealed metal grid installed in office, reception and conference room to give 1 hour fire resistance to underside of office balcony (see Fig. 7.18).
- Underside of former organ gallery lined with two layers of 12.7 mm plasterboard and skim finish to give 1 hour fire resistance.
- Three circular cast-iron columns supporting office balcony cleaned and treated with sprayed decorative intumescent coating to give 1 hour fire resistance.

(e) Services

- Eight Nor-Ray-Vac overhead gas fired radiant heating burners installed immediately below roof level to provide heating to main drawing office area and offices on balcony and organ gallery (see Figs 7.21 and 7.22).

Note: The Nor-Ray-Vac gas fired radiant heating system, marketed by Phoenix Burners Ltd, is a highly efficient and cost-effective method of heating buildings with large open interiors, and has been used extensively in churches, markets, galleries, museums, industrial buildings, etc., where providing effective space-heating to large interior volumes can prove extremely difficult.

- New lighting installation provided throughout building, including high intensity 'widespread' fittings to main drawing office area.
- New plumbing installation, sanitary fittings, etc. to toilet accommodation and food preparation room.
- New electrical installation.

Architects: The Gillinson Partnership, Leeds

7.5 ST PAUL'S HOUSE, PARK SQUARE, LEEDS

7.5.1 The existing building

St Paul's House, a Grade II listed building, was built in 1878 as warehousing for a Leeds clothing manufacturer. The existing four-storey building, rectangular on plan, and some 51 metres long × 22 metres wide, was widely recognized as the best example of an Hispano–Moorish architectural style in England. Its external brick elevations, with extensive ornamentation in terra-cotta, were surmounted by an ornate parapet, perforated by rondels and five terra-cotta minarets. In the early 1960s, the whole of this parapet, along with the minarets, had to be removed due to decay and instability. The external loadbearing walls were founded on strip footings of sandstone blocks, and the internal structure comprised cast-iron columns on a 3.900 × 5.490 metre grid, supporting steel main and secondary beams with substantial timber floors. The building is, like the first case-

157

study, located in one of Leeds' best preserved Georgian squares and is therefore of considerable historic and environmental importance.

The nature of Park Square, and its proximity to Leeds city centre, has resulted in it becoming an attractive area for office development, and this led the new owners of St Paul's House to seek permission to redevelop the building as prestige office accommodation. The building's Grade II listing, due principally to the architectural merit and attractiveness of its external envelope, precluded demolition. However, the uninteresting interior of St Paul's House contained little worth preserving, and the developers were therefore permitted to totally 'gut' the building and construct an entirely new structure behind the preserved facade.

7.5.2 The rehabilitation

This is an excellent example of drastic rehabilitation, far removed from the low-key schemes at the other end of the scale of redevelopment options (see Chapter 3) that have been described earlier. The complete demolition of the building's interior and erection of an entirely new structure behind its preserved facade, was a major exercise in constructional engineering, involving the use of a complex temporary support system to ensure the stability of the facade during the works.

A plan and cross-section of St Paul's House after its rehabilitation are shown in Figs 7.24 and 7.25, and Figs 7.26–7.28 show the work being carried out, and the completed building. The main operations involved in the rehabilitation of St Paul's House are itemized below.

- Temporary support system, comprising four structural steel towers and two levels of scaffold-tube flying shores erected within the existing building to provide support to the preserved facade during the demolition and new construction work. This provision is necessary with all facade retention schemes to prevent collapse of the facade walls during the

period between demolition of the existing interior structure and the tying-back of the facade to the newly erected structure behind.

The temporary support system's four structural steel towers were threaded through holes formed in the existing roof and floors, and the scaffold-tube flying shores were positioned between existing floor levels. Finally, the facade walls were tied to the ends of the flying shores by means of twin timber walings, which 'collared' the walls, timber packing pieces and wedges.

Figure 7.26 shows the temporary support towers, flying shores and walings after demolition of the interior structure.

- Interior of existing building demolished.
- New in-situ reinforced concrete structure, comprising flat plate floor slabs supported by square mushroom-headed columns on a 7.8 × 5.5 metre grid, constructed behind the retained facade.

This new structure provided two additional floors (see Fig. 7.25), one between the original ground and first floor levels, and the other at the original roof level, necessitating the addition of a new glazed mansard roof.

- Restoration of original parapet and minarets, which had been removed in the early 1960s as a result of their deterioration and instability. The cost of reinstating this important exterior feature of St Paul's House in terra-cotta (the original material) proved prohibitive, and this resulted in the highly successful use of glass-reinforced plastic replicas, produced by a craftsman specializing in the imitation of natural materials with GRP.
- Re-pointing of brick elevations as necessary.
- Repair and reinstatement of terra-cotta ornament to all elevations as necessary, using GRP specially pigmented to match existing.
- Brick and terra-cotta elevations cleaned with water spray and sealed.
- New bronze acrylic finished aluminium windows inserted into all existing window openings.
- New window inserted to replace original

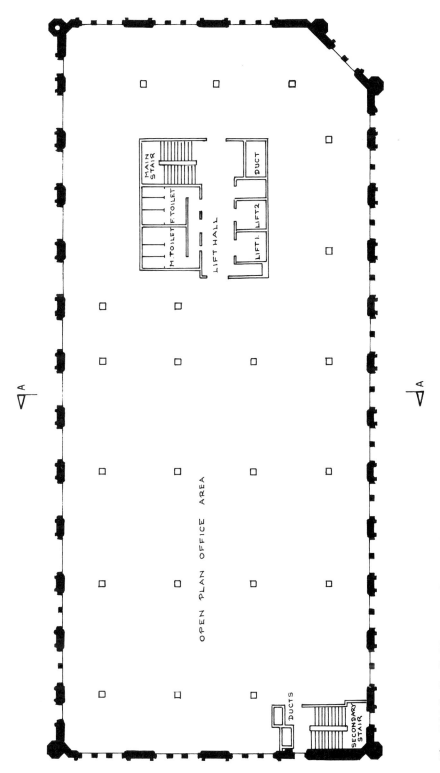

Fig. 7.24 St. Paul's House, Leeds: typical floor plan

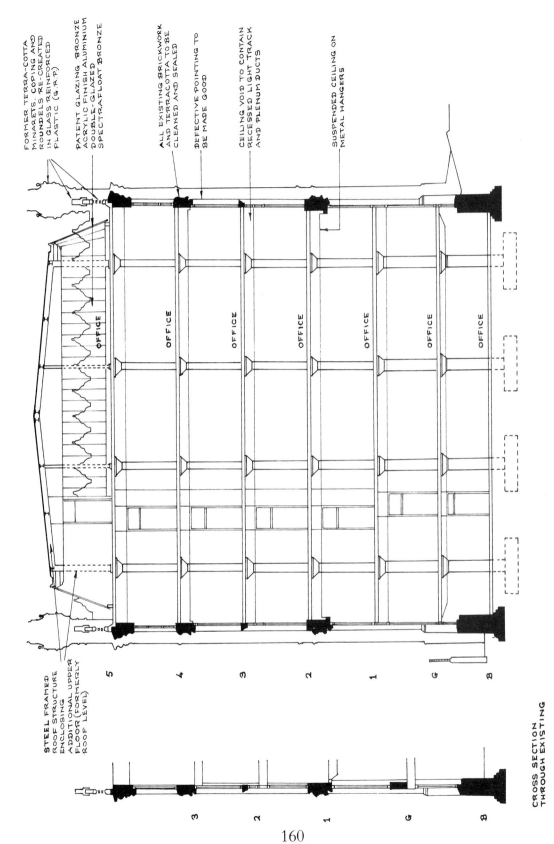

FORMER TERRA-COTTA
MINARETS, COPING AND
ROUNDELS RE-CREATED
IN GLASS REINFORCED
PLASTIC (G.R.P.)

PATENT GLAZING BRONZE
ACRYLIC FINISH ALUMINIUM
DOUBLE-GLAZED
SPECTRAFLOAT BRONZE

ALL EXISTING BRICKWORK
AND TERRACOTTA TO BE
CLEANED AND SEALED

DEFECTIVE POINTING TO
BE MADE GOOD

CEILING VOID TO CONTAIN
RECESSED LIGHT TRACK
AND PLENUM DUCTS

SUSPENDED CEILING ON
METAL HANGERS

STEEL FRAMED
ROOF STRUCTURE
ENCLOSING
ADDITIONAL UPPER
FLOOR (FORMERLY
ROOF LEVEL)

OFFICE
OFFICE
OFFICE
OFFICE
OFFICE
OFFICE
OFFICE

5 4 3 2 1 G B

CROSS SECTION
THROUGH EXISTING

3 2 1 G B

160

Fig. 7.25 St. Paul's House, Leeds: section A–A

Fig. 7.26 St. Paul's House, Leeds: view showing temporary support system after demolition of existing interior

Fig. 7.27 St. Paul's House, Leeds: exterior view during rehabilitation

161

Fig. 7.28 St. Paul's House, Leeds: interior view after rehabilitation

main entrance, and new main entrance with canopy formed to Park Square elevation.

The speculative open-plan office accommodation produced by the rehabilitation of St Paul's House was required by the clients to be of a high specification, designed to attract 'prestige' tenants and high rentals. This involved the provision of high quality interior finishes, self-contained sanitary accommodation at each floor level, a sophisticated heating, ventilation and air-conditioning system, and two passenger lifts. The high quality image of St Paul's House was completed by careful landscaping to the Park Square frontage, which incorporated the new main entrance of the finished building.

Architects: Booth Shaw and Partners, Leeds
Main Contractor: Fairclough Building Ltd, Leeds

7.5.3 Cost comment

As stated in Chapter 1, the majority of rehabilitation schemes, particularly those of a low-key

nature, produce modern accommodation more cheaply than new construction. However, it is clear that schemes like St Paul's House, which involved extensive and complex demolition and re-construction, cannot be as cost effective. In fact, such 'facade retention' schemes can be described as new construction that has been complicated and constrained by having to build behind or within an existing envelope. Generally, therefore the cost of schemes of this nature will be at least as much as, if not greater than, the cost of new construction. However, the greater costs incurred by opting for facade retention in comparison with carrying out a lower-key rehabilitation scheme, are often balanced by the following factors:

(i) It is usually possible to insert extra floors behind the retained facade. At St Paul's House, the original five floor levels were replaced by seven, therefore significantly increasing the lettable floor area.

(ii) It is easier to produce high specification, air-conditioned, well serviced accommodation

162

capable of attracting higher rentals, when the design is not constrained by an existing, obsolete interior.

(iii) The retention of an existing historic and architecturally attractive facade adds prestige, which can often be translated into higher rental income from tenants requiring this quality, such as banks, insurance companies, building societies etc.

7.6 ST LUKE'S CHURCH, HARROGATE

7.6.1 The existing building

St Luke's Church, built in 1897 in the Victorian Gothic style, is a Grade II listed building standing close to Harrogate town centre. The steady decline in the numbers attending St Luke's led to the church being declared redundant in 1980, and the congregation were 'rehoused' in a smaller, modern building nearby.

As with all redundant listed buildings, the key to preserving St Luke's Church was to find a new, viable use for the building, and this occurred when a local firm of builders and an architectural practice, in conjunction with the Yorkshire Metropolitan Housing Association, initiated a scheme to rehabilitate the church to provide flats and maisonettes.

With the exception of a severe attack of dry rot in the vestry area, the existing church was structurally sound and in a good state of repair. The rehabilitation scheme commenced in the spring of 1983 and took approximately one year to complete.

7.6.2 The rehabilitation

Plans and a cross-section of St Luke's Church are shown in Figs 7.29–7.33, and Figs 7.34–7.37 show the building during, and after completion of the work.

The large open internal volume of the church allowed a total of twenty-nine flats and maisonettes to be accommodated with minimal loss of the existing structure. This enabled all of the units, and the circulation areas, to incorporate some of the original architectural features, such as stone arches, carving, arched and circular windows, etc., all of which have been carefully used to preserve the existing building's character.

Following selective demolition of some internal walls, and excavation of the existing ground floor, four new floors were inserted, the lowest being slightly above the old nave floor, so as to provide a services void beneath the ground floor flats, connecting to vertical services ducts serving the flats on the upper floors. The new ground, first and second floors were constructed from precast concrete planks, supported by the load-bearing blockwork cross-walls which divided the flats (see Figs 7.33 and 7.35), and the third floor was of timber joisted construction.

The rehabilitation of St Luke's Church could reasonably be placed around halfway up the scale of re-development options (see Chapter 3) because, although it involved a considerable amount of new construction, very little demolition was required to accomplish it, the existing building comprising a voluminous shell, within which the new accommodation could be constructed. The twenty-nine flats and maisonettes produced by the scheme comprised seventeen single person bedsitter units, eleven single person/single bedroom units, and one two person/two bedroom unit.

The units are tenanted under a shared ownership scheme set up by the Yorkshire Metropolitan Housing Association, the building's owners. Shared ownership enables tenants to buy a portion of the property, and then rent the remainder until they wish to further increase their ownership 'stake'. Tenants can buy 25%, 50% or 75% of a property to begin with, and then increase their share of the ownership when able to do so, for example when their earnings increase.

The St Luke's Church scheme was financed by the Housing Corporation, now an important source of finance for producing 'new' housing

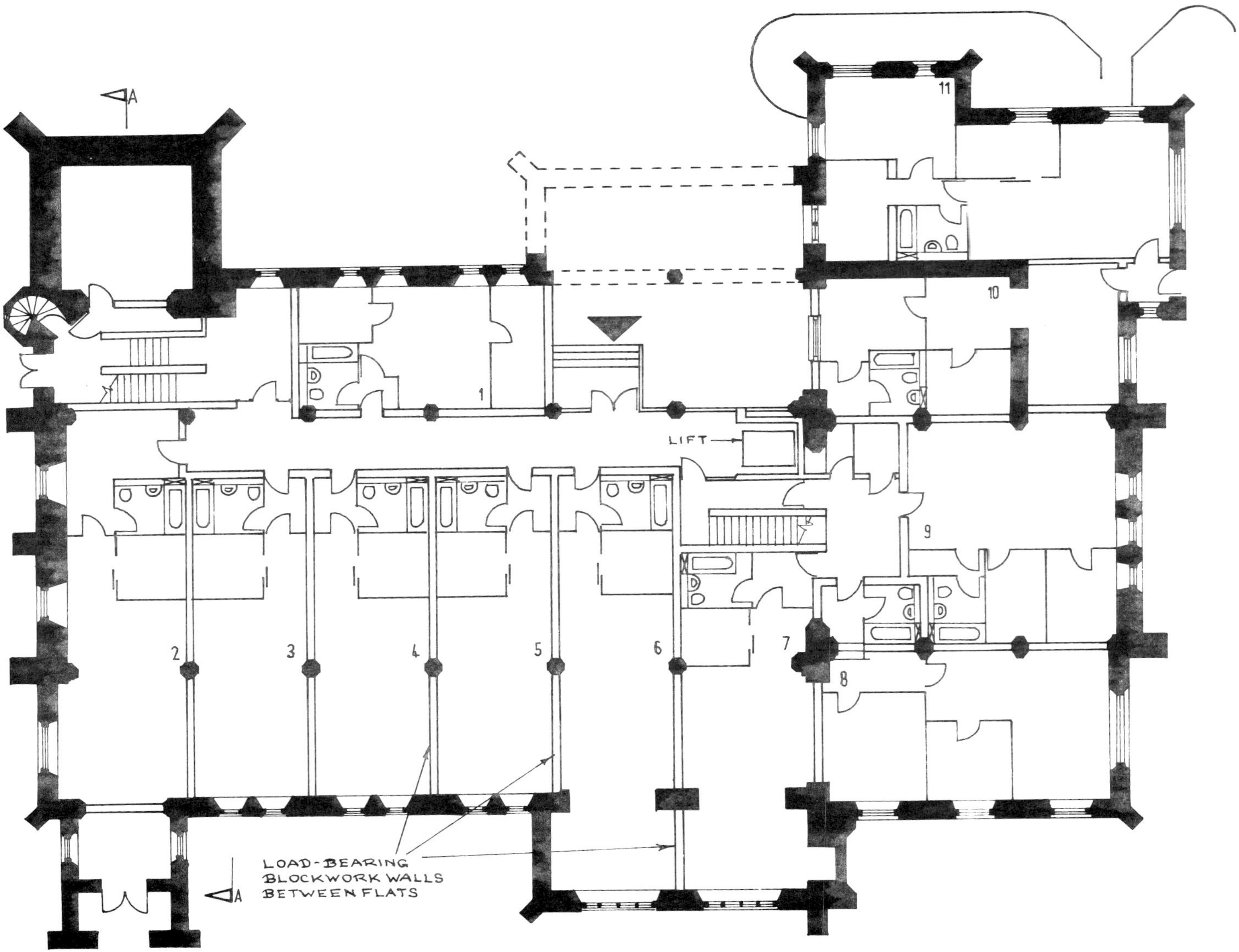

Fig. 7.29 St. Luke's Church, Harrogate: ground floor plan

LOAD-BEARING
BLOCKWORK WALLS
BETWEEN FLATS

LIFT

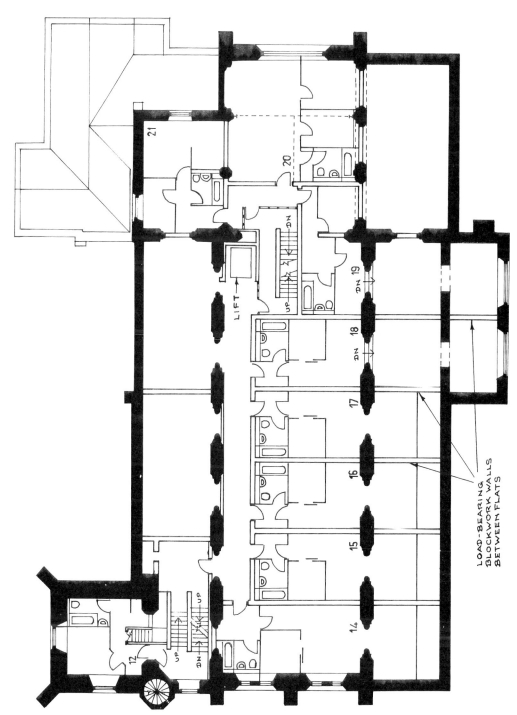

Fig. 7.30 St. Luke's Church, Harrogate: first floor plan

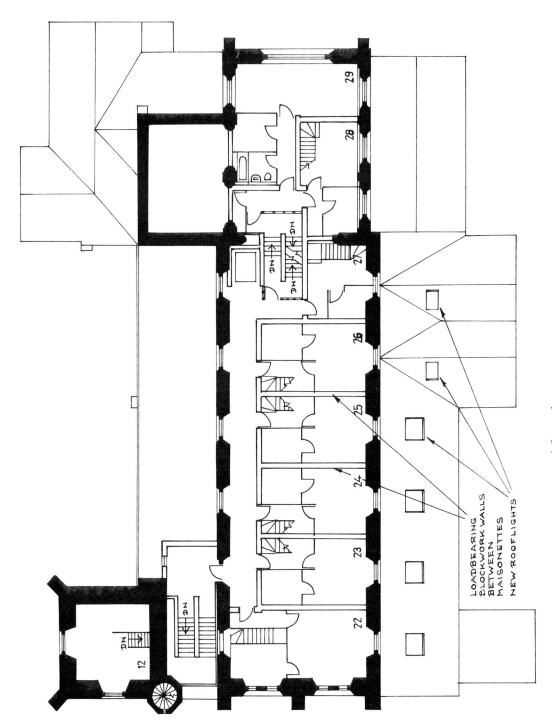

Fig. 7.31 St. Luke's Church, Harrogate: second floor plan

LOADBEARING
BLOCKWORK WALLS
BETWEEN
MAISONETTES

NEW ROOFLIGHTS

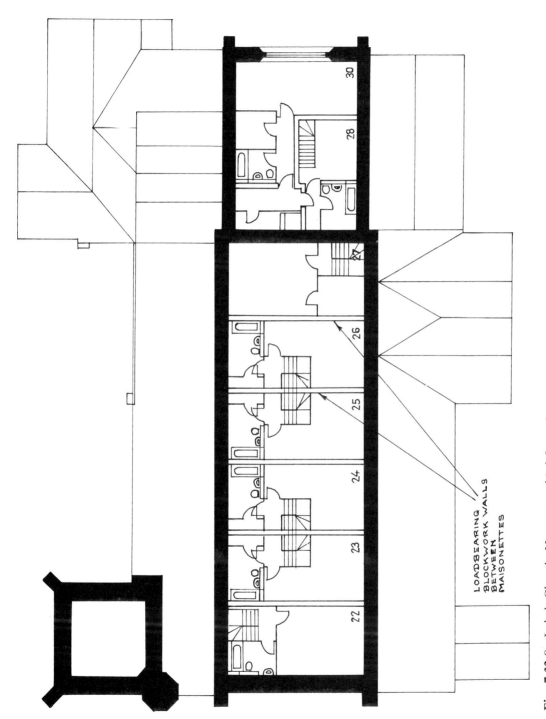

Fig. 7.32 St. Luke's Church, Harrogate: third floor plan

LOADBEARING
BLOCKWORK WALLS
BETWEEN
MAISONETTES

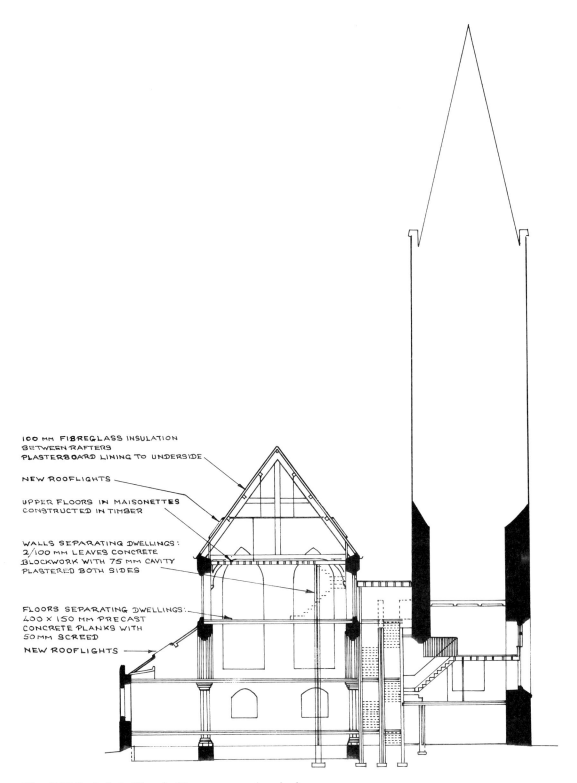

100 mm FIBREGLASS INSULATION
BETWEEN RAFTERS
PLASTERBOARD LINING TO UNDERSIDE

NEW ROOFLIGHTS

UPPER FLOORS IN MAISONETTES
CONSTRUCTED IN TIMBER

WALLS SEPARATING DWELLINGS:
2/100 mm LEAVES CONCRETE
BLOCKWORK WITH 75 mm CAVITY
PLASTERED BOTH SIDES

FLOORS SEPARATING DWELLINGS:
400 x 150 mm PRECAST
CONCRETE PLANKS WITH
50 mm SCREED

NEW ROOFLIGHTS

Fig. 7.33 St. Luke's Church, Harrogate: section A–A

168

Fig. 7.34 St. Luke's Church, Harrogate: interior view during rehabilitation

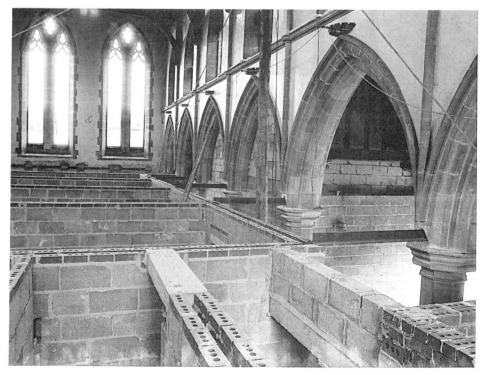

Fig. 7.35 St. Luke's Church, Harrogate: interior view during rehabilitation showing construction of separating walls between flats

Fig. 7.36 St. Luke's Church, Harrogate: interior view after rehabilitation

Fig. 7.37 St. Luke's Church, Harrogate: exterior view after rehabilitation

through the rehabilitation of existing buildings (see Chapter 6).

The financial details of the scheme, which should be read in conjunction with Section 6.2.13, were as follows: (figures approximate)

Total capital cost of project (covered by Housing Corporation loan)	£555 000
Total equity sold to tenants (in 25%, 50% or 75% shares)	£247 000
Total Housing Association grant	£220 000
Balance (covered by a long-term loan funded by the rental income)	£ 88 000
	£555 000

The main operations in the rehabilitation of St Luke's Church are itemized below.

(a) Demolition

- Selective demolition of internal walls, and part external wall in vicinity of new main entrance.
- Existing ground floor broken up and removed, and interior ground level lowered (see Fig. 7.34).
- All internal fixtures and fittings dismantled and removed.

(b) Structural work

- New ground, first and second floors constructed, comprising 400 mm wide × 150 mm deep precast concrete planks finished with 50 mm screed (see Fig. 7.33).
- New third floor (forming upper floor of maisonettes) constructed, comprising timber joists with chipboard sheet decking.
- New internal walls constructed, generally of two 100 mm leaves of concrete blockwork with 75 mm cavity (see Fig. 7.35) plastered both sides, to provide 1 hour fire resistance and sound insulation between occupancies.

- Two new in-situ concrete staircases constructed in blockwork enclosures.
- New blockwork lift shaft constructed.
- New main entrance formed, comprising arched entrance lobby.
- New internal partitions erected in flats and maisonettes.

(c) External envelope

- Minor repairs to stone elevations, roof and rainwater goods as required.
- Removal of stained glass from existing windows, and replacement with clear glass to achieve suitable natural lighting.
- Insertion of 15 new rooflights in existing slated pitched roofs to flats and maisonettes at first and third floor levels (see Figs 7.31 and 7.37).

(d) Internal finishes

- Existing pitched roof construction, where exposed in flats and maisonettes, insulated with 100 mm fibreglass between rafters, and finished with two 12.5 mm layers of plasterboard spiked to underside of rafters.
- Existing external walls, where exposed in flats and maisonettes, lined with Gyproc urethane laminate (see Section 4.4.1) fixed to pre-treated timber battens.
- Plasterboard and Artex textured ceiling finish to underside of new timber joisted and precast concrete floors.
- Plasterboard and skim finish to new internal partitions.
- Two-coat plaster finish to new blockwork walls.
- All common stair and corridor areas provided with carpet finish.
- Chipboarded timber floors, and screeded precast concrete floors within flats and maisonettes, left unfinished for tenants' own floorcoverings.

(e) Services

- Electric storage heaters, operated on off-peak

tariff, installed in all flats and maisonettes.

- Armsil prefabricated combination services units installed in all flats and maisonettes, comprising integral cistern, electric immersion heater and all water supply and waste pipework for kitchen and bathroom.
- New hydraulic eight person wheelchair lift installed.

(f) Treatment of damp penetration, timber decay, etc.

- Extensive attack of dry rot in vestry area treated by replacement of badly rotted timbers with new pre-treated timber, and fungicidal spraying of all existing timbers.
- All other timber throughout building checked for insect/fungal decay and treated where necessary.
- New silicone-resin pressure-injected damp-proof course provided to existing walls.

In 1985, the completed scheme received national and local housing design awards.

> Architects: Hill Mawson Partnership, Boston Spa, Yorks.
> Main Contractor: Walter E. Birch Ltd, Harrogate

7.7 HOUSING REHABILITATION, NEWCASTLE UPON TYNE

7.7.1 The existing buildings

This major scheme involved the rehabilitation of a severely run-down housing estate built for the local council in 1924.

Originally, all of the units were built as flats, but an earlier upgrading scheme resulted in some of them being converted to four-bedroomed maisonettes, and thus, when the developers took possession in mid-1984, there were 96 flats and 36 four-bedroomed maisonettes on the estate. All of the flats and maisonettes were of two storey traditional construction, comprising brick loadbearing cavity walls and tiled pitched roofs, without underfelt.

Because of the very poor condition of the estate, due to age, neglect and, more recently, vandalism, the local authority did not consider it worthy of rehabilitation, and was considering demolition. However, the estate's location, and the fact that the buildings were all structurally sound, led Bellway Urban Renewal Ltd to become interested. As a result, the company purchased the estate from Newcastle City Council with the aim of carrying out a large-scale rehabilitation scheme to provide modern two-bedroomed flats for sale to the public. The run-down condition of the estate prior to its rehabilitation is illustrated by external and internal views of typical houses, shown in Figs 7.38–7.41.

The scheme was made feasible by the award of a major, Government-funded, urban development grant, a relatively new form of financial aid aimed generally at stimulating the regeneration of run-down urban areas (see Section 6.2.11). The financial details of the scheme were as follows:

Houses purchased from local authority for	£160 000
Urban development grant	£938 000
Initial selling price of flats	£ 11 000

7.7.2 The rehabilitation

The scheme involved the rehabilitation and conversion of 96 two-bedroomed flats and 36 four-bedroomed maisonettes, to produce a total of 172 modern two-bedroomed flats for sale to the public. The variation in design of the existing buildings meant that every 'block' required a different treatment, and, in some, very little structural alteration was involved at all. Clearly, it would be unrealistic to attempt to describe the rehabilitation of every block, and so, for the purposes of this case-study, a typical block has been selected which included a mix of existing two-bedroomed flats and four-bedroomed maisonettes. Its rehabilitation is described below and illustrated in Figs 7.42–7.47, which show the existing and proposed plans, and

Fig. 7.38 Housing rehabilitation, Newcastle upon Tyne: exterior view before rehabilitation

Fig. 7.39 Housing rehabilitation, Newcastle upon Tyne: exterior view before rehabilitation

173

Fig. 7.40 Housing rehabilitation, Newcastle upon Tyne: interior view before rehabilitation

Fig. 7.41 Housing rehabilitation, Newcastle upon Tyne: interior view before rehabilitation

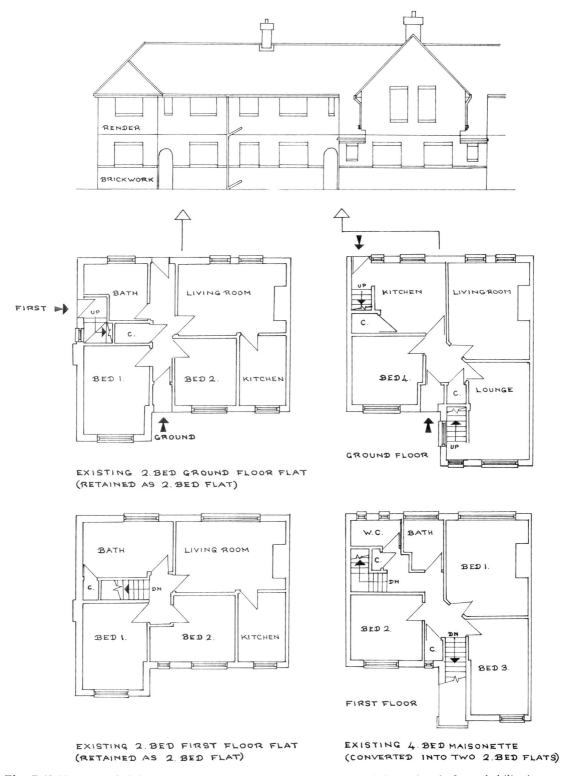

Fig. 7.42 Housing rehabilitation, Newcastle upon Tyne: elevation and floor plans before rehabilitation

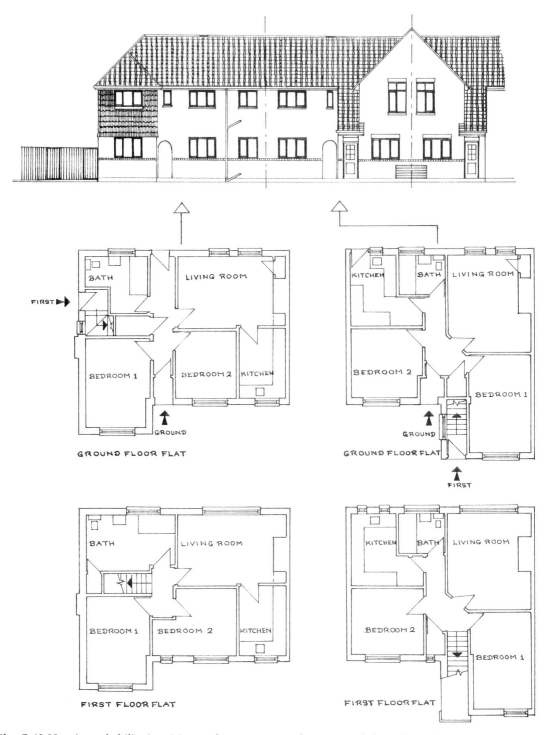

Fig. 7.43 Housing rehabilitation, Newcastle upon Tyne: elevation and floor plans after rehabilitation

176

Fig. 7.44 Housing rehabilitation, Newcastle upon Tyne: exterior view after rehabilitation

Fig. 7.45 Housing rehabilitation, Newcastle upon Tyne: exterior view after rehabilitation

Fig. 7.46 Housing rehabilitation, Newcastle upon Tyne: interior view after rehabilitation

views of the exterior and interior after completion.

(a) Demolition

- Existing rear staircase and associated partitions removed from four-bedroomed maisonette, and flooring made good to match existing (see Figs 7.42 and 7.43).
- Existing brick chimneys demolished and roof made good to match existing.
- Part front wall demolished to form new external door opening for main entrance to new first floor flat (see elevations, Figs 7.42 and 7.43).
- All existing fixtures and fittings removed, including built-in cupboards etc., sanitary fittings and kitchen fittings.

(b) Structural work

- Upgrading of existing staircase, and erection of new brick separating wall to provide access to new first floor flat (in former four-

bedroomed maisonette: see Figs 7.42 and 7.43).
- Erection of new internal partitions, comprising 75 × 50 mm softwood studding, finished with 12.5 mm plasterboard and skim, to form new bathroom and kitchen areas (in former four-bedroomed maisonette: see Fig. 7.43).

(c) External envelope

- New tile-hanging to part front and side elevations comprising plain tiles, fixed to 38 × 25 mm battens, on sarking felt, on 100 × 19 mm softwood bearers plugged to existing wall.
- Existing rendered surfaces repaired as necessary, and finished with approved decorative coating applied by roller.
- Existing brick surfaces re-pointed and repaired as necessary, and finished with approved decorative coating applied by roller.
- All existing rainwater goods removed and

Fig. 7.47 Housing rehabilitation, Newcastle upon Tyne: interior view after rehabilitation

replaced by new PVC guttering and down-pipes.
- All existing windows repaired or replaced with new timber units as required, and decorated.
- All existing entrance doors removed and replaced with new.

(d) Roof

- All existing roofs stripped down to rafters and, after repair or treatment as necessary, re-covered with reclaimed/new tiles on battens, on sarking felt.
- 150 mm glass-fibre insulating quilt laid in roof void between ceiling joists.

- Roof space ventilated by formation of 10 mm continuous gap at eaves, together with one ridge-vent per unit.

(e) Internal finishes

- Floors separating flats: existing lath and plaster ceilings replaced with two 12.5 mm sheets of plasterboard, to give 1 hour fire resistance, and decorated with Artex textured finish.
- All other ceilings repaired or replaced with 12.5 mm plasterboard as necessary, and decorated with Artex textured finish.
- Existing internal wall surfaces repaired and made good where necessary, and all wall

surfaces finished with woodchip wall paper and two-coat emulsion paint.

- All existing timber floors repaired and made good as necessary.
- Self-levelling latex screed (maximum 12.5 mm thick) applied to all timber floors in new kitchen and bathroom areas, and finished with 2 mm vinyl tiles.
- Existing concrete ground floors in former kitchen areas repaired and made good as necessary, and finished with two coats of asphalt, total thickness 19 mm.

(f) Interior fixtures and fittings

- New fitted bathrooms and kitchens installed in all flats.

(g) Services

- New gas-fired central heating systems installed in all new flats, comprising integral gas fire/boiler unit, small-bore pipework and pressed-steel radiators.

(h) Treatment of damp penetration, timber decay, etc.

- All existing timber elements, including ground and upper floors and roof, surveyed by specialist sub-contractor for fungal and insect attack.
- Defective timber cut out and replaced with new treated timber as necessary.
- All other suspect timber spray-treated with fungicidal/insecticidal solution as necessary.
- All timber ground floors spray-treated, regardless of condition.
- New silicone-resin pressure-injected damp-proof course provided to all existing walls, including hacking off of existing plaster to one metre above skirting level, and replastering with renovating plaster.

Architects: Bellway Homes Ltd, Newcastle upon Tyne

Main Contractor: Bellway Homes Ltd, Newcastle upon Tyne

FURTHER READING

Benson, J. *et al.* (1980) *Housing Rehabilitation Handbook,* Architectural Press, London.

Brandt, S. and Cantacuzino, S. (1980) *Saving Old Buildings,* Architectural Press, London.

Department of the Environment, Scottish Development Department, Welsh Office (1971) *New Life for Old Buildings,* HMSO, London.

Eley, P. and Worthington, J. (1984) *Industrial Rehabilitation: The Use of Redundant Buildings for Small Enterprises,* Architectural Press, London.

Highfield, D. (1982) *The Construction of New Buildings Behind Historic Facades: The Technical and Philosophical Implications,* M.Phil. thesis, University of York.

Highfield D. (1983) Keeping up facades. *Building,* **245** (39), 30 September 1983, 40–41.

Highfield D. (1984) Building behind historic facades. *Building Technology and Management,* **22**(1), January 1984, 18–25.

Powell, K. (n.d.) *Pennine Mill Trail,* SAVE Britain's Heritage, London.

Scottish Civic Trust (1981) *New Uses for Older Buildings in Scotland,* HMSO, Edinburgh.

Project Management

Beaven, L. and Fry, D. (1983) *Architects Job Book,* Royal Institute of British Architects, London.

Benson, J. *et al.* (1980) *Housing Rehabilitation Handbook,* Architectural Press, London.

Burgess, R. A. and White, G. (1979) *Building Production and Project Management,* Construction Press, London.

Chartered Institute of Building (1982) *Project Management in Building,* CIOB, Ascot, England.

Chudley, R. (1981) *The Maintenance and Adaptation of Buildings,* Longman, London.

Eley, P. and Worthington, J. (1984) *Industrial Rehabilitation: The Use of Redundant Buildings for Small Enterprises,* Architectural Press, London.

Green, R. (1986) *The Architect's Guide to Running a Job,* Architectural Press, London.

Lee, R. (1981) *Building Maintenance Management,* Granada, London.

Powell, J. (1980) *Handbook of Architectural Practice and Management,* RIBA Publications, London.

Walker, A. (1985) *Project Management in Construction,* Collins, London.

Building and Structural Surveying

Bailey, T. A. (1986) Timber Inspection and Diagnosis. *Building,* 17 January 1986, 41–3.

Bowles, R. (1986) Techniques for Structural Surveys. *Building,* 17 January 1986, 38–40.

Bowyer, J. (1984) *Guide to Domestic Building Surveys,* Architectural Press, London.

Eley, P. and Worthington, J. (1984) *Industrial Rehabilitation: The Use of Redundant Buildings for Small Enterprises,* Architectural Press, London.

Hollis, M. (1983) *Surveying Buildings,* Surveyors Publications, London.

Melville, I. A. *et al.* (1985) *Structural Surveys of Dwelling Houses,* Estates Gazette, London.

Seeley, I. H. (1985) *Building Surveys, Reports and Dilapidations,* Macmillan, London.

Staveley, H. S. (1983) *Surveying Buildings,* Butterworths, London.

Index

Index

Index